THE JUST CITY

THE JUST CITY

Susan S. Fainstein

CORNELL UNIVERSITY PRESS   ITHACA AND LONDON

First published 2010 by Cornell University Press
Printed in the United States of America

Library of Congress Cataloging-in-Publication Data

Fainstein, Susan S.
  The just city / Susan S. Fainstein.
    p. cm.
  Includes bibliographical references and index.
  ISBN 978-0-8014-4655-9 (cloth : alk. paper)

  1. City planning—Moral and ethical aspects.   2. Urban policy—Moral and ethical aspects.   3. Municipal government—Moral and ethical aspects.
4. Social justice.   I. Title.
  HT166.F245 2010
  303.3'72—dc22   2010004406

Cornell University Press strives to use environmentally responsible suppliers and materials to the fullest extent possible in the publishing of its books. Such materials include vegetable-based, low-VOC inks and acid-free papers that are recycled, totally chlorine-free, or partly composed of nonwood fibers. For further information, visit our website at www.cornellpress.cornell.edu.

Cloth printing   10 9 8 7 6 5 4 3

For Alexander, Julianna, and Jeremy

Contents

Preface

The idea for this book began at a conference organized by Andy Merrifield and Erik Swyngedouw in 1994 to commemorate the twentieth anniversary of David Harvey's extraordinarily influential work *Social Justice and the City.* My presentation there was the first of a series of conference papers, articles, and book chapters in which I addressed the theme of achieving justice through interventions at the metropolitan level. Until then my theoretical writings had not explicitly examined the question of the meaning of justice within the urban context even though it constituted the underlying question for my research. This book represents my effort to integrate the abstract and the practical; until now my theoretical and empirical investigations have largely proceeded on separate tracks.

Fifteen years after that initial Oxford conference the topic of justice is receiving ever greater attention among urban scholars. During the period beginning in the mid-1970s in which mainstream thought focused almost exclusively on stimulating growth, progressive urban scholars chiefly reacted to the accompanying neoliberal ideology through critique rather than the development of a counterideology. In part, this reluctance to specify values stemmed from neo-Marxian thinkers rejecting the use of explicit ethical formulations, which they regarded as ungrounded in an understanding of historical development. Increasingly, however, the latent normative judgments that had always underlain Left analysis have become manifest. It is my hope to add to this explication and to provide a set of principles that planners can apply in their activities.

I wish to express my gratitude here to the many institutions and individuals who have assisted me in this endeavor. I have received financial support from the Harvard Graduate School of Design and wish to thank former Dean Alan Altshuler for his encouragement, not just recently but throughout my career, beginning when I was just a graduate student. The Rockefeller Foundation provided a residency in the glorious Villa Serbelloni at Bellagio, where I began the writing of this book.

My doctoral students at Columbia, who participated in my theory seminars and organized a conference on the just city when I left that university, have been especially important to me in providing a forum and offering constructive criticism. James Connolly, Johannes Novy, Ingrid Olivo, Cuz Potter, Bruno Lobo, Matthew Gebhardt, Justin Steil, and Elizabeth Currid deserve particular mention. Members of the New York Right to the City Group, including James DeFilippis, Sharon Zukin, and Neil Smith, have continued to provide a forum for the discussion of ideas. Two members of that group, David Harvey and Peter Marcuse, have been enormous influences on my thought, as is evidenced by the number of times they are cited here. David and I are not always in agreement, but he has inspired me, as well as generations of urbanists, to ponder the major issues of our times. Peter has not only been a source of insights but has kindly read and critiqued much of my writing. When I was at Columbia, he was the most estimable of colleagues, forever raising interesting questions at the lunch table and making the Columbia planning program a place of intellectual ferment. Two other scholars, Richard Sennett and Dennis Judd, were not directly involved in this book but their ideas and friendship have nevertheless contributed to its development. Rainer Forst allowed me to sit in on his class on theories of justice at the New School and gave me a foundation in formal philosophy that I had previously lacked.

Sako Musterd, Willem Salet, Justus Uitermarck, Theo Baart, and Roger Taylor responded cheerfully to my requests for information regarding Amsterdam and London. A number of people read and provided helpful comments on parts of the manuscript. These include Léon Deben, Chris Hamnett, Sharon Meagher, Mark Purcell, Frank Fischer, and my editor at Cornell University Press, Peter Potter. Norman Fainstein read draft after draft and is responsible for improving its logic and readability. He has, of course, been a lifetime influence on my thinking, and it is difficult for me to disentangle my ideas from his.

I also wish to thank my Harvard students who provided me with research assistance. Sai Balakrishnan prepared the maps. Lior Gallili, Karolina Gorska, and Hieu Truong carried out many of the mundane chores that underlie any effort of this sort. Finally, I am grateful to Peter Wissoker, who for years encouraged me to write this book and who signed me with Cornell.

Some of the material herein was drawn from earlier published work, including:

"Planning and the Just City." In *Searching for the Just City,* edited by Peter Marcuse, James Connolly, Ingrid Olivo Magana, Johannes Novy, Cuz Potter, and Justin Steil, 19–39. New York: Routledge, 2009.

"Megaprojects in New York, London and Amsterdam." *International Journal of Urban and Regional Research* 32, no. 4 (2008): 768–85.

"Planning and the Just City." *Harvard Design Magazine,* no. 27 (Fall 2007/Winter 2008): 70–76.

"Planning Theory and the City." *Journal of Planning Education and Research* 25 (2005): 1–10.

"Cities and Diversity: Should We Want It? Can We Plan for It?" *Urban Affairs Review* 41, no. 1 (September 2005): 3–19.

"New Directions in Planning Theory." *Urban Affairs Review* 35, no. 4 (March 2000): 451–78.

"The Egalitarian City: Images of Amsterdam." In *Understanding Amsterdam,* edited by Léon Deben, Willem Heinemeijer, and Dick van der Vaart, 93–116. 2nd ed.: Amsterdam: Het Spinhuis, 2000.

"Creating a New Address I: Battery Park City." In *The City Builders,* 2nd ed., by Susan S. Fainstein, 160–74. Lawrence: University Press of Kansas.

"Creating a New Address II: Docklands." In *The City Builders,* 2nd ed., by Susan S. Fainstein, 175–96. Lawrence: University Press of Kansas.

"Governing Regimes and the Political Economy of Development in New York City, 1946–84." In *Power, Culture, and Place,* edited by John Hull Mollenkopf, 161–200. New York: Russell Sage Foundation, 1988.

INTRODUCTION: TOWARD AN URBAN THEORY OF JUSTICE

It has become a commonplace that deindustrialization and globalization have dramatically changed the fortunes of cities in the United States and Western Europe, causing leaders in these cities to respond by entering into intense competition for private investment.[1] Increasingly, urban regimes have focused narrowly on economic growth as their objective, essentially claiming that growth-promoting policies result in the greatest good for the greatest number. Justifications for projects in terms of enhancing competitiveness dominate the discourse of city planning; even the provision of amenities such as parks or cultural facilities is rationalized by their potential to raise property values and attract businesses and tourists. Decisions concerning where to locate facilities become warped by considerations of their economic, as opposed to their social, impacts. Thus, capital investments by city governments are intended to support development projects rather than improve the quality of peripheral neighborhoods, and rezoning for higher densities occurs in response to developer demands for more profitable investment opportunities.

---

1. The terms city, metropolitan area, and urban area are used interchangeably throughout much of this book except when issues of scale are under discussion. By all of them I mean a contiguous urban area that may be divided by jurisdictional lines. Where appropriate, however, as in discussions of metropolitan spatial divisions, analytic distinctions between neighborhood, city, and metropolitan area are made.

The principal mechanisms employed by governing regimes to create growth have involved investment in infrastructure, subsidies and regulatory relief to property developers and firms, and city marketing. These have been applied to a variety of schemes, with different emphases succeeding each other about every five years or so. Popular strategies have included office-led development, festive retail malls, sports facilities, "tourist bubbles," clustering of related industries, nurturing the creative class, and arts development. Except in wealthy enclaves, the desirability of growth is usually assumed, while the consequences for social equity are rarely mentioned.[2]

The overwhelming requirement that public expenditures be framed in terms of enhancing competitiveness was explained by the former mayor of London, Ken Livingstone, in discussing how he obtained a commitment from the U.K. central government for financing Crossrail, a railroad to be tunneled across central London:

> [I argued that] without Crossrail London would lose its edge in the competition [for financial firms] among global cities. As soon as you stop building you lose out. London land costs rule out virtually every business that isn't highly profitable. [To overcome concern over the cost] I showed that investment in London produces the highest rate of return for the country....If you couldn't show that a particular policy produced growth, you wouldn't get anywhere.[3]

Challengers to competitively oriented policies have sometimes questioned the need for growth, usually on environmental grounds; more typically they have accepted it as an aim but contested the distribution of benefits resulting from using public funds to leverage private investment or resisted the neighborhood transformation that would result. For

---

2. Fainstein (2001a) describes the enticements used in New York and London to promote office development; Frieden and Sagalyn (1989) chronicle the creation of festive retailing as a method of downtown revival; Rosentraub (1999), among many others, shows and critiques the enormous sums that state and local governments have showered on sports facilities; Judd (1999) uses the term "tourist bubble" to designate the group of structures such as convention centers and arenas that every mayor regards as critical for attracting visitors; Porter (1998) promotes clustering of related industries as key to inner-city revival; Florida (2002) identifies "the creative class" as the central element of urban regeneration; while Markusen (2006) and Currid (2007) point to the importance of culture in stimulating economic development.

3. Interview with the author, July 26, 2008.

example, opponents of the Atlantic Yards megaproject in central Brooklyn, New York, formed an organization called Develop Don't Destroy Brooklyn. The title reflected acceptance of economic development aims but disagreement with the high densities and use of eminent domain incorporated into the project.

Beginning in the 1960s, scholars of urban politics have criticized urban decision makers for imposing policies that exacerbated the disadvantages suffered by low-income, female, gay, and minority residents.[4] In particular, they have condemned policies that favor downtown businesses while ignoring neighborhood needs and giving priority to tourist facilities and stadiums over schools and labor-intensive industries. These critiques have implied a model of the just city—that is, a city in which public investment and regulation would produce equitable outcomes rather than support those already well off. Our knowledge of what constitutes injustice is virtually instinctive—it consists of actions that disadvantage those who already have less or who are excluded from entitlements enjoyed by others who are no more deserving.[5] Taking away housing, employment, or access to public space from the politically or economically weak seems fairly obviously to comprise injustice, albeit such action is usually rationalized as being in the long-run interest of the majority or deemed actually helpful to the poor. Thus, when New York's Mayor Edward Koch was accused of bias against the poor, he proclaimed: "I speak out for the middle class. You know why? Because they pay taxes; they provide jobs for the poor people" (Koch 1994, 221). In Chicago, where the Plan for Transformation had as its aim the destruction of all existing public housing units, thereby dramatically reducing the stock of housing affordable by low-income households, Mayor Richard Daley indicated that his purpose was dispersion of the poor in order to give them access to greater opportunity (Bennett 2006).

Although there is a rich literature in planning and public policy prescribing appropriate decision-making processes,[6] these process-oriented

---

4. See, inter alia, Jacobs (1961); Gans (1968); Mollenkopf (1983); Fainstein and Fainstein (1986); Logan and Molotch (1987); Stone (1989); Kohn (2004); Squires (1989); Dreier, Mollenkopf, and Swanstrom (2001).

5. Iris Marion Young (1990) provides a list of five forms of oppression experienced by people as a consequence of their group identity: exploitation, marginalization, cultural imperialism, and systematic violence.

6. As will be discussed later, proponents of communicative rationality and deliberative democracy expect that genuinely democratic processes will result in just outcomes. They

discussions rarely make explicit what policies would produce greater justice within the urban context.[7] At the same time most policy analysis concerns itself with best practices or what "works" in relation to specific goals such as producing more housing or jobs without interrogating the broader objectives of these policies. As Charles Taylor (1991, 19) comments, "Social science explanation…has generally shied away from invoking moral ideals and has tended to have recourse to supposedly harder and more down to earth factors."

Unlike social scientists, philosophers have long concerned themselves with the nature of justice.[8] Since the publication of John Rawls's *Theory of Justice* in 1971, philosophy has returned to the questions of values and governance that were central to it before the ascendancy of logical positivism.[9] The principal theories all posit an aspirational ideal according to which actual social policy can be formulated. The formulations, however, do not tell us what would be appropriate *urban* institutions and offer even less in terms of what actual programs would incorporate the criteria of justice that they propose.[10]

---

therefore focus on processes of participation and methods of negotiation rather than the content of policy or the character of the desirable city (Fainstein 2005a).

7. A few planning scholars have specified progressive institutions and policies, although most have typically not placed their recommendations within a broader theoretical context (see Clavel 1986; Mier and Alpern 1993). Fincher and Iveson (1988) do make such an attempt, and Kevin Lynch (1981) developed an argument concerning urban design incorporating justice. In a 1993 article in the *North Carolina Law Review,* which I coauthored with Ann Markusen, we attempted to specify particular urban programs that would increase social justice. Leonie Sandercock in her two books, *Toward Cosmopolis* (1998) and *Cosmopolis II* (2003), has sought to spell out the characteristics of a city responsive to difference. Gutmann and Thompson (1996), who attempt to provide substantive content to deliberative democracy, apply its principles to such specific policy areas as health care and earnings, which intersect with urban issues; however, they do not adopt a specifically urban perspective.

8. The dominant schemas developed in the last four decades are, first, Rawls's (1971) concept of justice as fairness; second, Jürgen Habermas's (1986–89) delineation of the ideal speech situation; third, communitarianism (inter alia, Sandel 1996; Walzer 1984); and fourth, Martha Nussbaum's (2000) and Amartya Sen's (1992) capabilities approach (see chapter 2 for a fuller discussion).

9. Within analytic philosophy values could not be discussed, and therefore investigation into the meaning of justice was shunted aside by mainstream philosophy (see H. Putnam 2002). In calling for a return to a value-oriented philosophy, Maeve Cooke (2006, 3) argues that critical social thinking would be impossible without a "more or less determinate, guiding idea of the good society." In other words, logical positivism left social reformers without any guidance.

10. The work of Iris Marion Young is the primary exception.

My aim in this book is to develop an urban theory of justice and to use it to evaluate existing and potential institutions and programs. I am not tackling a theory of the good city, one that would go beyond justice to create the conditions for human flourishing. In a comment on an earlier paper of mine, Sharon Meagher stated: "Widening the concept of justice [from Rawls's definition] without reference to the good life seems difficult, if not impossible, if only because of the power of naming—we simply haven't used 'justice' to refer to anything other than issues of fairness in a very long time."[11] Nevertheless, my effort, within the urban context, is to "name" justice as encompassing equity, democracy, and diversity and to argue that its influence should bear on all public decisions without going so far as to develop a theory of the good city.[12] Even though justice is only one, albeit a significant and necessary, component of a vision of the good, it raises enough questions and is so frequently traduced in the name of efficiency or the public interest as to constitute a sufficient subject for analysis here.

In addition, my analysis is limited to what appears feasible within the present context of capitalist urbanization in wealthy, formally democratic, Western countries. As such, it is susceptible to criticism for being too weak to deal with the injustices inherent in capitalism:

> This is…the point at which Fainstein's conception of the Just City falters. From the start, it delimits its scope to acting within the existing capitalist régime of rights and freedoms and is thus constrained to mitigating the worst outcomes at the margins of an unjust system.…Fainstein's emphasis on the discursive and inspirational role of the Just City avoids the necessity for outright conflict and struggle. (Harvey with Potter 2009, 46)

---

11. Personal communication, May 9, 2006. Similarly Spragens (2003, 601) insists that "however central the virtue of justice may be to political institutions, the ultimate concern of most citizens is with their capacity to lead what their moral compass recommends to them as a good life." Marcuse (2009, 91) also argues that a concept of justice alone is not enough: "The desired city…should not be a city with only distributional equity, but one that supports the full development of human capabilities for all. This requires more than Justice Planning."

12. Lefebvre's (1991 [1974]) arguments concerning the right to the city do extend beyond justice. The right to the city has become a mobilizing slogan for an urban-based social movement, the Right to the City Alliance, which in June 2008 encompassed twenty urban organizations in the United States. It presents as its aim "to develop a common frame and approach to unify our diverse struggles for housing, social wages, public space, and culture" (http://www.idealist.org/en/org/161513-236).

Although this critique is accurate in accusing me of accepting that urban policy making will continue within the "capitalist régime of rights and freedoms," I do not expect conflict to be avoided. Moreover, as will be argued below, I consider that the system itself will change incrementally as a consequence of continued pressure for justice. Forcing decision makers to make justice a principal consideration in urban policies would be more than a marginal change, and while in isolation such endeavors would not be structurally transformative, as a component of broader national and international movements they would add to overall pressure for restructuring capitalism into a more humane system. To the objection that a humane capitalism is an oxymoron, I have no answer.

Plan for this Book

My project differs from most of the urban literature in that, although I will do my share of critiquing, I would like to provide a guide to what to do if justice is the first evaluative criterion used in policy making. By and large, empirical analyses of urban programs and theoretical formulation have proceeded on separate tracks.[13] This book uses both deductive and inductive methods to create an argument for a normative framework promoting the (more) just city; develops an investigation and critique of present urban institutions and policies, especially as they apply to urban redevelopment; and concludes with a discussion of institutional and policy approaches to achieving greater social justice within cities.

My approach, after discussing the theoretical issues, is to consider urban development in the last thirty years within three metropolitan areas that I have previously investigated: New York, London, and Amsterdam.[14] Building on these investigations, I then identify the strategies and policies that result in more just outcomes. It has been pointed out to me

---

13. Urbanists have begun to formulate ethical theories concerning the appropriate criteria for evaluating urban development (inter alia, Sennett 1990; Forester 1993; Sayer and Storper 1997; Low and Gleeson 1998; Healey 2006, Meagher 2008; Purcell 2008), and some political theorists and philosophers have directly or indirectly concerned themselves with urban issues (inter alia, Fischer 2000; Hajer and Reijndorp 2001; Mouffe 2000; Mansbridge 1990a; Nussbaum 2000; Young 1990, 2000). The volume *Searching for the Just City* (Marcuse et al., 2009), comprised of papers initially presented at a Columbia University conference on urban justice, brings together both abstract and applied analyses.

14. See, inter alia, Fainstein (2001a, 1997); Fainstein, Gordon, and Harloe (1992); Fainstein and Fainstein (1978).

that education is a crucial aspect of policy to be considered under the rubric of the just city; although I do not disagree, I think that it, along with environmental policy, require separate and fuller examinations than I can provide here, although I do provide some discussion of the movement for environmental justice.

The three cities are examined in relation to their political regimes and development outcomes. They can be arrayed on a spectrum whereby, in terms of equitable material distribution, New York has been the least successful and Amsterdam the most. In regard to social integration of disparate groups, however, New York, while remaining racially segregated, has dealt relatively well with its immigrant population. London, under Labour rule, has occupied a middle position as it moved away from the antiplanning, trickle-down stance that characterized regeneration programs in the Margaret Thatcher/John Major period. Labour nonetheless retained the deregulatory/privatization strategy introduced by Thatcher. Amsterdam has supported strongly redistributive policies and has a long history of tolerance, but both orientations have been called into question since the midnineties. Examining the three cities and the causes of their varying trajectories allows the formulation and evaluation of strategies for revitalization that can be the program of urban social movements and the object of national and local policy.

Although the resources available to cities are determined largely by higher levels of government and the autonomous decisions of private investors, local public policy making still affects who gets what and is not fully constrained.[15] The choice of objects of investment (e.g., stadiums vs. housing; infrastructure vs. incentives to private developers; schools vs. convention centers) as well as locational decisions (e.g., where to put the bus station or public housing) is made by local governments. Particular policy areas in which municipalities have considerable discretion and thus the power to distribute benefits and cause harm include urban redevelopment, housing programs, zoning, racial and ethnic relations, open space planning, and service delivery. Whether the policy emphasis and budgetary priorities should be on physical construction or human capital

---

15. Logan and Swanstrom (1990) compile a collection of studies to demonstrate that variability among cities results from a degree of local autonomy. James DeFilippis (2009) shows that labor relations in most industries are locally rooted and are susceptible to regulation at the local level.

development, dispersion of low-income households or neighborhood improvement are decisions made locally.

Why Justice?

The choice of justice as the governing norm for evaluating urban policy is obviously value laden. It reacts to the current emphasis on competitiveness and the dominance in policy making of neoliberal formulations that aim at reducing government intervention and enabling market processes. Neoliberalism, somewhat confusingly to Americans who interpret liberalism as a leftist orientation, refers to the doctrine that market processes result in the efficient allocation of resources and provide incentives that stimulate innovation and economic growth. For the market to work, state action that distorts prices and interferes with rewards to investors must be minimized. Within metropolitan areas, functions that once were considered the prerogative of elected officials become the activities of public-private partnerships, quasi-autonomous authorities, and economic development corporations overseen by boards of business executives (see Purcell 2008). In David Harvey's words:

> The fundamental mission of the neo-liberal state is to create a "good business climate" and therefore to optimize conditions for capital accumulation no matter what the consequences for employment or social well-being.... [It] looks to further the cause of and to facilitate and stimulate (by tax breaks and other concessions as well as infrastructural provision at state expense if necessary) all business interests, arguing that this will foster growth and innovation and that this is the only way to eradicate poverty and to deliver, in the long run, higher standards to the mass of the population. (Harvey 2006, 25)

Even though the "Great Recession," still continuing at the time of this writing, has stimulated considerable public intervention into capital markets, relegitimated job creation programs, and reversed the trend toward deregulation, it has not undermined the emphasis on economic growth that has prevailed in urban policy. In fact, quite the opposite. Moreover, its effect on public revenue collection has, at least in the United States, forced extensive layoffs, hiring freezes, and salary reductions among local governing bodies, while program cutbacks have particularly affected the poor.

The justice criterion does not necessarily negate efficiency and effectiveness as methods of choosing among alternatives, but rather requires the policy maker to ask, efficiency or effectiveness to what end?[16] The measurement of outcomes in aggregate monetary terms leads to an apparent trade-off between efficiency and equity. If, instead of asking the *overall* benefit/cost ratio of a given project, we inquire as to the benefits and costs to those least well-off or those most directly and adversely affected, we are still concerned with efficiency.

Among planning theorists there is a debate between those who emphasize communication, negotiation, and democratic decision making as the principal normative standard for planning and those who instead opt for a substantive concept of justice (see chapter 1 for a more extensive discussion). In a recent reformulation of her ideas concerning collaborative planning, Healey (2003, 110) counters my argument that planners should intrude in the planning process and advocate for the application of normative concepts of the just city. She contends that

> concepts of the "good" and the "just" were themselves constructed through relations of knowledge and power.... [But] the processes of articulating values and the manner in which these might become embedded in established discourses and practices were important. In other words, substance and process are co-constituted, not separate spheres. In addition, process should not be understood merely as a means to a substantive end. Processes have process outcomes. Engagement in governance processes shapes participants' sense of themselves.

By this logic any assertion of a particular content simply regresses to the outcome of communication among participants, as all forms of knowledge are socially constructed (Healey 1996). This may be so, but it does not preclude the existence of such widespread consensus as to constitute a universal acceptance of certain values (e.g., justice) or require that intervention in the name of justice be forbidden on the grounds that it constitutes "imperialist" interference with participants' deliberations.[17]

---

16. Fischer (2009, 61) criticizes my focus on the three values of equality, diversity, and democracy for omitting efficiency: "Missing from the list... is the value of efficiency, which comes into play at the other end of the theory-action continuum. Without a measure of attention to efficient action, few problems can be solved."

17. Wendy Brown (2006) asserts that liberal tolerance actually depoliticizes structurally based difference and consequently represents cultural imperialism. Her argument implies that

Frank Fischer (2009) asserts that the debate is unproductive and that the two points of view can be brought together within a broader framework. In fact, the difference is more one of emphasis than fundamental disagreement. Nevertheless, the two sides do point to different metrics of evaluation: for the communicative theorists the test of policy depends on who is included in its formulation, on the existence of an open, fair process, and on better argument as the deciding factor. For just-city theorists the principal test is whether the outcome of the process (not just of deliberation but of actual implementation) is equitable; values of democratic inclusion also matter, but not as much. Moreover, as will be discussed in chapter 1, the logic of Habermasian communicative rationality means that if the process of deliberation conforms to the ideal, then the outcome will necessarily be equitable. On the ground, however, we can never expect that the ideal will be met; thus, the question of emphasis on process or outcome remains.

Within the philosophical literature two rationales exist for the decision to center a discussion of urban policies on a substantive concept of justice:[18] (1) reference to a general consensus; and (2) Rawls's explanation of why individuals would opt for it in the original position. These are discussed in the next section.

General Consensus

The emphasis on justice can be defended in terms of a communicative consensus at the highest level of articulation; it then becomes a universal principle rather than one negotiated in each interaction. As David Harvey rightly contends (1996, 362), "Universality can never be avoided, and those who seek to do so...only end up hiding rather than eliminating the condition. But universality must be construed in dialectical relation with

---

most calls for justice based within the Western liberal tradition do not transcend the context in which they are made and are based on a sense of cultural superiority. Gellner (1992, 27), questioning the postmodern antipathy to traditional social science, wonders whether "the objectivism aspired to or invoked by traditional...social science was [in actuality] covertly a means of imposing a vision on men, which constrained those dominated to accept their subjection. It is not entirely clear whether the violation [perceived by postmodernists] consisted of imposing a certain *particular* vision, confirming the established order, on its victims, or whether the main sin was the imposition of the very ideal of objectivity. Is the aspiration to objectivism as such the cardinal sin?" Or, is any attempt to have one's vision prevail morally objectionable?

18. These two justifications are chosen from many possibilities. They are, however, those which seem most influential at the present moment.

particularity. Each defines the other in such a way as to make the universality criterion always open to negotiation through the particularities of difference." In an article countering the relativizing thrust of postmodernist thought, Harvey accepts that the content of the term justice takes on different meanings depending on social, geographical, and historical context. At the same time he insists that the word retains usefulness as a mobilizing concept because of shared interpretations:

> Justice and rationality take on different meanings across space and time and persons, yet the existence of everyday meanings to which people do attach importance and which to them appear unproblematic, gives the terms a political and mobilizing power that can never be neglected. Right and wrong are words that power revolutionary changes and no amount of negative deconstruction of such terms can deny that. (Harvey 2002, 398)

Although Harvey indicates that it is not possible for him to formulate an abstract definition of justice, he nevertheless develops precepts that are, presumably, the ones on which "people" can agree.[19]

One way of dealing with the universalism/particularism debate is to apply Karl Mannheim's (1936, 281) argument in his essay on "The Sociology of Knowledge." Here he calls for the "acquisition of perspective" so as to overcome the "talking past one another" of groups in conflict. Mannheim is arguing that the historical situatedness of concepts does not preclude the possibility of a transcendent ethic, for this ethic will be reshaped and reinterpreted within differing historical realities. Consciousness derives from group identification *and also* from rational formulations. Mannheim assumes that when history is taken into account by all participants, thinking individuals can find a common ground. His is essentially a Hegelian exercise in its acceptance of the concept of the rational subject who is capable of making comparisons and learning. Unlike Hegel, however, he does not contend that history is reason revealed, and he takes material as well as mental forces into account.

---

19. He derives from the work of Iris Marion Young six propositions to govern a just planning and policy practice that incorporate these "everyday meanings." These are, in brief, the nonexploitation of labor power, the elimination of forms of marginalization of social groups, access to political power and self-expression by oppressed groups, elimination of cultural imperialism, humane forms of social control, and mitigation of the adverse ecological impacts of social projects (Harvey 2002, 400–401).

Within Mannheim's conceptualization we can continue to hold up fairness as the key to social justice while developing its content differently depending on our social position and historical location. Such an activity requires both self-criticism and criticism of the other. In particular, there is no "other," whether high or low on the social hierarchy, so privileged as to be immunized from outside criticism. If the concept of social justice acquires a sociohistorical content, the meaning of freedom incorporated within it switches from the liberal formulation of "freedom from," as well as from the Foucaultian notion of resistance, to a more complex idea incorporating the concept of self-development. Freedom then includes the acceptance of obligations for which, in Nancy Hirschmann's (1992, 235) words, "consent is not only unavailable but of questionable relevance." Equality likewise shifts its connotations and is measured not by sameness of condition but by reciprocity, communication, and the mutual acceptance of obligation, especially for the raising of children. Indeed, some inequalities of power or benefits, stemming from rewards for merit, response to need, or the provision of general welfare, can be interpreted as just (Runciman 1966; Simmel 1950, 73–78).

At this time there is sufficient consensus on the value of justice, if not its particular manifestations, to support its application to all public policy decisions. But, as Brian Berry asserts (2005, 10), "the absence of an explicit conception of social justice in political life has the result that arguments about public policy are made without any attempt to explain from the ground up what is their justification." Those who instead give first priority to the efficiency principle,[20] to democratic deliberation, or to culture and tradition would not deny the importance of justice but instead either see it as subsumed by these other values or of lesser importance. My argument, which will be detailed later, is that there is not always a trade-off between justice and efficiency, but when there is, the demands of justice should prevail. Beyond that, I accept that its actual content requires debate; Benhabib (2002, 39) terms such a view "a historically enlightened universalism." It is my intention to formulate and defend a set of principles that constitute the core of just urban policies that can be developed

---

20. In a rather extraordinary rhetorical move, economists use the term "moral hazard" to refer to inefficiencies caused by groups or individuals taking on risk or receiving benefits for which others bear the costs. One frequently used example is the overuse of health facilities by insured individuals. It is never applied to labor exploitation or other forms of injustice that noneconomists might regard as presenting a greater moral hazard. It is an interesting formulation for a discipline that normally wholly eschews considerations of morality.

at the local level. For the moment the key point is that making justice the first principle by which to evaluate urban planning and policy is essential and *is not met without ascribing to it a substantive content:*

> The whole point of a universalistic conception of justice is that it provides a basis on which both those inside and those outside a country can criticize practices and institutions that reflect local norms, which typically endorse discrimination, exploitation and oppression.
>
> In every society, the prevailing belief system has been largely created by those with the most power—typically, elderly males belonging to the majority ethnic and religious groups. (Berry 2005, 27)

Cornel West (1991), who like Harvey draws from the Marxian philosophical tradition, perceives values as historically developed within a community. Thus, he similarly avoids the Kantian position of the categorical imperative and regards morality as socially constructed. Nevertheless, he stresses that communally held values form the basis of critique of existing power relations and of human progress. He argues that "the point is not to lift oneself out of the flux of history…but rather to immerse oneself more deeply into history by consciously identifying with—and digesting *critically* the values of—a particular community or tradition" (West 1991, 3).[21] The purpose for him, as for Harvey, is to use commonly held values as the basis for mobilizing publics toward the end of a more just society. If a definition of justice can be applied broadly, then it represents what Maeve Cooke (2006, 22) calls a "context-transcending view," according to which "the concept of ethical progress can be applied across historical and social contexts."

The thesis that the application of a concept of substantive justice can be based on consensus draws on a Habermasian formulation of what people would be persuaded to desire were they in a situation governed by norms of sincerity, truth-telling, and rationality.[22] In the words of Iris Marion Young (2000, 30), "A process of public deliberation under these ideal conditions provides both the motivation to take all needs and interests

---

21. Unless otherwise indicated, italics are in the original.

22. This is Hilary Putnam's (2002, 113) summary of the Habermasian norms of communicative action.

into account and knowledge of what they are.... Each understands that his or her best interests will be served by aiming for a just result."

Similarly, in his discussion of the inseparability of fact and value, Hilary Putnam (2002, 45), while recognizing that there can be no absolutist concept of morality, nevertheless argues that people can "discuss and try things out cooperatively" to arrive at a set of principles. From this starting point he (2002, 44) posits that these principles will include "the welfare of others regardless of national, ethnic, or religious boundaries." Although he does not use the same terminology, concern with the welfare of others equates with Young's statement regarding "aiming for a just result." Likewise, Frank Fischer (1980, 194) considers that there exists a general consensus on certain values: "Widespread agreement exists on the general primacy of ideals such as ... the reduction of human suffering, the protection of human life ... and social reciprocity."[23] Again the implication is that, while ideals arise out of discourse, justice is one that is widely held and not limited to citizens of liberal democracies.

Even Martha Nussbaum (2000, 151), who takes a Kantian, deontological position in favor of universal values, considers that ultimately "*people from a wide variety of cultures,* coming together in conditions conducive to reflective criticism of tradition, and free from intimidation and hierarchy, *should agree* that this list [of capabilities] is a good one" (emphasis added).[24] She comments that "relativists tend ... to understate the amount of attunement, recognition, and overlap that actually obtains across cultures" (Nussbaum 1993, 261). Although her list of capabilities goes beyond simply justice, justice is one of the fundamental dimensions of her ethical position and, she asserts, is supported by commonly held ideals as well as philosophical deduction.

Thus, justice can be seen as the consensual outcome of deliberation under hypothetical ideal conditions. As mentioned above and to be discussed in more depth later, the concept of truthful communication is an insufficient guide to producing justice in actual policy making, but it does support a higher order argument for employing justice, however defined, as an evaluative criterion.

---

23. Fischer includes political freedom in his list. Although this value does permeate democratic societies, it is much less universally endorsed than the others he names.

24. Nussbaum's theory of capabilities will be discussed later. The point here is that she does not take a purely universalist moral position but also recognizes the importance of agreement on values.

The Rawlsian Argument

John Rawls's argument for a just distribution of primary goods begins with a formulation based on rational responses to a hypothetical situation. His work constitutes the dominant foundation for contemporary discussions of justice and its relation to equality.[25] As is well known, Rawls begins by positing an original position in which individuals, behind a veil of ignorance, are unaware of their status in whatever society to which they will belong. In the original position individuals will act fairly and therefore articulate the elements of a just society. Rawls's first principle is liberty and his second, subsidiary principle is "difference," by which he means that there should be equality of opportunity and that any inequality should be to the benefit of the least-advantaged member of society (Rawls 2001, 42). His argument is that free individuals, acting rationally, will choose a rough equality of primary goods so as to assure that they will not end up in an inferior position. In his most recent formulation, he states that this involves "a framework of political and legal institutions that adjust the long-run trend of economic forces so as to prevent excessive concentrations of property and wealth, especially those likely to lead to political domination" (Rawls 2001, 44).

Rawls has been so influential because, within a vocabulary acceptable to proponents of rational choice theory, he presents a logical argument that defends equality of primary goods as the basis of justice without resorting to natural law, theology, altruism, Marxist teleology, or a diagnosis of human nature. Rawls's original position is comparable to Habermas's ideal speech situation; in both instances the outcome is a theory of justice formulated under conditions that ensure fairness. Rawls, however, does not base his argument on communication, and in presenting the difference principle, he deduces that equality of primary goods constitutes the content of justice. Disagreement arises over the principles that should define what is just and unjust rather than the precedence of justice itself (Rawls 1971, 5).

Questions Raised

Based on the arguments from consensus and fairness, justice becomes a primary criterion for evaluating public policy. Because these are arguments

---

25. The original formulation is contained in Rawls (1971). A revised and edited version that takes into account some of the responses since the original publication is in Rawls (2001).

at the highest level of generality, the choice to employ this criterion need not be remade in each instance of decision making, and it can be applied whether or not the decision is made through a democratic process.[26] Once we accept the criterion of justice, we then face the following questions in applying it to the urban milieu:

1. What are the qualities comprising a just city within the wealthy Western world?[27] If the content of justice is defined by a community, and the city is made up of diverse communities, whose definition should prevail, particularly if diversity, democracy, and sustainability, not just equitable material distribution, are constitutive of justice?

2. To what extent have the qualities of a just city been realized in the recent history (1970–2009) of Western cities, as represented by New York, London, and Amsterdam? Issues to consider include the components of redevelopment programs, the character of public space, the extent and character of property rights, the extent of redistributional programs, and the relations among and spatial distribution of different social groups.

3. What are the economic and social forces, politics, planning, and policies that have shaped this history? What has been the interaction between social forces and governmental activity, and to what extent has the public sector been able to act autonomously? How constrained is the city by its national context and by the forces of global competition?

4. What strategies can be followed at the subnational level to improve social justice and what are the institutions/social movements that might bring them about? Is there reason to expect that a benevolent state, guided by a competent bureaucracy, will be the leader in promoting progressive change? Do social movements carry with them the hope of transformation toward a more just

---

26. See Fischer (1980) for an argument concerning the different levels of normative judgment in policy analysis. Although the concept of the just city is a social construction and originates in discourse, it is developed at a different level of analysis from the consideration of whether a particular policy promotes justice (see Fischer 1980 and 2003). Goals are not simply there to be "discovered" in the form of preferences, but neither are they redeveloped *ad hoc* in each interchange (Lindblom 1990; Giddens 1990).

27. I do not consider myself in a position to treat cities in developing countries, although some of the arguments to be presented are applicable to them as well.

society?[28] Is it possible to promote growth and equity simultaneously (i.e., what is the relationship between competitiveness and cohesion)?

Crosscutting these broad, historically rooted questions are the issues of process versus outcomes and specificity versus universality. To what extent does the character of the decisional process influence the justice of its outcomes and do certain kinds of procedures favor particular groups? Does enhancing citizen participation produce more just results? Can the conclusions drawn from cases in one place be applied to others? This book only examines cases in the developed world. My unwillingness to tackle the issue of urban justice in developing countries arises from my view that, even while the principle of justice should apply everywhere, approaches in relatively affluent locations cannot be simply reproduced in poor cities.

Nonreformist Reforms

Proposing strategies for reform of urban programs raises two general issues. One concerns the amount of urban autonomy. The extent to which cities can engage in strongly redistributive programs is limited by the welfare policies of their national governments.[29] Cities cannot be viewed in isolation; they exist within networks of governmental institutions and capital flows. Robert Dahl, in a classic 1967 article, referred to the Chinese box problem of participation and power: at the level of the neighborhood, there is the greatest opportunity for democracy but the least amount of power; as we scale up the amount of decision-making power increases, but the potential of people to affect outcomes diminishes. The city level therefore is one layer in the hierarchy of governance. But the variation that exists among cities within the same country in relation to values such as tolerance, quality of public services, availability of affordable housing,

---

28. Giddens (1990) and Castells (2000a) both see the basis of structural transformation in broad-based social movements such as environmentalism and feminism rather than in class-based parties.

29. In Fainstein (2001b) I argue that the most egalitarian city-regions exist within nations that have a highly active welfare state and that city governments can opt for more redistributive policies when they are less dependent on their own revenue base. Paul Peterson (1981) asserts that localities cannot afford redistributive policies because supporting welfare measures with high taxation would drive out capital investment.

segregation/integration, points to a degree of autonomy. This is especially the case in the United States, where the federal system, traditions of home rule, and national withdrawal from urban programs have intensified local differences. Even in the United Kingdom, however, despite a highly centralized governmental system, local leadership has caused cities to follow different paths (see Judd and Parkinson 1990).

Thus, although the amount of support from other levels of government constrains the capacity of urban regimes to redistribute resources, it is still possible to develop a concept of justice relevant to what is within city government's power and in terms of the goals of urban movements (Fainstein and Hirst 1995). Castells (1977) does not consider cities to be the spatial formation that defines production, but he regards them as the locus of collective consumption—that is, the place in which citizens can acquire collective goods that make up for deficiencies in earnings. Consequently he considers that urban social movements can potentially produce a municipal revolution even if they cannot achieve social transformation (Castells 1983). According to this logic, then, *urban movements do have transformative potential despite being limited to achieving change only at the level in which they are operating.* It is this level that comprises the concern of this book.

The second, and more problematic, issue is the extent to which redistribution and recognition (i.e., respectful acknowledgment of culturally different groups) are possible under capitalism. Nancy Fraser (2003, 70–82) distinguishes between affirmative and transformational strategies for addressing injustice. The former corrects inequitable outcomes without disturbing the underlying social structure, while the latter works by changing the social framework that gives rise to injustice. She notes that although transformative strategies may be preferable in principle, they are difficult to achieve in practice. She finds a middle ground by calling for "nonreformist reforms," which would operate within existing social frameworks but "set in motion a trajectory of change in which more radical reforms become practicable over time" (Fraser 2003, 79).[30]

The concept refers back to the debate over a century ago among socialists regarding whether reform was possible within capitalist democracies and is particularly associated with Eduard Bernstein. In contrast to orthodox Marxists, "democratic revisionists shared an emphasis…on

---

30. The term originated in Gorz (1967).

morality and ethics as opposed to science and materialism, and on human will and cross-class cooperation rather than irresistible economic forces and inevitable class conflict" (Berman 2003, 121). As many commentators have observed, Karl Marx's argument concerning the inevitability of capitalism's collapse under the weight of its own contradictions and of a socialist revolution led by an empowered proletariat both lacks historical support and leaves opponents of capitalist inequality with little to do short of revolution.[31] Consequently transformational movements aimed at a more egalitarian society must find a rationale based in human motivation rather than historical inevitability and, if not committed to or expecting revolution, must seek to achieve their aims through politics. The development of practical alternatives to the status quo and neoliberal hegemony becomes the primary task for those with a moral commitment to human betterment: "reforms as well as radical actions may be working towards profound and far-reaching changes in the expectations which govern [structural] relationships" (Marris 1987, 148). As Erik Olin Wright contends: "[Alternative] institutional designs can become part of pragmatic projects of social reform within capitalist society. There are many possible capitalisms with many different ways of interjecting non-capitalist principles within social and economic institutions" (Wright 2006, 22).[32]

This then is the purpose of this book—to recommend nonreformist reforms directed at improving the lives of residents of cities within Western Europe and the United States. It is my hope to shift the conversation within discussions of planning and public policy toward the character of urban areas, lessen the focus on process that has become dominant within planning theory,[33] and redirect practitioners from their obsession with economic development to a concern with social equity. Unquestionably there is a relationship between the types of procedures employed

---

31. Marxist critique leaves planners seeking justice with few opportunities since, in Peter Hall's (2002, 371) words, they "could never hope to divert the course of capitalist evolution by more than a millimeter or a millisecond....The Marxian logic is strangely quietist: it suggest that the planner retreats from planning altogether into the academic ivory tower." See also Fainstein and Fainstein (1979).

32. See also Cooke (2006), chap. 3; Fraser (1997); Fung (2005).

33. Although the concern of communicative rationality planning theorists is with public officials who have the responsibility for city planning, they do not discuss the merits of actual policies for cities but instead dwell on the interactions among planners, politicians, and stakeholders. See Fainstein (2005b) and Beauregard (1990) for a discussion of the loss of the city as the object of planning.

and social outcomes, between institutional forms and the distribution of benefits, between growth and the possibility of improvements for those at the bottom. Nevertheless, democratic procedures do not always produce egalitarian outcomes, technical/scientific ones incorporate disguised normative biases, growth does not necessarily trickle down, and popular preferences may be misguided.

If the just city becomes the object of planning theory, how then should we approach theory development? Leonie Sandercock presents one strategy in her book *Towards Cosmopolis*. Her definition of the just city is one that is socially inclusive, where difference is not merely tolerated but treated with recognition and respect. She thus asserts that she wishes to connect "planning theory with other theoretical discourses—specifically debates around marginality, identity and difference, and social justice in the city—because these are debates which empower groups whose voices are not often heard by planners" (Sandercock 1998, 110). John Friedmann (2002, 104) presents a utopian vision and relates it to critique: "Moral outrage over an injustice suggests that we have a sense of justice, inarticulate though it may be....If injustice is to be corrected...we will need the concrete imagery of utopian thinking to propose steps that would bring us a little closer to a more just world."[34] In an argument concerning how utopian thinking can influence history, Hajer and Reijndorp (2001), in a book that examines how the goal of environmental sustainability has gradually penetrated society, delineate the interweaving of coalition politics, discourse, and concern with outcomes. The relating of politics to vision, of policy to justice, constitutes the form of realistic utopianism that is the purpose of this book.

Organization of the Book

The next chapter elaborates on the philosophical approaches to the problem of justice briefly touched on here. In particular, it examines conflicting views on the issues of equality, democracy, and diversity. The question of

---

34. Similarly Maeve Cooke (2006, 162) supports a utopianism that locates "emancipatory potentials within existing historical reality that can be actualized by autonomously thinking and acting human beings." She contrasts this both to the abstract finalism of detailed utopian visions, on the one hand, and the Marxist conception of historical inevitability on the other. David Harvey (2009) also rejects a utopianism of spatial form while calling for a dialectical utopianism.

sustainability will also be raised, but this will be a subsidiary discussion—not because of its lack of importance but simply because it is too difficult to encompass within a single book. Chapter 2 focuses on the moral issues raised by programs aimed at urban revitalization and the applicability of theories of justice to their implementation. This discussion is followed by three chapters devoted to case studies of revitalization efforts in New York, London, and Amsterdam. Chapter 6 examines a number of the issues raised by the case studies, including the commodification of urban life, the impact of tourism as a leading industry, the right to the city as it plays itself out in public space, relations among urban subareas and between city and suburb, and participation in planning. Finally the book concludes with a series of principles to govern policy with the aim of furthering the goal of the just city.

1

PHILOSOPHICAL APPROACHES TO THE PROBLEM OF JUSTICE

Developing a vision of the just city requires coping with the vast outpouring of scholarship on justice that has followed on the publication of John Rawls's foundational work, *A Theory of Justice* (1971). The issues most germane to urban policy in these writings center on what constitute criteria of justice. I have therefore distilled the discussions in the philosophical literature and planning theory down to the four topics that seem most relevant to my concerns: (1) the relation of democratic processes to just outcomes; (2) the criterion of equity; (3) the criterion of recognition; and (4) the tensions among democracy, equity, and diversity.

My contention is that the tendency of recent theory in both political philosophy and planning to emphasize democratic processes as key to justice overly idealizes open communication and neglects the substance of debate. After defending the priority I give equity, I go on to interrogate the usefulness of respect for difference as defining urban justice then argue for the merit of Sen and Nussbaum's capabilities approach in relation to formulating the value basis of the just city. I agree with David Harvey's argument, referred to in the introduction, that the content of the term justice takes on different meanings depending on social, geographical, and historical context. Thus, my discussion, while based on an overarching concept of justice, is intended to address its meaning at the beginning of the twenty-first century in cities of the wealthy, Western world, where neoliberal formulations have become powerful influences on urban policy.

Democratic Processes and Just Outcomes

Much of the recent critical theory within planning and public policy focuses on the decision-making process.[1] Demands for transparency, inclusion, and negotiation in public decisions were a reaction to the top-down, technocratic approach underlying governmental programs such as urban renewal, exclusionary zoning, and placement of toxic-producing facilities. The premise of the critique, leading to a call for open processes, is that the inequitable impacts of urban programs resulted from blocking the voices of affected publics. The logic of this analysis caused an intense focus on the process of communication. Much of this critique is in my view appropriate but the remedy proposed—a more open, more democratic process—fails to confront adequately the initial discrepancy of power, offers few clues to overcoming co-optation or resistance to reform, does not sufficiently address some of the major weaknesses of democratic theory, and diverts discussion from the substance of policy.

Two somewhat different routes, one epistemological (or postpositivist), and the other practice oriented, led to the development of arguments establishing the communicative model as the normative standard for planning and policy making. The epistemological approach is primarily concerned with how alternative policies are derived and expressed; the practice-oriented approach examines the process of choosing among alternatives. In the remainder of this chapter I lay out the basic arguments supporting the communicative model according to each approach. Then I present my reasoning in criticizing the communicative model's assumption that a just process necessarily produces a just result.

Epistemological Approach

The communicative model calls for knowledge that is situated contextually and that relies on reasoning, empathy, and a variety of kinds of evidence to support policy proposals. Its methodology shuns positivist policy analysis as both biased and based on disingenuous claims of being value-free or objective. Positivism is defined as requiring social science investigation to conform to the same procedures as the natural sciences: "Because only empirically based causal knowledge can qualify social science as a genuine 'scientific' endeavour, social scientists are instructed to

---

1. See, inter alia, Healey (2006), Fischer and Forester (1993), Forester (1999), Innes (1995).

eschew normative orientations and to limit their research investigations to empirical or 'factual' phenomena" (Fischer 2003, 122). In contrast, the epistemology of communicative rationality is based on the postpositivist thesis that no identifiable objective reality exists but rather only interpretations of reality. Consequently the marshaling of facts and the measurement of costs and benefits, presented in the form of testable hypotheses and usually represented quantitatively, obfuscates the assumptions and normative framework that underlie the analysis. For example, the decision to allocate funds for highway construction typically uses calculations of the monetary value of time savings as the metric by which to evaluate the relationship between project costs and public benefits. Other sorts of considerations—such as the possibly greater good of diverting funds to health care or education, the subjective value of the time of nonearners such as parents caring for children, the greater safety of public transit, and the polluting effects of auto transport—are not part of the calculation. They could, of course, be attributed monetary value and be included in the analysis, but the prices attached to each element and the weightings of the different considerations would be subjective. In other words, the calculation of what matters and how much weight to place on each consideration is necessarily value-based and includes a number of important considerations that may have been excluded from the start.

Because, in the postpositivist approach, appropriate decisional procedures involve a mix of value statements, empirical evidence, and subjective perceptions, its proponents consider that we should regard policy making and planning as argumentative practices not as quasi sciences (Fischer and Forester 1993, 2). As such, the process is socially constructed and its resolution is the result of the interaction of the parties involved. Within a democratic community each party should have its say, and no privileged hierarchy, whether based on power or technical expertise, should exist. The epistemology of postpositivism thus leads to a concern with how knowledge is communicated and to an acceptance of a variety of ways of conveying an argument, including especially the construction of a narrative that may include logical argumentation, anecdotes, and emotional responses as well as quantitative measurements.

Practice Orientation

Planning theorists identifying themselves with the communicative model derive their position from the philosophical traditions of Deweyan pragmatism and Habermasian rationality. Whereas John Dewey's work comes out of Anglo-American philosophical realism and empiricism, Habermas's philosophy traces back to Hegelian idealism and Marxist critical analysis and proceeds to encompass Wittgenstein's scrutiny of language. Communicative rationality and neopragmatism converge in planning theory when used to provide a guide for action, as both emphasize the importance of process in determining the rightness of choices and shy away from providing abstract criteria for evaluating the content of decisions. The concept of communicative planning thus starts with the proposition that decisions should be reached "by an intersubjective effort at mutual understanding…[that] refocuses the practices of planning to enable purposes to be communicatively discovered"[2] (Healey 1996, 239).

Neopragmatists tend toward empiricism, searching for instances of best practices from which generalizations can be drawn:

> The big question for the pragmatic analysts is how practitioners construct the free spaces in which democratic planning can be institutionalized. The idea…is to uncover examples of planning that are both competent and democratic, and then to explore who the practitioners were who did it, what actions they took to make it happen, and what sorts of institutional conditions helped or hindered their efforts. (Hoch 1996, 42; see also Innes 1995)

Although the "best practices" approach of pragmatism would seemingly imply a judgment as to outcomes, it finesses the issue by avoiding the development of a guide to what is "best" or, as Hoch puts it, "competent."

Communicative planning theory parallels the ideas that political scientists have originated around deliberative democracy.[3] Within planning

---

2. The expectation of consensus or mutual understanding does not characterize all contemporary democratic theorists. Thus, I. M. Young (2000) expects irresolvable conflicts of interest; Chantal Mouffe (2000, 2005) develops a theory of "agonistic democracy," where the only consensus is on acceptance of basic democratic institutions; Mark Purcell's (2008) "radical pluralist" version of democracy likewise sees the continuation of clashing, particularistic interests. Patsy Healey (2003, 114) herself writes that the results of argumentative processes can be "liberating and creative, but they may also be oppressive."

3. Freeman (2000, 382, emphasis added) summarizes the precepts of deliberative democracy as follows: "Conceived as an ideal of political relations, a deliberative democracy is one in which political agents or their representatives (a) aim to collectively deliberate and vote (b) their sincere and informed judgments regarding (c) measures conducive to the common good of citizens. (d) Political agents are seen and see one another as democratic citizens who are politically free and equal participants in civic life. (e) A background of constitutional rights

theory the idea of planning as pluralistic, requiring negotiation among opposed interests, was spelled out in Paul Davidoff's (2003) famous article on advocacy planning. Originally published in 1965, the piece called on planners to work for the benefit of disadvantaged groups rather than as impartial technicians. Davidoff made an analogy between legal and planning advocacy and essentially proposed that planners frame briefs on behalf of their clients. His argument derived directly from J. S. Mill's (1951, 108) contentions regarding the importance of testing ideas against each other: "He [a human being] is capable of rectifying his mistakes, by discussion and experience....There must be discussion, to show how experience is to be interpreted."

Demands by the New Left for participatory democracy during the 1960s and '70s, as well as the revolt against top-down planning mounted by urban protest movements of that time, inspired social scientists on the left to reconsider democratic theory. They were searching for concepts that would support a vision of democracy extending beyond periodic voting and simple preference aggregation. The social movements of the 1960s and '70s had made them aware that the model of representative democracy wherein politicians chose policies and bureaucrats simply executed them deviated from reality—a reality in which bureaucratic and planning decisions took place in a realm of considerable autonomy (Lipsky 1980). Despite the decline of urban movements in the last part of the twentieth century, expectations of citizen participation and its institutionalization (along with the decentralization of governmental functions in many cities) meant that the issue of democratic procedures remained

---

and *all-purpose social means* enable citizens to take advantage of their opportunities to participate in public life. (f) Citizens are individually free in that they have their own freely determined conceptions of the good, and these conceptions are publicly seen as legitimate even though they are independent of political purposes. Moreover, (g) free citizens have diverse and incongruous conceptions of the good, which are constitutionally protected by basic rights. Because of this diversity (h) citizens recognize a duty in their public political deliberations to cite public reasons—considerations that all reasonable citizens can accept in their capacity as democratic citizens—and to avoid public argument on the basis of reasons peculiar to their particular moral, religious, and philosophical views and incompatible with public reason. (i) What makes these reasons public is that they are related to and in some way advance the common interests of citizens. (j) Primary among the common interests of citizens are their freedom, independence, and equal civic status." "All-purpose social means" refers to the background condition of relative equality. Similarly Ackerman (1980, 28) specifies material equality as a prerequisite for "liberal political dialogue." See also, inter alia, Dryzek (1990) and Gutmann and Thompson (1996).

pertinent. During those years community activists continued to challenge the legitimacy of insulated technocratic decision making by planning authorities (Scott 1998), and a variety of citizen groups were integrated into governmental practices.

The theory of deliberative democracy emerged within political science to counteract the dominance of the interest-based public choice paradigm and its conservative tendency. Theorists in this vein deny that individuals have fixed preferences, based on self-interest, that can simply be registered; instead they claim that people's views are informed through interaction with others. As a riposte to economistic thinking within social analysis, this represents a progressive move, but it does not adequately confront the constraints on democracy in a society where resources are privately owned and controlled.

Relationship between Inclusive Deliberation, Equity, and Justice

In its reliance on good will, communicative planning theory typically passes over structural conflicts of interest and shrinks from analyzing the social context that blocks consensus building.[4] Socialist theory and practice, on the other hand, do concern themselves with the question of equity. In its Marxist form socialist theory called for public ownership of the means of production. As socialism operated in the Soviet Union and Eastern Europe, it involved state ownership of economic enterprises; for the social democratic parties of Western Europe the collective ideal was pursued by redistributing privately generated revenues through the state sector. The socialist dream, however, faded with the fall of the Soviet bloc and ceased to offer the lodestar it once presented for leftist thinkers. The failures of socialism as it really existed, along with the heightened

---

4. In their critique of network theory, which comprises one strand within communicative planning theory (see Albrechts and Mandelbaum 2005), Moulaert and Cabaret (2006, 60) comment: "Overemphasis on the role of interpersonal relations and trust in institution building obscures the role of structures and institutions, and the danger looms that the network is idealized as a form of social organization." Mark Purcell (2009, 141) asserts: "What the neoliberal project requires are decision-making practices that are widely accepted as 'democratic' but that do not (or cannot) fundamentally challenge existing relations of power. Communicative planning, insofar as it is rooted in communicative action, is just such a decision-making practice." In other words communicative planning is essentially conservative in relation to existing structures.

individualism, consumerism, and decline of traditional working-class occupations in Western Europe, caused the social democratic parties to moderate their egalitarian programs. It also called into question the potential of the state, if it had total economic control, to embody the interests of its citizens.

Demands for greater democracy, undistorted discourse, and recognition of difference seemed to promise greater equity as a consequence of the stronger representation of the interests of nonelite groups: "The deliberative democrat thinks that the best way to limit political domination and...to promote greater social justice through public policy is to foster the creation of sites and processes of deliberation among diverse and disagreeing elements of the polity" (Young 2001, 672).[5] This approach, however, depends on a benign hope that reasoned discussion will produce just outcomes without any predetermined program indicating the content of justice or designating which participants in the discussion hold the moral high ground. As Nancy Fraser (1997, 2) asserts: "No new comprehensive progressive vision of a just social order has emerged to take socialism's place. Proposals to elevate 'radical democracy' and 'multiculturalism' to that status express the desire in some quarters for such a vision." Or, as Bronner (1999, 18) has less sympathetically put it, "democracy has become the answer to every question and the solution to every problem."

The ideal that everyone's opinion should be respectfully heard and that no particular group should be privileged in an interchange is an important normative argument. But it is not a sufficient one, and it does not deal adequately with the classic conundrums of democracy. These include ensuring adequate representation of all interests in a large, socially divided group, protecting against demagoguery, achieving more than token public participation, preventing economically or institutionally powerful interests from defining the agenda, and maintaining minority rights. Political theorists have endlessly disputed these issues, and they remain unresolved.

Democratic thought is theoretically weak when it is not tied to an economic program. If pressed, advocates will admit that deliberative democracy operates poorly in situations of social and economic inequality and indicate that background conditions of equal respect and undistorted speech must be created in order for it to function well. Yet, oddly,

---

5. Young (2000) herself calls for a social-movement-based approach to democracy, wherein protest and civil disobedience are acceptable methods of participation.

discussions within political and planning theory focus on democratic procedures without tackling the thornier problem of overcoming enormous inequalities of wealth and power when argument alone comes up short. To put this in other words, the analysis is purely political rather than political-economic: "Liberalism assumes the autonomy of the political in a very strong form. Liberal political theory assumes that it is possible to organize a democratic form of political life on the basis of socioeconomic and sociosexual structures that generate systemic inequalities" (Fraser 1997).

In an unequal society democracy and justice are frequently at odds. My criticism of the proceduralist emphasis in planning theory is not directed at its extension of democracy beyond electoral participation but rather at a faith in the efficacy of open communication that ignores the reality of structural inequality and hierarchies of power.[6] Moreover, it slides over the question of whether in an existing historical context citizens are good judges of their own interests or the public good. After deliberation has run its course, people may still make choices that are harmful to themselves or to minorities.[7] As Nussbaum (2000, 135) notes, the "informed-desire approach...[to democratic decision making depends on] the idea of a community of equals, unintimidated by power or authority, and unaffected by envy or fear inspired by awareness of their place in a social hierarchy." Gutmann and Thompson (1996, 348) likewise specify necessary conditions for meaningful deliberation: basic liberty, basic opportunity, and fair opportunity (see also Freeman 2000, 414). They state that their conception of the deliberative perspective "explicitly rejects the idea, sometimes identified with deliberative democracy, that deliberation under the right conditions...is sufficient to legitimate laws and public policies" (Gutmann and Thompson 1996, 200). In other words, democratic deliberation functions properly only in situations of equal opportunity (see also Cohen 1996).

There is an element of circularity or infinite regress in these arguments. Communicative theorists assume that processes with unjust consequences must not have been genuinely open or else participants

---

6. For critiques of communicative planning theory in regard to its overemphasis on process, its disregard for questions of the implementation of agreements, and its overlooking of what Yiftachel calls "the dark side of planning," see Fainstein (2000); H. Campbell (2006); Watson (2006); and Yiftachel (1999).

7. Mill (1951, 89) was fearful of "the tyranny of the prevailing opinion and feeling."

were inadequately informed as a result of distorted communication. The model assumes that participants know their own interests, or at least will discover them through the process of debate, and that by discussion they will transform the structures producing the background conditions necessary for deliberation. Marx's concept of false consciousness, in which unequal social relations structure people's perceptions, and Antonio Gramsci's description of a hegemonic ideology come into play. Individuals may be free to express their thoughts to each other yet remain prisoners of existing social relations, institutions, and ideologies that cause them to accept programs contrary to their own long-term interests.[8] This is especially so when dominant elites control communications media.

Iris Marion Young, Chantal Mouffe, Mark Purcell, and others, while supporting strong democracy, break with the form of the communicative model developed within planning theory. They maintain that a pluralistic, decentered form of democratic participation, in which social movements press strong demands, will incorporate equity goals and thereby reduce injustice. Everything, however, depends on the content of those demands. If we look, for example, at the bases of anti-immigrant sentiment in the United States and Europe or the antiabortion movement, we find illiberal social movements with a broad base of popular support. The response that if populist views are misguided, the cause is distorted communication is fatuous when the path to political power lies precisely in making emotional appeals, especially since many communicative theorists break with Habermas's emphasis on rationality in discourse, instead endorsing rhetoric and storytelling modes of persuasion (Sandercock 1998, chap. 3).

False consciousness is not only a left-wing concept. Conservative theorists contend that the mass of people, out of ignorance or the influence of demagogues, will act contrary to the public interest. In terms of social issues capitalist elites may be more tolerant than mass publics. The notion that policy makers could be above the political fray and make decisions based on an abstract formulation of the public good arose from a perception that people will choose policies based on short-range selfish considerations. It is used to justify protecting bureaucracies from

---

8. Wolff, Moore, and Marcuse (1969) argue that as a consequence of capitalist hegemony, tolerance—that is, allowing the free play of ideas—can be repressive through marginalizing all discourse outside the mainstream. This view has more recently been taken up by Wendy Brown (2006).

political input. Although this viewpoint obviously can provide a rationale for authoritarianism and privileging the interests of elites, it cannot be simply dismissed. Citizens, like elites, can be misguided and self-serving, as indicated by the prevalence of NIMBYism within forums of popular participation.

In their rejection of autocratic policy determination, communicative theorists disregard the possibility that paternalism and bureaucratic modes of decision making may produce desirable outcomes. Yet, various studies of the European welfare states and of the New Deal in the United States have concluded that the principal programs for ensuring health and security were generated by state officials with little reference to interested publics.[9] Even though these measures would not have been approved without supportive constituencies and the threat of oppositional social movements, the actual formulation of policy (i.e., the planning of it) occurred without much stakeholder input. Although a commitment to democratic values for their own sake counters a call for benevolent despotism and leads us to wish for citizen input, we cannot deny out of hand that insulated decision making may produce more just outcomes than public participation. The gains won by the American civil rights movement initially were the product of judicial decisions, not legislative enactments. Contemporary Singapore could be classified as a benevolent despotism, and despite the limits it places on liberty, and especially on democracy, it produces a very high quality of life for its citizens. On the other hand, we can probably think of many more instances where authoritarian decision making caused outcomes strongly biased toward upper class interests.

The indeterminate and variable quality of bureaucratic decision making points to the character of the state as an important contextual variable that needs to be accounted for in any prescription for deliberation:

> The connection of planning to spatial policies of the state is what gives the practice of planning its specificity, whether we talk about governance, governmentality, or insurgent planning. The practices of urban/spatial/environmental/community planning are connected in diverse and changing ways to the state, its powers and resources deployed in projects of spatial management.

---

9. See Flora and Heidenheimer 1981; Mencher 1967; Evans, Rueschemeyer, and Skocpol 1985.

Theories ignoring this context risk losing their explanatory potential for prescriptive utility. (Huxley and Yiftachel 2000, 339)

When state power is mobilized for elite interests, effective democracy can
counter its unjust effects; when reformers manage to hold state power, justice might be best achieved by allowing officeholders to make decisions.

A further problem of the deliberative approach arises from the relationship between speech and action. Major changes in social consciousness require deeper transformations than mere verbal assent (Lukács
1971). Even if perceptions of interest are biased or misdirected by distorted speech and even if structures are socially produced, changing
speech alone does not transform the structures that shape consciousness.
Karl Marx and Friedrich Engels (1947), in their critique of the Hege-
lians, assert that the world was changed through struggle, not the force of
ideas. They do not mean, as they are often misinterpreted, that economic
structures automatically determine outcomes and that human agency is
helpless to affect them. But they do mean that words will not prevail if
unsupported by a social force carrying with it a threat of disruption.

An intervening stage of mobilization is required between the formulation of ideas and social action, and the two are dialectically related. Ideas
can give rise to social movements that in turn change consciousness, ultimately resulting in the adoption of new public policy, but this is more
than a matter of negotiation and consensus building among stakeholders.
In the instances of feminism, environmentalism, antitax programs, and
neoliberalism—the most effective social movements of the last decades
in the West—discontent among influential fractions of the population
became a social force when mobilized by ideas that defined both a reason
for feelings of dissatisfaction and a set of goals to overcome them. The
aroused consciousness that puts ideas into practice requires leadership
and the mobilization of power, not simply people reasoning together.
Even within a social movement common consciousness arises not only
from discussion among people with similar values and interests but also
from visceral response. Thus, transformative social movements, whether
conservative, like neoliberalism, or progressive, like environmentalism,
contain distortions and unsupported arguments and depend on emotional appeals. Communicative theorists, to the extent that they concern
themselves with how to overcome structural impediments to democratic
processes, promote the establishment of institutions that are conducive to open interchange. But they will not evoke much enthusiasm for

institutional transformation unless they can point to a substantive outcome beyond democracy itself as a consequence.

The power of words depends on the power of the speakers. To quote
Bent Flyvbjerg (1998, 234), "When we understand power, we see that we
cannot rely solely on democracy based on rationality to solve our problems." John Forester (2001, 269), in a review of Flyvbjerg's book, wonders
at his "sense of breathless surprise" that power and politics should affect
planning. Forester considers Flyvbjerg's discovery a commonplace and
wishes to get past a critical approach that concerns itself with revealing
power but proposes no way to deal with it. His remedy for discrepancies
of power is to change people's minds. As Chantal Mouffe (1999, 752)
argues, however:

> What is really at stake…is the need to acknowledge the dimen-
> sion of power and antagonism *and their ineradicable character.* By
> postulating the availability of [a] public sphere where power and
> antagonism have been eliminated and where a rational consensus
> would have been realized, this [deliberative] model of democratic
> politics denies the central role in politics of the conflictual dimen-
> sion and its crucial role in the formation of collective identities.
> (Emphasis added.)

There is a naïveté in the communicative approach, in its avoidance of the
underlying causes of systematic distortion and its faith that reason can
prevail (Neumann 2000).[10] As Flyvbjerg (1998) points out, much that is
accepted as reason is simply rationalization promulgated and repeated by
the powerful.

Mark Purcell (2008)develops a model of democratic planning that
takes into account the weaknesses of the deliberative approach by recognizing the inevitability of speech distortions and power relationships.
He explicitly rejects "the argument that the proper aim of democratic
decision-making is to achieve consensus and/or the common good." Instead he opts for "a social-movement model where disadvantaged groups
come together to pursue democratic outcomes that best meet their particular interests," arguing that only through such action is it possible to
redress inequality (2008, 77). His theory echoes the argument made by

---

10. This is less the case for Habermas's own work, where the ideal speech situation is a critical standard against which processes are evaluated, as it is for many of the scholars who have
attempted to use communicative action as a guide for practice.

Ross Zucker, who develops a substantive theory of democracy in which "the just distribution of economic resources is a defining characteristic of democratic rule."[11]

The problem with this formulation, with which I am otherwise in agreement, is that by conflating democracy with economic equality, it redefines democracy away from its normally accepted meaning. Purcell and Zucker are imposing equity rather than participation or deliberation as the criterion by which to judge decision making. Their argument, which is similar to T. H. Marshall's (1964) in his characterization of the meaning of citizenship, derives from a logic that says without fairly substantial economic equality, formal democracy excludes the disadvantaged (whether by income or personal attribute) from genuine influence.[12] The intention is to counter the proceduralist conception of democracy. Analytically, however, it is clearer if the terms democracy and equity (or justice) are differentiated, thereby allowing process and structural situation to be considered separately.

The contemporary concern with deliberative processes and public participation both stimulates and reflects a move toward greater openness in policy making. Yet, even though public decision making has become more participatory than in the past and authority is increasingly decentralized, we have seen inequality grow, at least in part as a consequence of governmental actions. This trend underscores the importance of applying the criterion of equity to policy evaluation if we wish to see greater justice. The next section develops the argument for employing it.

Equity

I choose to use the word equity rather than equality when proposing a standard for evaluating public decision making. Equity, as I employ the

---

11. Zucker (2001, 1). Ian Shapiro (1999) goes even farther in ascribing a substantive content to democracy, arguing that participation is valuable but nevertheless a subordinate good to justice, which he defines as overcoming domination.

12. Marshall categorizes citizenship rights as legal, political, and social, with each type preceding the other historically. Only with full social rights can legal and political rights be fully exercised. In a similar argument Rousseau contends that equality is the prerequisite to liberty: "If one enquires into precisely wherein the greatest good of all consists,... one will find that it boils down to the two principal objects, *liberty* and *equality*....equality because liberty cannot subsist without it" (Rousseau [1987 edition], 170).

term, refers to a distribution of both material and nonmaterial benefits derived from public policy that does not favor those who are already better off at the beginning. Further, it does not require that each person be treated the same but rather that treatment be appropriate. In this interpretation distributions that result from market activities are included; they are considered to be within the realm of public policy since the choice of leaving allocations to the market is a policy decision. Relative disadvantage may be defined in terms of class or group characteristics.

There are two reasons to prefer the term equity over equality. First, the goal of equality is too complex, demanding, and unrealistic to be an objective in the context of capitalist cities. It acts as a magnet for all the objections based on rewards to the most deserving, on questions of the obliteration of incentives, on the trade-off between growth and equality, and on the unfairness of penalizing everyone above the median in the name of the greater good. Since the effects of more just policies within cities would never be sufficient to radically change the income distribution, there seems no need to establish a target to be shot down. My purpose in developing a concept of the just city is to provide an evaluative standard by which to judge urban policies and to express the goals of urban movements. Changes at this level may be sufficient to impel what Castells has termed a "municipal revolution," but only power mobilized at the national and international level is sufficient to force major transformation.

Still, applying the criterion of equity in urban decision making would elevate the standing of weaker, poorer groups in terms of the impacts of specific decisions without implying the claim that these policies have sufficient scope to bring about equality. For the most part, urban policies, which are typically under the control of pro-growth regimes, have favored the well-off over the disadvantaged. Instead, pro-equity regimes would require that the distributional outcomes of programs be measured in terms of (a) who benefits from them, and (b) to what extent? A pro-equity program favors the less well off more than the well-to-do. That is, it should be redistributive, not simply economically but also, as appropriate, politically, socially, and spatially.

Second, equity is the term commonly used in policy analysis for describing the impacts of a program. It implies fairness, which is a more broadly accepted value than equality. It has the power to gain wider political support than terms that explicitly target the better-off. Thus, demands for civil and human rights, access to education and health, and protection from loss of one's home have greater currency than calls for reparations or job quotas. Consequently equity is a more politically strategic term, even though underlying it is, in fact, a move toward greater equality.

Distributional equity represents a particular concept of fairness in which policy aims at bettering the situation of those who without state intervention would suffer from relative deprivation. It is, however, at odds with the utilitarian framework based in liberal political theory that forms the usual basis for policy analysis, since the doctrine of the greatest happiness of the greatest number says nothing about the happiness of those not among the majority. Nevertheless, giving priority to equity accords with the strand of liberal theory represented by Rawls's interpretation of justice as fairness and also with one possible interpretation of Marxian thought. The following sections discuss the issues raised by liberal political theory and find support for a concept of distributional equity in Rawls's critique of utilitarianism as well as in neo-Marxist theory.

Liberal Theory

The contract theory of government, as exemplified by the writings of John Locke, sets forth the principles for democratically forming a government that protects the rights of the individual; it is the basis for the liberal tradition of political theory. Utilitarianism, as originally depicted by Jeremy Bentham and elaborated by John Stuart Mill, provides guidance within that tradition for governmental decision making. It incorporates an ideal of equity through establishing the public interest, calculated in terms of the utilitarian formulation of the greatest good of the greatest number, as the appropriate standard for policy evaluation:

> The impact of utilitarian streams of thought on progressive public policy-making in general…has been enormous.…Bentham's central proposition was that the only consistent way to achieve rational choice is to assess the consequences of action open to us in terms of the pleasure or pain they bring. The assessment is achieved by summing individual utilities. Each person in the calculation counts for one and no more than one (the impartiality principle). A good public policy is one which maximizes individual pleasure or, to employ the catch-phrase of utilitarianism, which achieves "the greatest happiness of the greatest number."

> In theory, the selection of the "best" policy is a simple matter of calculation. (Campbell and Marshall 2006, 242)

Within utilitarianism equity means benefiting the majority. In the context of eighteenth and nineteenth century Europe, it constitutes a progressive move consonant with a democratic theory based on electoral majorities and incorporates a rational approach to satisfying democratic demands. It assumes a capability of calculating the relationship between means and ends, present value and future benefits, and then assessing the total sum of satisfaction among individuals in a society resulting from choosing a particular set of actions.

As argued by Rawls (1971, 26), however, "the striking feature of the utilitarian view of justice is that it does not matter, except indirectly, how this sum of satisfactions is distributed among individuals."[13] Thus, to take the example of urban redevelopment programs, it does not matter, according to the utilitarian view, if some people lose their homes, as long as they receive compensation for their loss.[14] This means that, in the case of owner-occupied housing, the compensation is based on the assessed value of the loss rather than the replacement value. For displaced renters the only compensation may be moving costs, even if no comparable rental property is available. No reparation at all is provided for whatever emotional loss is involved (see Fullilove 2004). If displacement arises from the creation of a physical environment that provides others with a benefit commensurate with the cost to the displaced and offers aesthetic pleasure to the broader public, the sum of satisfaction will exceed that of the status quo.

Exacerbating the issue of distribution is the question of whether, as long as total satisfaction increases, it matters that the material gains are directed to specific individuals (e.g., developers) while the public benefits are diffuse (e.g., economic growth or the presence of a major league ball

---

13. Low and Gleeson (1999, 34) further criticize utilitarian individualism for producing alienation: "This view [of humans] pervades the common sense of our time. Persons as 'customers' or 'consumers' have replaced persons as 'citizens' in the language of modern policymaking. But this narrowed perspective leads to an overwhelming sense of helplessness and alienation, which is self-reinforcing." Their point is that possessive individualism destroys feelings of identification with a larger whole.

14. Cost-benefit analysis, although operating within a utilitarian framework, is constrained by Pareto optimality from making one group worse off in order to produce betterment. Policy analysts get around this constraint by assuring the losers compensation supposedly equal to their losses, assurances that in real life are often not honored.

team). Further, how does one measure benefits and losses (utiles in the language of the early utilitarians) to determine net satisfaction? When measurements are quantified monetarily, it is virtually inevitable that any replacement of an existing use by a more valuable one will produce net positive benefits.[15] If they are calculated based on subjective responses, then consensus on value usually becomes impossible.[16]

Although Rawls also works within the tradition of liberal contract theory, he avoids the pitfalls of utilitarianism through his development of the difference principle. Whatever the lacunae in the difference principle relative to cultural diversity, communal values, and historical context, it convincingly sets up a counterposition to the greatest good of the greatest number calculation, which is equally ahistorical. Much debate has centered on the meaning of primary goods in Rawls's terminology as well as on the relationship between equality of opportunity and equality of condition. For my purposes the applicability of Rawls's conception of justice to the just city lies in the assertion that a fair distribution of benefits and the mitigation of disadvantage should be the aims of public policy. Rawls's use of the phrase "prevent excessive concentrations of property and wealth" implies a realistic utopianism—the expectation is not of eliminating material inequality but rather of lessening it. Thus, the criterion for evaluating policy measures, according to Rawlsian logic, is to ensure that they most benefit the less well off. Although we can add to that, as will be discussed below, additional nonmaterial values, *at the same time, the economic impact of policies should never be forgotten.*

---

15. This is the objection raised by Justice Sandra Day O'Connor in the U.S. eminent domain case, *Kelo v. New London* (June 23, 2005). In her dissenting opinion, she declared: "Nothing is to prevent the State from replacing any Motel 6 with a Ritz-Carlton, any home with a shopping mall, or any farm with a factory." Analyses supporting the construction of sports venues and convention centers, despite their resulting in a net loss to the public fisc, typically justify them as contributing to overall welfare through job creation and enhancement of the city's image.

16. In a further criticism of utilitarianism, Iris Marion Young (2000, 101) argues that even beyond the (mal)distributional effects of its calculus, its assumption that each person's interest should be given equal weight even when some have greater needs should also be faulted. Similarly Amartya Sen (1992, 14) comments that utilitarianism, even while allowing inequality of outcomes, "attaches exactly the same importance to the utilities of all people...and...guarantees that everyone's utility gains get the same weight in the maximizing exercise." It is only in this sense impartial, as it cannot take into account that some groups' needs are greater than others (Nussbaum 2006). There is also an underlying assumption that measurable, objective interests exist (see Balbus 1971 for a discussion of the concept of objective interest). Moreover, it relies on the fact/value dichotomy that H. Putnam (2002) effectively discredits.

Marxian Interpretations

The emphasis on distribution that arises from the work of Rawls and his followers breaks with the precepts underlying Marxian socialism. Marx consistently maintains that the relations of production rather than those of distribution or reproduction[17] are the source of exploitation and inequality. Thus, for Marx no real change is possible without restructuring production. He denies taking a moral stance but rather insists that historical forces arising out of the contradictions of capitalism and the creation of a politically conscious working class (a class "for itself") would result in social transformation, ultimately providing a material distribution to each according to his or her needs.

David Harvey (1996, 331), in his interpretation of Marx and Engels on justice, first quotes Plato, who in *The Republic* has Thrasymachus declare: "Each ruling class...defines as 'right' for their subjects what is in the interest of themselves." He then presents a quote from Engels:

> Justice [expressed in legal terms] is but the ideologized, glorified expression of the existing economic relations....While in everyday life...expressions like right, wrong, justice, and sense of right are accepted without misunderstanding even with reference to social matters, they...create the same hopeless confusion in any scientific investigation of economic relations as would be created, for instance, in modern chemistry if the terminology of the phlogiston theory were to be retained. (Quoted in Harvey 1996, 331)

Although Harvey (1996, 332) agrees that justice as embodied in the law within capitalist states reflects the interests of the ruling class, he nevertheless believes the term can create a powerful mobilizing force for political action.[18] He regards it as erroneous to see any concept of justice as independent of time and place, but nevertheless argues that one can construct a utopian ideal of social relations although not of spatial form. Such an ideal is not approached through communicative interaction—he explicitly rejects Habermasian theory—but rather through a transformation of the class structure, which itself depends on a revolutionary consciousness

---

17. One of the feminist objections to Marxism is its devaluing of reproduction, both in the sense of the birthing and rearing of children and of maintaining conditions necessary for sustaining human life.

18. In using the term justice, Harvey intends more than simply economic justice, but he sees economic relations as fundamental to the elimination of oppression.

among the exploited. Although he refers to justice, not equity, the argument he is making can serve to provide a justification for equity.

In making the distinction between social relations and form, Harvey contrasts them too sharply, as by form he is referring to the elaborate schemes for cities laid out by utopian socialists and by social relations he is talking about "a relational theory of justice" (332) that does not depend on philosophically derived universals. A relational theory that takes into account situatedness in time and place can, however, give content to social relations without going so far as to lay out the streets of the ideal city and without wholly abandoning transcendent normative criteria. Marx and Engels themselves are contradictory in that, as Norman Geras points out, they frequently use the language of morality to condemn capitalism:

> The conclusion I defend is this: that Marx's work, whatever else it may be, and his disclaimers to the contrary notwithstanding, is an indictment of capitalist society in the light of transhistorical principles of justice (amongst other moral values); an indictment, that is to say, in the light of non-relative normative standards, pertaining to the social distribution of benefits and disbenefits, resources and burdens. (1992, 39)

Geras's claim is based on the following logic:

> First,…in characterizing exploitation as robbery, Marx was impugning the justice of it. Second, I qualify this claim in the light of his own disavowal of a critique of capitalism in the name of justice. Third, I argue that…at the heart of his very critique on behalf of…other values, [is] a concern for distributive justice. (Geras 1985, 65)

If one accepts Geras's interpretation, as I do, then both the liberal tradition, represented by Rawls, and the Marxian one support using the equity criterion as the moral basis for deriving policy prescriptions. The problem raised by Marx becomes less one of whether or not distributional equity is the appropriate metric but rather whether any effort that begins with distribution instead of production can made a real difference in the lives of the relatively disadvantaged.

In the *Urban Question* (1977), Manuel Castells argues that, under the aegis of the Keynesian welfare state, antagonism within the workplace has become displaced into the urban arena. Here the working class is partially supported by the social wage, achieved through taxation and distributed by the state. Conflict is over control of collective consumption (i.e., what the state provides) and its allocation, rather than over workplace hierarchy and wages. By this logic, then, once the local state becomes an arena for class antagonism—and for cross-class alliances within urban social movements—the analytic distinction between the relations of production and reproduction (or consumption) dissolves. The capitalist economic system continues to generate crisis and inequality, but the state has within its capacity the ability to mitigate their effects. Mobilizations making demands on the capitalist state, including at the urban level, thus have the potential for increasing equity of outcomes.

Arguments from liberalism and Marxism alone, however, no longer suffice as validations for a position regarding justice. In the postmodernist/poststructuralist era, critics on the left have attacked liberals and Marxists for their failure to identify sources of oppression intrinsic to both liberal individualism and Marxist class analysis. The terms recognition, diversity, multiculturalism, cosmopolitanism, and the politics of difference describe the starting point of their critiques. The next section discusses claims that the socially excluded are marginalized by the discourses of both liberalism and Marxism and that the argument for economic redress fails to take account of nonmaterial forms of oppression.

Recognition/Diversity/Difference and the Contribution of Poststructuralist Theory

Poststructuralist thought, in its attention to group-based difference, correctly challenges liberal individualism and Marxian class analysis. In using the term poststructuralist, I encompass those approaches that see social differentiation as based on multiple foundations, including race, ethnicity, gender, religion, and culture. As a political formula it gives rise to demands for language autonomy and acknowledgment of particular customs such as holiday celebrations or styles of communication. In its call for recognition of difference it is emancipatory in pressing for the end of discrimination and acknowledgment of the positive aspects of maligned cultures.

Nancy Fraser (2003), in her debate with Axel Honneth concerning redistribution or recognition, regards the two as analytically separable but both necessary components of a just society. The identification of individuals with family, religion, and culture is so inherent to the human condition that the failure of liberal and Marxist theory to take it into account seems perverse. Marx's expectation that capitalism and globalization would dissolve national and sectarian loyalties was far off the mark; in fact, globalization, although in some ways making all places more alike, also intensifies particularistic commitments as a consequence of reactions to alleged cultural imperialism and also because of the way in which modern technology facilitates the spread of doctrine.[19]

Liberal Atomism

The most common criticism from feminist and cultural perspectives of liberal and Marxist arguments is that they are unconcerned with recognition of "the other."[20] The thesis is presented most strongly by Axel Honneth (2003, 114), who asserts that "even distributional injustices must be understood as the institutional expression of social disrespect—or, better said, of unjustified relations of recognition." In *Justice and the Politics of Difference,* perhaps the most influential book within the discipline of philosophy regarding the significance of group differences and the inadequacy of liberalism in dealing with them, Iris Marion Young states: "I believe that group differentiation is both an inevitable and a desirable aspect of modern social processes. Social justice...requires not the melting away of differences, but institutions that promote reproduction of and respect for group differences without oppression" (1990, 47). She considers that a social group is defined by a sense of shared identity and that a liberal contract model of social relations only conceives of associations based on common interests and fails to take account of groups arising from shared identity (Young 1990, 44). Under this conception the argument for justice shifts from a fair distribution to "social differentiation without exclusion" (238). Emancipation, for Young, lies in the rejection of the assimilationist model and the assertion of a positive sense of group difference wherein the group defines itself rather than being defined from the outside (172).

---

19. See Castells (2004) and Robertson (1992). Ayatollah Khomeini was able to influence the Iranian Revolution through recording audiotapes sent to Iran from Paris. More recently Osama bin Laden has used video to broadcast his views. Religious and political movements of all persuasions make use of the Internet to promulgate their views.

20. See Benhabib (2002, 49–81) for a discussion of the origins, meaning, and contradictions of the concept of recognition.

Liberal democratic theory, by treating individuals atomistically, ignores the rootedness of people in class, gender, cultural, and familial relationships. In doing so and by placing liberty at the top of its pantheon of values, it fails to recognize the ties of obligation that necessarily bind people to one another and also the culturally based antagonisms that separate them. In her feminist critique of the liberal tradition, Nancy Hirschmann (1992, 10) comments:

> To assert that all men are inherently free and equal was an important contribution to political thought....But it is one thing to conclude from this that divine right and patriarchy are illegitimate; it is quite another to conclude that each separate and individual human being must decide for herself which obligations—political and otherwise—she will assume.

Hirschmann's point—one that communitarian and conservative theorists share—is that necessary obligations exist, and a political philosophy based on voluntarism fails to recognize the moral dilemmas of human existence. Jean-Jacques Rousseau, a contract theorist but not a liberal in the Anglo-American tradition, did not, in *The Social Contract,* call for the freedom enjoyed by natural man. Instead, he asked what could make social bonds legitimate. In recognizing the benefits of civilization, Rousseau was leading up to the stance taken by multiculturalists—that people do not exist outside of culture and that stripping them of their social relations is both denying history and robbing individuals of their existential security.[21]

A further objection to much of liberal thought, arising from feminist and multiculturalist viewpoints, is that the concepts of reason and of rights, defended by theorists ranging from Locke to J. S. Mill to Rawls, are based on a masculinist conception of adversarial democracy.[22] This body of theory, it is argued, unselfconsciously universalizes the standpoint of white males, values disputation, and defines interests solely in selfish terms:

---

21. Rousseau, however, rather than opting for cultural pluralism, considered that genuine democracy could only exist within small communities of like-minded people.

22. The critique applies partially to Habermas, whose concept of intersubjectivity is consonant with the views of these critics but whose emphasis on rationality in discourse is at odds with them.

> The procedures of adversary democracy have the great advantage of making decisions possible under conflict. But the theory has both prescriptive and descriptive weaknesses. Because adversary democracy takes preferences as given, and because it assumes both self-interest and irreconcilable conflict, it does not meet the deliberative, integrative, and transformative needs of citizens who must not only aggregate self-interests but choose among policies in the name of a common good. (Mansbridge 1990b, 9)

Mansbridge's critique represents a modification within liberalism that retains liberty as a first principle but redefines human nature in terms of altruism rather than selfishness. In its feminist form, however, it makes nurturance rather than freedom the governing standard of human relations (Held 1990).

Thus, the feminist/culturalist critique of the liberal tradition condemns it on the grounds of atomism, assumptions of homogeneity, and belief in the desirability of assimilation. The attack on the Marxist position (and its various political-economic derivatives) faults its economism, which tends to delineate social stratification entirely in class terms and which defines interests wholly materially.

Economism

Poststructural analysis identifies three serious problems with the logic that economic inequality subsumes all forms of subordination. First, both theory and empirical evidence point to the contrary argument. Thus, as Simmel (1950) alleges, even after the introduction of socialism, individuals would continue to express "their utterly inevitable passions of greed and envy, of domination and feeling of oppression, on the slight differences in social position that have remained."[23] Group enmities likely would also endure. Recollections of persecution of one group by another or feelings of group superiority based on color, nationality, or religion will not disappear simply because of economic equality. Socialism as it really existed demonstrated that abolition of private property does not dissolve

---

23. Simmel's forebodings, of course, precede the development of poststructuralist theory and take a less benign view of the implications of socially constructed difference. Ralf Dahrendorf (1959) similarly argues that hierarchies of power and social differentiation are inevitable.

ethnic and gender antagonism and may even increase the importance of symbolic differences.

Whereas liberal political theory has sought ways by which people with differing interests or life styles can remain dissimilar and live peacefully together, socialist thought has typically aimed at dissolving differences and thus has not been concerned with the problems of governing antagonistic groups.[24] Liberal thinkers are always vulnerable to the argument that their institutions and procedures function to perpetuate and disguise inequality. But showing that the governance systems of liberal democracies are biased against the poor and minorities does not mean that greater equity would result from their dissolution. The liberal aim of finding the means for individuals to live peacefully together may incorporate biases against the powerless, but some method of maintaining order must be found and, as the quotation from Simmel above indicates, greater equality does not eliminate hostility. Harvey (1992, 600) recognizes this issue when he declares that "a just planning and policy practice must seek out non-exclusionary and non-militarized forms of social control to contain the increasing levels of both personal and institutionalized violence without destroying capacities for empowerment and self-expression." His simple statement of the problem, however, does not suggest any simple solution.

Critique of Poststructural Analysis

Poststructuralist analysis provides a needed corrective to both liberal and Marxist theory by incorporating context and group difference into the understanding of the meaning of justice:

> Equal recognition is not just the appropriate mode for a healthy democratic society. Its refusal can inflict damage on those who are denied it … The projecting of an inferior or demeaning image on another can actually distort and oppress, to the extent that it is interiorized. Not only contemporary feminism but also race relations and discussions of multiculturalism are undergirded by the premise that denied recognition can be a form of

---

24. This criticism was most strongly expressed by Max Weber (1958) in "Politics as a Vocation," when he contrasted the ethic of responsibility with the ethic of absolute ends.

> oppression.... The demands of recognizing difference themselves take us beyond mere procedural justice. (Taylor 1991, 49–50, 52)

Nevertheless, poststructuralism can lead to essentialism, unproductive conflict, and new forms of oppression rather than to the mutual respect and reduction of surplus repression prescribed by its more enlightened philosophers. In some versions, it leaves little room for individual deviation from group norms,[25] bringing back some of the rationales for feudal tyranny that liberal absolutism combated in the eighteenth century.[26] As in feudalism, associational ties rather than common purpose become the desired framework for social relations. Most discomforting is the tendency of poststructuralist thought in its feminist and ethno-culturalist manifestations to take a critical stance toward other groups but to avoid self-criticism (see Moi 1985). Thus, we have an acceptance of the privileged position of the oppressed, identified by their color or national origin, and the incapacity to deal with oppression carried out by members of groups that are themselves oppressed. Examples abound, from defense of the subordination of women in religious communities to black anti-Semitism to extreme stereotyping of Western thinkers and traditions by critics of Orientalism. It raises difficult issues if subordinated cultures are themselves internally repressive.

When seen through the lens of economic egalitarianism, poststructuralism seems to have abandoned the socialist dream of a working class united in its common commitment to justice and equality. Indeed it may be counterproductive, for even though economic grievance may underlie group complaint, pressure for economic advantage based on group rather than class attributes is divisive.[27] Philosophers like Young, Fraser,

---

25. Young's 1990 book seems to allow little leeway for individuals to construct their identities outside their group affiliations; she, however, modifies this position in *Inclusion and Democracy* (2000). Fincher and Iveson (2008), although making diversity a central aim of planning, argue for a form of thinking that "unsettles" fixed identities.

26. Louis Hartz (1990, 29), in his brilliant analysis of the dialectics of political theory, comments: "The novel proposition [of the monarchical state] that individuals are genuinely autonomous, and equal within the state, meant that human beings could successfully become unraveled from the meaning of their prior associations. Formerly [i.e., in the feudal era] corporate attachment had defined personality; in the breakdown of the old order individuals would be redefined."

27. A 2009 U.S. Supreme Court case points to the tensions created. The City of New Haven chose to discard the results of a promotion test for firemen because minorities fared poorly on it. White firemen who qualified for advancement by dint of their test scores sued, and after

and Seyla Benhabib aim at enlarging the concept of justice to accommodate group affiliation without neglecting economic inequality. The combining of the goals of material equity and recognition of difference has led to the vocabulary of social inclusion and exclusion, which acknowledges multiple forms of oppression and which has become part of the language of the European Union. In the United States the terminology shifts from recognition to diversity. Inclusion and diversity, however, are trickier concepts than equity, because their multiple dimensions can be in contradiction and, when carried too far, can undermine other forms of justice.

Tensions among Democracy, Equity, and Diversity

The goals of democracy, equity, and diversity are difficult to combine in the real world of politics, where majority sentiment for the latter is often lacking. By defending strong group identifications and simultaneously opposing spatial exclusion, poststructuralism endorses a situation in which antagonisms are openly expressed and may easily result not in increased understanding of the other, but in cycles of hostile action and revenge. A democratic transition to the desirable end state of tolerance and diversity is extraordinarily difficult to achieve, even in American cities where the melting pot remains a potent ideal and immigration still commands considerable appeal. In Europe, where national cultures are more defined and deeply rooted, the juxtaposition of differing cultural traditions is fraught with tension. The enduring irredentism of Northern Irish Catholics, Spanish Basques, and Bosnian Serbs dispels any illusion that proximity necessarily leads to understanding.

Richard Sennett (1970, 194) seeks to overcome this problem by dismissing the desire of groups to segregate themselves as resulting from lack of experience with a heterogeneous situation: "If the permeability of cities' neighborhoods were increased, through zoning changes and the need to share power across comfortable ethnic lines, I believe that working-class families would become more comfortable with people unlike themselves." His argument implies that people will consent to new arrangements if they are required to experience them. To force the experience, however,

---

losing in a lower-level court, had their suit upheld by a 5–4 decision of the Supreme Court. *Ricci et al. v. DeStefano et al.*, U.S. Supreme Court, June 29, 2009.

is to override democratic considerations and possibly to cause a ratcheting up of animosities. Sennett uses the example of South Boston's Irish Catholic enclave to demonstrate the xenophobia that ensues from spatial isolation. After he wrote *The Uses of Disorder,* in which this discussion appears, the substance of his fears for South Boston, in fact, became manifest, as that area became the locus of extremely aggressive opposition to school desegregation. This more recent history both supports his argument concerning the effects of isolation and undermines his contention that people should be required to confront the other—forced to be free, as it were. For the court-mandated attempt to break down racial isolation proved largely counterproductive, stimulating massive white flight and leaving a sullen legacy that militated against the genuine integration of the Boston schools (Lukas 1985).

Arguments for equity and democracy are frequently elided—nineteenth-century opponents of extending the franchise feared expropriation of property would follow as an inevitable result, while contemporary democratic theorists consider greater democracy will lessen inequality: "In actually existing democracies there tends to be a reinforcing circle between social and economic inequality and political inequality.... One means of breaking this circle ... is to widen democratic inclusion" (Young 2000, 17; see also Purcell 2008).

The theoretical move toward a deliberative rather than an aggregative form of democracy (i.e., for direct citizen participation in policy making rather than majority rule expressed through periodic elections) reflects a perception that, as well as reinforcing inequality, mass democracy frequently leads to demagoguery, chauvinism, and the trampling of minority rights. Unfortunately, the argument supporting Young's view that widening democratic inclusion will break the vicious circle supporting inequality seems overly sanguine, as there is no necessary link between greater inclusiveness and a commitment to a more just society.

Urban Populism

Although holders of both the equity-oriented and poststructuralist viewpoints stumble over majoritarian opposition to their aims, forcing them to allege various contentions of false or untutored consciousness, urban populism begins with popular preference. Populist demands for greater democracy encompass two intertwined but sometimes separate strands. The first consists of a thrust toward economic democracy, aimed in particular at bringing down plutocratic elites. In Todd Swanstrom's words, "the political analysis offered by urban populism was essentially a streetwise version of elite theory: a small closed elite, stemming from the upper economic class, uses its control over wealth to manipulate government for its own selfish purposes" (1985, 129). Historically this outlook was dominant in both the urban and agrarian strands of nineteenth-century American populism, which vilified bankers and "robber baron" industrialists. In Europe it has manifested itself recently in tax resistance movements in Britain and France.

The second, culturalist strand is reflected in the writings of Herbert Gans, who attacks the schemes of planners that deviate from mass taste: "The planner has advocated policies that fit the predispositions of the upper middle class, but not those of the rest of the population" (Gans 1968, 21). He disparages Jane Jacobs's glorification of diversity and her contention that spatial arrangements are significant determinants of attaining that aim. In a critique that applies also to writings by, among others, Sennett, Christine Boyer, and Michael Sorkin, he maintains:

> [Jacobs's] argument is built on three fundamental assumptions: that people desire diversity; that diversity is ultimately what makes cities live and that the lack of it makes them die; and that buildings, streets, and the planning principles on which they are based shape human behavior....Middle-class people, especially those raising children, do not want working-class—or even Bohemian—neighborhoods. They do not want the visible vitality of a North End, but rather the quiet and the privacy obtainable in low-density neighborhoods and elevator apartment houses. (Gans 1968, 28–29)

Gans's accusation thus is that Jacobs—and by extension later poststructuralists—succumbs to an undemocratic desire to impose on others her predisposition to bohemian color.

Other writers in the same vein emphasize the elitism of planners and intellectuals in disregarding the traditional affiliations and desires of ordinary people. Harry Boyte (1980, chap. 1), while committed to the aims of diversity and economic equality, attacks Marxists for failing to appreciate the contribution of religion, family, and ethnicity to people's security and well-being. Peter Saunders, incensed by the failure of the British left to comprehend the desire of ordinary people for homeownership, defends Margaret Thatcher's "Right to Buy" program in the name of democracy: "It can plausibly be argued that such intensely personal forms of ownership perform important psychological functions for the individual, whether in socialist, capitalist or precapitalist societies" (Saunders 1984, 219).

Gans, Boyte, and Saunders, while seemingly susceptible to charges that they support a majoritarian effort to suppress deviant minorities, explicitly argue that their form of populism respects minorities. Thus, Gans (1973, 139), while demanding that planners respect popular taste, also proposes "*a more egalitarian democracy*" that responds to the needs of minorities. Boyte (1980, 38–39) declares that "democratic revolt requires…an important measure of cultural freedom, meaning both insulation from dominant individualist, authoritarian patterns and also openness to experimentation and diversity." Saunders (1984, 223) calls for the development of "a coherent socialist theory of individual property ownership" that would abolish relations of exploitation.

These authors fail to confront the genuine inconsistency that afflicts democratic theory in its effort to preserve minority rights. They extol neighborhood homogeneity, citizen activism, religion, family, ethnic ties, and home in the name of democracy, and even of equality, but their arguments can easily lead to a strongly illiberal, exclusionary politics that does reinforce inequality and minority exclusion. If democratic participation is the principal value underlying the antielitist orientation of urban populism, how is it possible to repudiate the injustices perpetrated by homeowner movements in the United States and community-based anti-immigrant mobilizations in Europe? Social theorists who foresaw "the revolt of the masses" as destructive of civilized values have had endless corroboration in history (Ortega y Gasset 1932).[28]

The recourse of democrats who fear the intolerance that can result from majority rule is a theory of rights. As embodied in the first ten amendments of the U.S. Constitution and the Universal Declaration of Human Rights of the United Nations, such a theory protects individuals by attributing to them inalienable rights. The vesting of rights in individuals derives intellectually from concepts of natural law and offers

---

28. There is a stream of elitist political theory stretching from Niccolò Machiavelli to Vilfredo Pareto, Gaetano Mosca, and Robert Michels in the prewar period to Bernard Berelson and other analysts of voting behavior after the war who see elite domination of society as inevitable, even in democracies. They vary as to whether they regard this as morally acceptable or not.

a logical resolution to the problem of imbuing a democratic philosophy with a transcendent ethic that limits the outcomes of democratic processes. Without this sort of recourse, minority rights must otherwise be justified by faith that deliberation, whether in the original position or the ideal speech situation, would produce an agreement on tolerance.

Virtually by definition a view of society as consisting of multiple, dissimilar cultural groupings produces a conception of politics as based on coalitions. This is, of course, the standard perception of liberal pluralism, and within that context it is wholly desirable. From a Left perspective, however, such an approach is problematic. Where exclusion and oppression are identified as prevailing social characteristics of capitalist democracies and hopes for social emancipation come to rest with a coalition of out-groups that share little but their antagonism to the extant social hierarchy, expectations for a coherent alternative political force are shaky.[29] Even the identification of the components of such an alliance is difficult. In Harvey's (1992, 599) attempt to devise a program sensitive to post-structuralist arguments, he declares that "*just planning and policy practices must empower rather than deprive the oppressed.*" But who decides who is the oppressed? Without a universalistic discourse, oppression is in the eyes of the beholder. Many members of the American middle class would accept Harvey's dictum but consider themselves oppressed by welfare cheats and high taxes, while their European counterparts construe immigration as representing a similar imposition. Identification of oppressed groups within a pluralistic framework is hardly a simple matter.

Trade-offs and Contradictions

Any attempt to maximize the values of equity, democracy, and diversity simultaneously presents vexing problems of reconciling their multiple meanings and conflicting agendas as well as identifying a coherent social force to press for them. My discussion so far has not even dealt with the

---

29. Robert Putnam (2007, 150–51), based on an extensive survey of American attitudes, concludes that, in the short run, "inhabitants of diverse communities tend to withdraw from collective life, to distrust their neighbours, regardless of the colour of their skin, to withdraw even from close friends, to expect the worst from their community and its leaders, to volunteer less, give less to charity and work on community projects less often, to register to vote less, to agitate for social reform *more*, but have less faith that they can actually make a difference, and to huddle unhappily in front of the television.…Diversity, at least in the short run, seems to bring out the turtle in all of us."

issue of equity in relation to environmental questions, which raise even more problems with regard to the other values discussed here:

> Viewing social justice as the striving towards a more equal distri-
> bution of resources among social groups across the space of cities
> and nations [is] a definition of "fair distribution....The envi-
> ronmental movement expands the space for this "equity" in two
> ways: (1) intergenerationally (present versus future generations)
> and (2) across species....The two added dimensions of equity
> remain essentially abstractions, however, since no one from the
> future or from other species can speak up for their "fair share" of
> resources....
>
> This expansion of socio-spatial equity to include future gen-
> erations and other species not only makes the concept more com-
> plex; it also creates the possibility for contradictions among the
> different calls for "fairness." Slowing worldwide industrial expan-
> sion may preserve more of the world's resources for the future
> (thereby increasing intergenerational equity), but it may also
> undermine the efforts of the underdeveloped world to approach
> the living standards of the west (thereby lowering international
> equity). (S. Campbell 2003, 445)

The arena of environmental policy raises particularly difficult questions of equity and democracy. Thus, Maarten Hajer (1995) calls for progress in achieving environmental quality through openness and reframing of the discourse surrounding ecological issues to expose harmful practices and propose radical solutions. But, as he himself notes, the introduction of more open and participatory procedures in the United States produced primarily symbolic results (1995, 284). Hajer concerns himself with eq-uity issues in the sense that he perceives an antagonism between industrial polluters and the public, but he avoids discussing the differing interests within the public itself in relation to who should sacrifice present op-portunities in the name of environmental protection—who should suffer unemployment in order to close a polluting factory and go without hous-ing in the name of environmental conservation.

The environmental justice movement has addressed the tension be-tween equity and the location of environmentally hazardous facilities. Its goals, however, are to ensure that undesirable uses are fairly allocated and employment growth is stimulated rather than attaining intergenerational or species equity. And indeed, groups calling for environmental preservation have often used this aim as a rationalization for exclusionary policies. At the same time trade-offs undeniably exist between present consumption and future well-being. In environmental policy, as in so many areas, often the most efficient way to achieve objectives is to invest in programs that primarily benefit the well-off—that is, programs to remove land from potential development, thereby raising the price of available housing sites, or subsidizing new, higher-density construction in inner cities that promotes gentrification.

The environment, then, constitutes another complicating factor in defining equity. It will come up again later in the book, in the case studies of actual planning. It is not, however, the primary focus of my discussion, which, in the next chapter, examines questions of equity, democracy, and diversity as they play out in strategies for urban transformation. The remainder of this chapter examines the capabilities approach as the most fruitful of the various philosophical strategies regarding justice applicable to urban governance.

The Capabilities Approach

There is no general solution to the tensions among and within the values of democracy, equity, and diversity that I regard as the basic elements of justice. Nevertheless, we can start with them as broadly applicable norms and attempt to spell them out as appropriate to particular circumstances. The capabilities approach, originally adumbrated by Amartya Sen (1992, 1999) and fleshed out by Martha Nussbaum (2000), offers a way to devise rules that can govern the evaluation of urban policy and provide content to the demands of urban movements.[30] Nussbaum goes beyond Sen's generalized and deliberately open-ended description of capabilities to provide an explicit list; Sen (1993, 47), while indicating that he has "no great objection to anyone going on that route," rejects it as overspecified. For my purposes, it is Nussbaum's elaboration of actual content that is most helpful.

The capabilities approach can be considered an extension of liberalism in its emphasis on the development of the individual and its ahistoricism— like liberalism it begins with a set of normative assumptions rather than

---

30. My list of rules is stated in chapter 6.

an analysis of the historical dialectic, as Marx does. It builds on liberalism, however, in its concern with group recognition and emotional relationships. In other words, it places the individual within a network of affiliations rather than regarding him or her as an atomized entity whose well-being is defined by personal freedom and realizing a defined set of preferences. In its sociological understanding, it therefore does not assume that governance occurs within the context of a blank slate.

Capabilities do not describe how people actually function (i.e., end state) but rather what they have the opportunity to do. One need not exercise one's capabilities if one chooses not to (e.g., one can choose asceticism), but the opportunity must be available, including a consciousness of the value of these capabilities. According to this reasoning, each person must be treated as an end, and there is a threshold level of each capability beneath which human functioning is not possible. Nussbaum (2000) argues that capabilities cannot be traded off against each other. She lists, inter alia, life, health, bodily integrity, access to education, and control over one's environment (political and material) as necessary capabilities. Translated into a communal rather than individualistic ethic, the capabilities approach would protect urban residents from having to sacrifice quality of life for financial gain. Hence, for example, communities desperate for an economic base should not have to accept toxic waste sites because they lack any other form of productive enterprise. In contrast, conservative economists who support establishing market systems in pollution controls see such trade-offs as rational and desirable.

The capabilities approach can be usefully applied to urban institutions and programs. Judgments would be based on whether their gestation was in accord with democratic norms (although not necessarily guided by the strictures of deliberative or deep democracy), whether their distributional outcomes enhanced the capabilities of the relatively disadvantaged, and whether groups defined relationally achieved recognition from each other. In Sen's attack on utilitarianism (1999, chap. 3) he argues against the analysis typically employed by cost-benefit accounting as it is used to justify urban capital programs in most cities. These analyses tend to exaggerate benefits and underestimate costs, rely on aggregates, and ignore distributional outcomes.[31] A more sensitive form of analysis asks the questions: Who benefits and who assesses what

---

31. See Flyvbjerg, Bruzelius, and Rothengatter 2003; Altshuler and Luberoff 2003.

outputs each group in the population receives? Then, applying the difference principle amplified by the capabilities approach, such that our concern extends beyond primary goods, we should opt for that alternative that improves the lot of the relatively disadvantaged or minimally does not harm them. The definition of disadvantage, however, is subjective and is usually categorized according to social group affiliation. What we do know is that groups most lacking in political and financial power and most subject to disrespect are least likely to be included in deliberation or to prevail in the outcome. A commitment to justice over technical efficiency in evaluating the content of policy would shift the balance in their favor.

2

JUSTICE AND URBAN TRANSFORMATION: PLANNING IN CONTEXT

Much of planning theory dwells on planning processes and the role of the planner without analyzing the socio-spatial constraints under which planners operate or the object—urban space—that they affect. Such a narrow focus results in theoretical weakness arising from the isolation of process from context and outcome. Instead, in my view, planning theory should address the following questions: (1) What is the relationship between the urban context and planning activity? In other words, what are the background conditions that facilitate and constrain planning for a just city? (2) How does planning affect city users, including residents, commuters, and visitors?[1] (3) What principles should guide plan formulation, content, and implementation? Although responses to these questions do require examination of the planner's role and strategies, they also demand exploration of the field of forces in which planners function and a formulation of what a better city might be in relation to justice. This chapter and the three that follow explore the context and evaluation of urban policy by examining some of the broad issues that arise in planning

---

1. Guido Martinotti (1999) notes that, with increased travel, cities are host to large numbers of transients ("users"). Their legitimacy is often challenged by critics of the commodification of urban space. Visitors and commuters, however, are significant elements in modern urban development and constitute a large cross-section of the population; thus, they too should be considered when formulating a concept of justice in the city.

practice and analyzing them in terms of the dilemmas involved in producing a more just city. Chapter 6 addresses the third question of guidelines for just urban planning. The discussion does not go so far as to investigate the broader concept of the good city. Justice is only one component of the good city, but it is the focus of this book, which restricts itself to local approaches to achieving greater justice in wealthy countries. The analysis is limited to the relations between equity, diversity, and democracy, which I indicated earlier to be the principal components of urban justice. Thus, in looking at these questions I do not focus on some of the considerations—for example, good city form or environmental sustainability—that would be encompassed in a more expansive investigation.

The Tradition of City Planning

The impetus for the development of planning lay in a critique of the industrial city and a desire to re-create cities according to enlightened design principles. Whether the focus was on greenfield sites, as in Ebenezer Howard's garden city model, or on redeveloping the existing city, as in Georges-Eugène Haussmann's Paris and Daniel Burnham's City Beautiful, planning devoted itself to producing the desired object. Early planners proceeded without much reflection about the process by which the ideal city was formulated—its implicit theoretical arguments dwelled on the nature of the good city instead of how one derived either the ideals or the means to attain them. It was taken for granted that the function of planning was to impose a consciously chosen pattern of development upon the urban terrain; the method of making the necessary choices was not problematized. Rather, good planning was assumed to be guided by experts who, on the basis of study and experience, would devise plans in the public interest. Beyond Patrick Geddes exhortation to "survey then plan," little attention was directed toward methodology and the result was embodied in a physical design (Hall 2002, 355–56). The public interest constituted the moral basis of planning, but its content was taken for granted rather than analyzed, and it was assumed that its realization would benefit all.

To be sure, there was, during the first part of the twentieth century, some attention to process, as American progressive reformers, in their effort to rid government of bias and corruption, successfully pressed for independent planning commissions and European governments incorporated planning into meritocratic bureaucracies. These moves, a part of a general impetus to divorce public policy determination from political influence, rested on a view that a sharp line separated politics from administration and a belief that experts could develop policies in isolation from selfish interests. Here, as among the later theorists discussed below, the content of good policy was expected to be a result of good procedures and did not need to be analyzed in advance. Later, historical deconstructions of the period revealed the biases of technocratic professionals and their business supporters, showing that insulated decision making and allegedly meritocratic selection procedures favored upper- and middle-class interests.[2]

The development of an explicit theory directed at prescribing the planner's modus operandi began with the publication of Karl Mannheim's *Man and Society in an Age of Reconstruction* in 1935.[3] It laid the philosophical foundations for later theorizing by describing a democratic planning process that would enable experts to plan under the guidance of the public through their elected representatives. Mannheim's ambition exceeded that of *city* planning—inspired by the ideals of reform liberalism, he envisioned the national state's participation in economic and social planning. He argued that, if the planning bureaucracy was subject to parliamentary control, it could apply its technical expertise to the solution of social problems without impinging on freedom:

> The new bureaucracy brought with it a new objectivity in human affairs. There is something about bureaucratic procedure which helps to neutralize the original leanings towards patronage, nepotism, and personal domination. This tendency towards objectivity may, in favourable cases, become so strong that the element of class consciousness, still present in a bureaucracy which is chosen mainly from the ranks of the ruling classes, can be almost completely superseded by the desire for justice and impartiality. (Mannheim 1940, 323)[4]

---

2. See, for example, Hays (1995) and S. Cohen (1964) for a discussion of the Progressive period in the United States and Crozier (1964) for discussion of the impact of public bureaucracy in Europe.

3. This book was written in German and published in Holland. The English-language edition appeared in 1940 and was substantially revised and enlarged by the author.

4. Polanyi (1944) similarly argued that freedom, rather than being limited by state planning as contended by extreme liberals such as Friedrich Hayek, required planning.

In his acceptance of the role of impartial expertise and of legislative control of planning goals, Mannheim laid the foundation for the direction taken by academic planners during the postwar period:

> The subject [of physical planning] changed from a kind of craft...into an apparently scientific activity in which vast amounts of precise information were garnered and processed in such a way that the planner could devise very sensitive systems of guidance and control....Instead of the old master-plan or blueprint approach, which assumed that the objectives were fixed from the start, the new concept was of planning as a *process*....And this planning process was independent of the thing that was planned. (Hall 2002, 360–62)

Famous for transforming city planning from primarily a design profession into a social science after the Second World War, theorists at the University of Chicago and the University of Pennsylvania and their followers laid out the rational model and methods for testing policy alternatives (Sarbib 1983; Hall 2002, 359–63). They incorporated the thesis that general goals could be stipulated in advance within a democratic political process, and that the formulation of the means to reach those goals and the process of implementing those means could be conducted impartially by disinterested appointed officials (Dror 1968; Faludi 1973). Democracy constituted the value content of the strategy. Presumably goals democratically derived were inherently equitable, and the means for achieving these ends could be scientifically discovered.

Along with rationality, planners' claim to influence was increasingly based on an ideal of comprehensiveness—by looking at the region, city, or neighborhood as a whole, they could coordinate the different elements of urban development: land use, transportation, production facilities, and so forth, which otherwise were the domains of separate, noncommunicating bureaucracies (AIP 1959). Using the tools of modern statistical and economic analysis, experts could measure the interactions among different subsystems precipitated by alternative policies and then evaluate the extent to which each development scheme maximized achievement of the specified goals.

Ironically, however, the vision of achieving agreement on general priorities and then applying planning expertise expressed through the rational model wholly ignored the devastating attack on positivism mounted by Mannheim himself in his essay on the sociology of knowledge. Here, in a striking foreshadowing of postmodernist/poststructuralist critique, he stated:

> For each of the participants [in a discussion] the "object" [of discourse] has a more or less different meaning because it grows out of the whole of their respective frames of reference, as a result of which the meaning of the object in the perspective of the other person remains, at least in part, obscure.... [This approach] does not signify that there are no criteria of rightness and wrongness in a discussion. It does insist, however, that it lies in the nature of certain assertions that they cannot be formulated absolutely, but only in terms of the perspective of a given situation.... Interests and the powers of perception of the different perspectives are conditioned by the social situations in which they arose and to which they are relevant. (Mannheim 1936, 281, 283, 284)

As applied to urban planning, Mannheim's assault on universalism jettisons the notion of a value-free, unbiased methodology and denies that forecasters can assume that past experience will simply repeat itself in a new historical context. Thus, the assumptions underlying the use of quantitative cost-benefit analysis to weigh alternatives within the rational model are undermined. Furthermore, the notion that a singular choice among alternatives will prove generally beneficial rather than creating winners and losers becomes questionable. Mannheim proposes instead the use of reason and comparative analysis rather than a formally rational methodology. Such an approach is necessarily value-laden and calls for various forms of knowledge, not simply the expertise acquired through scientific training. His thesis is a clear precursor of Habermas's concept of rationality. Mannheim differs, however, from contemporary communicative theorists in that he expects an educated elite, working within his flexible definition of reasoned reflection, to plan on behalf of society at large. His views perhaps find their most recent echo in the work of Anthony Giddens (1990). In both his explanation of people's willingness to trust expertise and in his description of reflexivity, by which knowledge circles in and out of society, Giddens presents an approach to knowledge that is neither relativist nor positivist, but, as he puts it, "relationist" (or, one might say, dialectical).

As discussed in chapter 1, the belief that fact and value can be separated, which underlies the application of the rational model, has been strongly attacked. The ideal of comprehensiveness has also sustained much criticism. Thus, Alan Altshuler (1965) notes that comprehensiveness requires planners to rank all the manifold interests within the city into a single set of goals and have available the technical capacity to find the means to reach those ends. He doubts that they possess this capability. Charles Lindblom (1959), whose work echoes the skepticism of such management theorists as Herbert Simon, argues that the combined desire for rationality and comprehensiveness is both impractical and undesirable. He characterizes the actual planning and policy-making process as incremental, based on a strategy of "muddling through." As reflected in his oxymoronic title, "The Science of 'Muddling Through,'" he declares this cautious method of "partisan mutual adjustment" to be more effective in reaching desirable outcomes than the synoptic planning method idealized within the rational model.

In the 1960s and '70s, the intellectual current that had questioned the claims of planning to rationality and comprehensiveness was strengthened by theorists who regarded the presumption of disinterestedness as a mask for the power of property developers and upper-class groups.[5] In response to the social agitation of the times, a dissident but nonetheless influential movement within the profession forced planners and urban policy makers to become more concerned with the impacts of decisions on the politically powerless—especially those displaced by highway and urban renewal programs (Hoffman 1989). For this group of thinkers the underlying moral justification for planning shifted to remedying the disadvantages produced by poverty and racial discrimination instead of producing a plan that would maximize an alleged public interest.

These critics of planning were in agreement over the causes and consequences of planning actions but differed as to the potential of planning to effect desirable change, given the power of capital. One group, operating within a neo-Marxist paradigm, emphasized the structural underpinnings of the system and basically argued that equitable planning could only occur after a complete transformation of the system of private property.[6] Needless to say, this conclusion proved very discouraging to progressive planners who by then were also working for community-based

---

5. Among the most influential were Herbert Gans (1968), who revealed the social-class composition of the supporters of planning and showed the depredations of urban renewal; David Harvey (1978), who argued that the "ideology of planning" was simply a rationalization of the class interests of developers; and Manuel Castells (1977), who regarded environmentalism as instrumental in protecting upper-class privilege.

6. See Castells (1977); Harloe (1977); Harvey (1978); Foglesong (1986).

organizations rather than solely for city governments and business groups.[7] One response to this seeming impasse was to chart courses whereby planning could, in fact, achieve fairer outcomes.[8] The more practice-oriented attempts presented exemplary policies but without describing and justifying their underlying value positions or a deep probing of the strategies and conditions that could produce their desired results.[9]

There are now growing efforts to develop middle-range theory that embeds planning practice within a larger, postpositivist theoretical framework that is more in accordance with Mannheim's relationist strategy than a purely technical approach (Fischer 2003).[10] I use the term middle range here because, although some of these works extend to countries at various stages of political and economic development, the primary focus is on norms governing policy within democratic Western metropolises in the first part of the new millennium. In other words the arguments are not at a global level of generalization. Thus, while, as argued in the introduction, broad concepts of justice have a universal resonance, their specific content is restricted in relation to both place and time rather than applying to all cities in an entire historical epoch. The remainder of this chapter discusses some of the issue areas most significant to a conceptualization of the just city based on the three principles of democracy, diversity, and equity as forming the moral basis of planning and policy.

Democracy

Calls for democratic control of decisions made within urban bureaucracies arose in the 1960s and '70s in response to two perceptions: that

---

7. See Fainstein and Fainstein (1979); Hall (2002), chap. 10; Brooks (2002).

8. See Clavel (1986); Krumholz and Forester (1990); Mier and Alpern (1993); Hartman (2002). Many of the communicative planning theorists (e.g., John Forester, Judith Innes, Patsy Healey, James Throgmorton) use actual cases as the basis for their theorizing concerning the ways in which progressive planners can improve the negotiations around divisive issues. They refrain, however, from offering policy prescriptions except in regard to the mode by which planners interact with other stakeholders.

9. Fainstein (1999) and Sayer and Storper (1997) comment on the failure of most left-wing writing on urban policy to specify the values beneath their analyses.

10. This has particularly been the case for discussions of communicative rationality, but it is increasingly so also for consideration of the just city as the concept applies to participation (Purcell 2008; DeFilippis 2004), public space (Kohn 2004; Mitchell 2003), infrastructure (Flyvbjerg 1998), the environment (Low and Gleeson 1998), and tourism (Hannigan 1998; Fainstein and Gladstone 1999).

"street-level bureaucrats," including planners and social welfare workers, made decisions affecting urban residents without regard to their knowledge, opinions, and interests (Lipsky 1980); and that public agency staff came out of sharply different social strata from those affected by their decisions. The latter view led, in the United States, to accusations of "internal colonialism," particularly in the case of white personnel operating in black neighborhoods (see Blauner 1969). Citizen participation was to overcome the injustices caused by lack of responsiveness and failures of empathy, as well as being a value in its own right through its furtherance of democracy.[11]

In an article that is still frequently cited, Sherry Arnstein develops a "ladder of citizen participation." She argues that the stronger the role of disadvantaged groups in formulating and implementing policy, the more redistributional will be the outcomes: "In short, it is the means by which they ['have-not citizens'] can induce significant social reform which enables them to share in the benefits of the affluent society" (Arnstein 1969, 216). Arnstein (224) recognizes that the minority communities demanding control are not monolithic and that there are well-founded critiques of community power: it can encourage separatism, inefficiency, opportunism. Nevertheless, she concludes that without a redistribution of decisional power, there will be no redistribution of benefits. In line with Arnstein's argument, community groups demanded power based on the view that only by gaining control over policy could local citizens ensure that governmental actions would benefit them. Thus, "community control" became a central goal of urban activists during the 1960s and '70s.

Subsequently, however, highly mobilized protests faded in both Europe and the United States, causing pressure for citizen involvement to diminish. Programs such as Model Cities in the United States and the Community Development Project in the United Kingdom, which required community participation, disappeared, while public-private partnerships between business and government flourished.[12] In the United States planners who had been moved to neighborhood offices and advocated

---

11. See the overview provided by Altshuler (1970).

12. Frieden and Kaplan (1975) describe and evaluate the Model Cities program; Marris (1987) analyzes the Community Development Project. Ceccarelli (1982) and Fainstein and Hirst (1995) trace the rise and decline of urban political movements. Mayer (2003) shows the ways in which activists have been co-opted by participatory institutions under neoliberal approaches.

on behalf of community groups lost their jobs (Needleman and Needleman 1974). Planning was largely recentralized in American city halls, although some cities continued to experiment with various forms of citizen empowerment. In the United Kingdom all sorts of partnership arrangements that called for citizen participation proliferated, but it was unclear how much real influence community groups actually had. The situation varied substantially in continental Europe—in Amsterdam, for example, there has been considerable local consultation, while in Paris the top-down tradition has continued. The strongest model, where citizens actually determined budgetary expenditures, was until recently extremely rare.[13]

One such example, the Neighborhood Revitalization Program (NRP) in Minneapolis, where capital budget funds were allocated to community organizations under a twenty-year program, illustrates both the strengths and weaknesses of the citizen participation model. Under this program existing community groups were required to become more broadly inclusive of their neighborhoods and, through a series of meetings, to devise a neighborhood plan. After more than a decade of operation, an extensive evaluation of the program concludes that it was quite successful in achieving its principal objective of neighborhood revitalization. Unsurprisingly, its achievements, in terms both of eliciting widespread participation and obtaining results, varied from neighborhood to neighborhood. In relation to the crucial issue that concerns us here—the creation of just outcomes—the evaluators find that, although more affluent homeowners tended to dominate deliberations, some wealthy communities did support construction of low-income rental housing. On the other hand, the authors admit, in response to critics who accused community groups of insensitivity to low-income residents, especially in regard to affordable housing, that "the NRP has not substantially addressed the preoccupations of many activists concerned with equity and justice" (Fagotto and Fung 2005, 60). They argue, however, that more active intervention by program staff could have oriented participants to a stronger concern with equity.

---

13. The most frequently cited instance of participatory budgeting, often held up as a model, is that of Porto Alegre, Brazil. An estimated one hundred European cities had adopted the concept by 2008; an evaluation of them concludes that only a minority genuinely empowered the participants; in these cases institutional change was accompanied by "social mobilization" (Sintomer, Herzberg, and Röcke 2008, 175)

The NRP case points to two conclusions. First, the equity outcomes of citizen deliberations are unpredictable and are likely to vary according to the particular values of the active participants. Second, planners can affect the character of deliberation and move participants toward a greater commitment to just outcomes. In Minneapolis, planning department staff tended to play a passive role, inhibited by their belief that democratic planning precluded their taking initiatives and shaping people's opinions (Fainstein and Hirst 1995). Their normative position rested on the primacy of democratic deliberation as the governing value. The tension between democracy as practiced and equitable outcomes arises because citizen participants usually prefer policies that benefit owners more than renters. In general, middle-class homeowners are more likely to participate than lower-income renters and are more effective in doing so.

The initial demands for citizen participation in bureaucratic decision making originated with low-income groups wanting increased benefits. As time passed, however, participatory mechanisms primarily became a vehicle for middle-class interests. As such, they represented a move toward democratizing the planning process but not usually in the direction of redistribution, and they always posed the threat of co-optation. Since participation is typically organized by areas, it draws together people with only limited common interests. Moreover, neighborhood activists are never more than a small proportion of a community; thus, their claim to legitimacy is always suspect. Sometimes they may genuinely reflect a broad constituency, but they may also become a narrow clique unwelcoming to outsiders and serving their own personal desire for prominence.

Usually the achievements of neighborhood participatory bodies are limited to modifications of preexisting development schemes, small-scale improvement programs, blocking funding cutbacks, and symbolic recognition. They may act as springboards for individuals aiming at citywide political power, but successful neighborhood-based elected officials often reorient their affiliations after gaining office. Context matters—if participants are not backed by widespread mobilization, they are unlikely to carry much weight. Moreover, in cities suffering from a withdrawal of capital investment, neighborhood participants are no more able than the mayor to stem the tide and often yield to the logic that only through subsidies to developers are any investments likely to happen. In cities under development pressure they may be able to gain concessions in terms of community spaces, social services, and affordable housing; their ability to halt gentrification, however, is restricted by their lack of control over private-market activities.

What we can say in general about institutionalized citizen participation is that it increases the information available to policy makers by providing local knowledge (Corburn 2005); it makes decision making more democratic and open but not necessarily more equitable; it can lead to parochialism and corruption but in that respect it may not be any more dangerous than traditional modes of governance. It is rarely transformative, but it does, like the old-fashioned political machine, provide a training ground for developing leadership skills and a path of upward political mobility.

Diversity

My use of the term diversity as denoting one of the three criteria of urban justice is problematic. In addition to the tensions between diversity and other values that will be discussed below, claims for diversity can be challenged as simply strategic rather than in themselves germane to justice. Thus, Chris Hamnett argues that

> diversity has been pushed as a positive quality in its own right by [London Mayor Ken] Livingstone amongst others, but I think this is dubious and was simply a tactic/strategy to portray London as diverse and therefore a richer city culturally. I think tolerance is a much better criterion, as it embodies implicit positive qualities that different groups are either accepted or valued equally or are seen as having a right to exist and to access resources. This could apply to tolerance of the homeless or other groups, not simply different ethnic groups.[14]

I take his point and could have used the term "recognition" or "openness to others"—the word "tolerance," which he proposes, implies a certain patronizing quality. Diversity, however, is a convenient shorthand, encompasses reference to the physical environment as well as social relations, and refers to policy ambitions that go beyond encouraging acceptance of others to include the social composition of places.

---

14. Personal communication, June 4, 2009.

Peter Marcuse also questions whether diversity has a transcendent value beyond its political usefulness:

> Diversity is only a value for the outs, not the ins. The classic case is education today [in the United States]. What we want is decent education for blacks. Separation is unequal, because they're screwed in separate schools. So we want to bring them into the same schools as whites, so they'll be treated equally. But we can't say that, given the [decisions of the] present Supreme Court [on affirmative action and quotas]. So we argue that we want diversity [and everyone will benefit from the exposure to others]. It's a euphemism for equality. We don't want Donald Trump in...the ghetto; we want ghetto residents to have a chance to live wherever they want. If they live in a great working-class neighborhood, why do we want middle class people there too?[15]

Marcuse thus differs from those who regard a diverse society as inherently preferable to a more homogeneous one; rather, he sees it as only providing leverage in the drive for equality.

Marcuse's argument is difficult to rebut, because the term as it is employed in the United States is often used instrumentally when equality of access to privilege is really meant. In Europe social inclusion takes on a similar instrumental quality. My response is that diversity is a lesser value than equity; however, in an era of massive spatial mobility and consequent heterogeneity as streams of migrants move into urban areas around the world, diversity at the metropolitan scale becomes a necessary virtue. At the same time, this is not always the case at the level of small areas. As discussed in chapter 1, Iris Marion Young's formulation of relatively homogeneous neighborhoods with porous boundaries rather than proportionality in each precinct is a perfectly acceptable formulation.

As used by urbanists, the term diversity has a variety of meanings. Among urban designers it refers to mixing building types; among planners it may mean mixed uses or class and racial-ethnic heterogeneity in a housing development or a public space; for sociologists and cultural analysts it primarily takes on the latter meaning. During the 1960s advocates of physical and social heterogeneity constituted dissident voices against

---

15. Personal communication, September 22, 2008.

the prevailing doctrine of functional zoning and homogeneity. Most influential among them within the discipline of planning is Jane Jacobs's, whose call for a cityscape based on multiple uses resonated widely. She argues that physical heterogeneity would promote economic and social diversity:

> One principle emerges...ubiquitously, and in so many and such complex different forms [that]...it becomes the heart of my argument. This ubiquitous principle is the need of cities for a most intricate and close-grained diversity of uses that give each other constant mutual support, both economically and socially. The components of this diversity can differ enormously, but they must supplement each other in certain concrete ways. (Jacobs 1961, 14)

Jacobs urges planners to look at the real cities that people love and which are characterized by congestion, multiple interactions among strangers, short streets, and mixed uses. In later works she contends that diversity not only makes cities more appealing but is the source of economic productivity. Her reasoning anticipates the recent, widely publicized argument of Richard Florida (2002, 30), who asserts that urban diversity stimulates creativity, which in turn causes economic growth. Eventually what had been a counterargument to the dominant strand within planning became a new orthodoxy, at least within central cities. Modernist urban renewal, with its stark buildings arrayed on superblocks, came to be seen as a serious error, and mixed use became the guideline for new developments. The relationship in these new projects between physical and social differentiation, however, is not clear.

Toward the end of the twentieth century the concern among philosophers with recognition of the other, as discussed in chapter 1, converged with planning's new emphasis on diversity. The planning theorist Leonie Sandercock (1998, 2003) terms her ideal city *Cosmopolis*. Like Iris Marion Young she links recognition of the other with justice. She describes a metropolis that allows people from a variety of ethnic and racial backgrounds equal rights to city space, calls for a multiplicity of people that facilitates "the pleasures of anonymity,"[16] which she asserts is closely

---

16. Whether most people actually do consider anonymity pleasurable is questionable.

related to sexual desire and fantasy, and claims that the function of city planning should be to create urbanity.[17]

The diversity that remains the goal of theorists such as Sandercock is not the local color appealing to Jane Jacobs and creative-class cosmopolitans but rather one captured by Lefebvre's phrase "the right to the city." It refers to the inclusion of all city users within the space of the city, regardless of their cultural differences. Margaret Kohn makes an impassioned argument that the creation of citadels of exclusivity, to borrow a term from Peter Marcuse (see Marcuse and van Kempen 2002), not only restricts enjoyment of urban amenities to the affluent but prevents recognition of the situation of others.[18] In discussing the relations between well-to-do passersby and the homeless, she comments:

> There is no guarantee that encountering a panhandler on the street will elicit sympathy....Democracy does not guarantee that society will advance specific values such as the recognition and celebration of difference or heterogeneity. Some people, perhaps the majority, may feel nothing more than aversion when confronted with a panhandler or bench squatter....Nevertheless, as a society we cannot make decisions about how to solve the problem of homelessness if most citizens are unaware of the nature and scope of the problem. (Kohn 2004, 181)

Still, despite the seeming unanimity of urban theorists on the merits of diversity, they differ substantially concerning the kinds of environments planners should aim to produce—and how and whether conscious planning can create them. Thus, Richard Sennett, commenting on the widely praised development of New York's Battery Park City, laments: "Battery Park City...is planned according to current enlightened wisdom about mixed uses and the virtues of diversity. Within this model of community, however, one has the sense...'of an illustration of life' rather than life itself" (Sennett 1990).

---

17. Numerous urban historians have regarded the sharp separations between public and private space that have been demanded in most of city planning as a method of isolating women and thereby protecting them from sexual temptation (see Fainstein 2005a for a discussion of feminist critiques of planning).

18. Fincher and Iveson (2008, 13) doubt that provision of large, heterogeneous public spaces encourages "inclusionary interaction."

Planned communities designed with the goal of diversity, whether within inner cities or in New Urbanist or neotraditional greenfields developments, seem inevitably to attract accusations of inauthenticity, of being simulacra rather than the real thing. Thus, planners appear caught in an insoluble dilemma—either leave the market to take its course or impose an oxymoronic diverse order. Although in the past market-driven development produced highly differentiated landscapes as a consequence of local custom, small-plot ownership, minimal regulation, and incremental development, today's large developers, enmeshed within a globalized architectural and property market, build on a grand scale and repeat the successful formulas of everywhere else. The paradox is that the internally diverse character of festival marketplaces, entertainment districts, and live/work environments replicates itself, so that places lose their individuality just as much as had been the case under high modernism.

The relationship between diversity and equity as components of justice is not straightforward. Richard Florida's (2002) argument, referred to above, finds a happy reconciliation between the values of economic growth and social diversity. Thus, diversity, until recently a value associated more with politically left cultural critics than progrowth coalitions, has become a mantra for public officials aiming at fostering urban resurgence. Florida, however, is misinterpreted if he is taken to imply that diversity promotes equity as well as growth. He explicitly states: "While the Creative Class favors openness and diversity, to some degree it is a diversity of elites, limited to highly educated, creative people. Even though the rise of the Creative Class has opened up new avenues of advancement for women and members of ethnic minorities, its existence has certainly failed to put an end to long-standing divisions of race and gender" (Florida 2002, 80). He could have added that it not only has failed to end racial and gender divisions, but it has seemingly exacerbated income inequality.[19]

---

19. Sassen (2001) regards the existence of a large, low-wage labor force and the decline of middle income groups as the direct consequence of growth in high-end creative occupations. Although her thesis has been much debated in regard to the causal linkage, it is nevertheless the case that the prosperity of global cities such as London and New York has not spread downwards and these cities display very high levels of income inequality. Hamnett (2003) finds growing maldistribution of income in London, but he attributes it to a combination of growth at the top and unemployment rather than low-wage labor at the bottom.

Recognition, as discussed in chapter 1, is analytically distinct from re-distribution and must be regarded as a separate component of the just city. For planning it requires special attention to the creation and gover-nance of public space, but it does not necessarily mandate that each space be open to everyone all the time. We customarily see signs on playgrounds indicating that access is restricted to children and their caregivers; sepa-rating rowdy teenagers from toddlers does not transgress our sense of justice. Quiet cars on trains and parts of parks reserved for contempla-tive activities likewise are not offensive. The key is to limit behavior, not people, and to apply only reasonable limitations. The meaning of "rea-sonable," of course, is debatable, and here planning intervention ought to be on the side of the most liberal interpretation.

The objection to this argument is that certain kinds of behavior are correlated with certain kinds of people. Skateboarding, loud music, and hanging out are behaviors more likely to be displayed by teenagers and are the sorts of activities that others often find offensive or threatening. Restrictions directed at behavior can become interpreted as discrimina-tion, particularly if people of color are the ones responsible. Although there are no easy resolutions to these kinds of conflict, some amount of spatial segregation offers the best method of coping with clashing styles of behavior, provided that sufficient space is allocated to each group. Spa-tial segregation is, however, at the cost of a wholly shared environment that forces people to deal with difference.

The issue of diversity is also significant for the designing of neigh-borhoods. Requiring housing in any area to encompass a broad income range and forbidding discrimination on the basis of race, ethnicity, or disability constitute standards conducive to justice. However, requiring people to move against their will in order to achieve racial balance or dispersion of poverty is counterproductive and an infringement on lib-erty.[20] The example of Chicago is instructive here. Beginning at the turn of this century the Chicago Housing Authority (CHA) embarked on a plan to demolish its large high-rise projects and disperse their occupants. It gave most of them housing vouchers to use in the private market and promised a minority the right to return to the mixed-income projects built on the vacated sites. The CHA had for years been under court orders

---

20. Goetz (2003) argues that involuntary dispersal fails in its aims and exacts severe costs on those dispersed.

(the *Gautreaux* decisions starting in 1966) to desegregate public housing and had made some effort to relocate residents toward that end. It could point to (weak) evidence from studies of resulting moves to the suburbs that identified employment, housing, and educational improvements among African Americans who left voluntarily, using resources provided as remedies required by the court. In the 1980s, with public housing widely considered a failure, social science theories blamed geographical concentrations for the persistence of poverty over generations.[21] CHA officials and the mayor of Chicago justified their destruction of public housing and the displacement of residents by citing these theories: "Since the early 1990s CHA officials have sustained a strikingly consistent articulation of their main policy aims: to reduce the 'social isolation' of the 'distressed communities' that CHA developments had become; to employ the 'mixed-income model' of community development to save public housing; to humanize affordable housing through the use of new urbanist design techniques" (Bennett 2006, 293).

If we put aside for the moment the question of whether the Chicago regime's real aim was actually gentrification, and its justifications of its land-clearing efforts as intended to benefit the poor wholly cynical, we can in the name of diversity favor the goal of reducing social isolation and humanizing affordable housing. The effects of the policies intended to achieve this result, however, are at best mixed. The conclusions that Goetz (2005, 409) reaches concerning a similar program in Atlanta apply equally here: "Against the modest set of benefits experienced by original residents, we must keep in mind the millions of dollars spent on the demolition and redevelopment of the sites, the disruption to households and social support networks by displacement and relocation, and the permanent loss of thousands of units of low-cost public housing."

We see in this example, therefore, that the achievement of diversity may come at the cost of other values. If people are moved against their will, then democracy and equity are not served. If neighborhoods

---

21. William Julius Wilson's (1987, 1989) arguments concerning the negative effects of concentrated poverty have been especially influential. See also Wacquant (2008), who identifies causes for geographically concentrated urban marginality in the United States and France in shifts within the capitalist political economy and thus moves away from the cultural causes that are prominent in Wilson's portrayal.

FIGURE 1.   Cabrini-Green replacement housing (Chicago). Photo by Susan S. Fainstein.

become diverse as a consequence of gentrification, then the remaining
low-income residents may lose their sense of ownership of the area even
if they receive improved services:[22]

> Changing the spatial distribution of the population or remedying
> fiscal or service disparities may create a more optimal and equi-
> table spatial allocation, but in some ways it fails to acknowledge
> basic human aspirations to live in security, in community, or in a
> revitalized core. In the case of regionalist dispersal programs, the
> attempt to achieve greater equality has even destroyed human
> dignity, in an uncanny replay of the urban renewal era. (Chapple
> and Goetz 2008, 18)

The touchiest and most difficult aspect of the question of forcing
diversity comes in terms of requiring exclusionary places to welcome

22. Freeman (2006) depicts the ambivalence of poor people who remain in gentrifying
neighborhoods.

people who are different. On the one hand it is simply unethical (and usually illegal) to practice discrimination based on ascriptive characteristics like skin color or nationality; on the other, heavy-handed forced integration contravenes democratic procedures and provokes a backlash. The most positive cases are those such as Shaker Heights, Ohio, where, as Dennis Keating (1994) chronicles, elements in the receiving community facilitate the in-migration of people of a differing race. Yet even in the good examples, where the process of obtaining diversity does not transgress other values, diversity in itself is inadequate to override hostility. In a review of Keating's book, Elizabeth Lasch-Quinn (1996, 229) comments:

> Keating's faith that "interracial contacts will reduce racial conflict or discrimination" determines his ultimate promotion of "greater racial diversity among homeowners living in neighborhoods that otherwise are mostly homogeneous." That contact is needed is undeniable; that it will address the deep divisions in…society without attention to the economic sources for the perpetuation of such divisions, as well as the widespread doubt about the justice of special privileges [like mortgage assistance to those integrating neighborhoods], is belied by the evidence Keating gives of continuing hostility and neighborhood segregation even in those suburbs considered models of racial diversity.

The above comment points to a further troubling aspect of the push to further social diversity: the tension between heterogeneity and community. Robert Putnam (2007, 137) is concerned to find that "immigration and ethnic diversity tend to reduce social solidarity and social capital. New evidence from the US suggests that in ethnically diverse neighbourhoods residents of all races tend to 'hunker down.' Trust (even of one's own race) is lower, altruism and community cooperation rarer, friends fewer." Putnam expresses faith that in the long run these negative effects will diminish, resulting in new forms of social solidarity and more inclusive identities, but he offers no evidence that this will transpire.[23] Community

---

23. In their study of a neighborhood group in the Netherlands that had the fostering of diversity as a primary aim, Uitermarck and Duyvendak (2008, 130) comment: "It seems incredibly difficult to first identify ethnic differences and then to bridge them. The scenario is rather that they are not mentioned, yet bridged, or that they are mentioned but not bridged.…What

itself is, of course, a double-edged value. Although affording members social support, it is exclusionary:

> "Community" has ever been one of the key sites of social control and surveillance, bordering on overt social repression. Well-founded communities often exclude, define themselves against others, erect all sorts of keep-out signs (if not tangible walls).... As a consequence, community has often been a barrier to rather than facilitator of progressive social change, and much of the populist migration out of villages (both rural and urban) arose precisely because they were oppressive to the human spirit and otiose as a form of sociopolitical organization. (Harvey 1997, 1)

Even while contemporary planners, including the New Urbanists against whom Harvey's critique is directed, praise diversity as adding to the appeal of locales and contributing to social inclusion, they simultaneously seek to promote stronger community ties. But can people who perceive little commonality among themselves produce the bonds that give rise to mutual assistance?

Supporters of increased diversity are made uncomfortable by the seeming irreconcilability of community and diversity. Peter Marcuse (2002, 111) tries to overcome the difficulty by distinguishing between ghettoes and enclaves: ghettoes are involuntary spatial concentrations of a particular population group, while enclaves are voluntary and promote economic, social, political, and cultural development. When the enclave cluster is an ethnic minority or gender-identified group seeking to protect its way of life or overcome disadvantage, the term has a positive spin. In fact, by offering sanctuaries for cultural difference, enclaves, while being homogeneous on the micro level, contribute to diversity at the metropolitan level. Citadels, on the other hand, defined as exclusionary areas dominated by the privileged, conform to the negative description offered by Harvey, as quoted above. Thus, urban neighborhoods characterized by lack of diversity may or may not be desirable, depending on their contribution to equity and culture (Marcuse 1997).

In sum, diversity as a planning doctrine reflects an aspirational goal; at the same time the desirability of pressing for it depends very much on

---

we...see is that people develop the competence to interact together during brief moments and then return to their own network, which can be more or less segregated."

the process by which it is achieved and the class and racial/ethnic context in which it operates.

Equity

Planners face equity issues most directly when devising policies for housing and urban regeneration.[24] In relation to housing policy, the questions of income and ethnic diversity discussed above frame one significant set of decisions and will not be repeated here. Others arise from the extent to which housing is considered a right; determination of appropriate forms of tenure (private market rental; public, nonprofit, or cooperative ownership; individual ownership); and the linkage between housing and regeneration.

Early housing reformers in both the United States and Europe reacted against the insalubrious living conditions of industrial cities. After World War II government took an active role in housing provision on both sides of the Atlantic. As is well known, European states invested extensively in mass-produced rental housing that was built and operated by public entities; in contrast, the United States primarily emphasized the construction of single-family homes and developed public housing only for the poorest segment of the population. The European approach, even when governments were led by relatively conservative Christian Democratic parties, was based on an equity-oriented philosophy of mass public provision.[25] The United States, on the other hand, used demand-side subsidies, including tax deductions and mortgage guarantees, to encourage home ownership. While U.S. policy succeeded in providing decent housing to a substantial proportion of the working class, it contributed to suburban sprawl, discriminated against minorities, and caused public housing to be considered as a shelter of last resort, thereby isolating and stigmatizing its low-income occupants.[26]

---

24. Transportation is not discussed in this chapter. However, it is an area under local planning jurisdiction that also has strong equity implications. Investment choices between commuter rail and bus and decisions about fare and route structures have very different impacts on low- and high-income riders.

25. See Harloe (1995) for the definitive comparative study of social housing provision in the United States and Europe.

26. Housing scholars use the term "residualized" to refer to social housing that only serves a narrow, low-income band of the population.

By the beginning of the twenty-first century European and American approaches increasingly converged, as Europe moved away from supply-side strategies and American cities gentrified in the core. Public-sector housing production declined on both continents, while private developers of large housing complexes were being asked to include a proportion of units for low-income households. Existing social housing was restructured—in the United States the HOPE VI program replaced many public housing projects with mixed-income developments under various forms of ownership and management; in Europe governments also demolished existing estates, converting them into mixed-income developments or transferring them to housing associations (Van Kempen et al. 2005). Public subsidies to nonprofit organizations (community development corporations in the United States; housing associations in Europe) or private developers now provide the principal means by which new affordable housing gets built. Market forces rather than democratic decision making determine the size and location of housing investment except in those Northern European countries where the government uses land banking to control property investment; even in those places developer interest is usually key to the release of land. A system of rent supplements has increasingly become the norm in both North America and Europe. In the United States, however, rental assistance is not assured to those qualifying by income, while in most European countries all eligible households receive help.

The abandonment of government-owned housing as the European solution to the housing question does not necessarily represent a move away from regarding housing as a basic right. If the rent supplement is guaranteed and there are units available in which it can be applied, then demand-side subsidies offer the recipient greater choice than was the case in public housing. Although the monotony and bureaucratic ossification that characterized much social housing was not inevitable, they were common enough characteristics to make a move toward mixed-income complexes under a variety of auspices welcome to many. Also, as a larger proportion of the population aspired to ownership, the demand for social housing, which had once encompassed a broad spectrum of the population, diminished. All this meant that the right to housing as it had been implemented in Europe needed to be reconceptualized and served in new ways:

> Social democratic parties struggled but failed to come to terms with the politics and economics of the [post-Fordist] era .... They

failed to move from an increasingly ineffective defence of the economic and social framework of the post-war welfare states to a
new set of principles and ideas that might have challenged the
ideological dominance of the New Right, and provided a basis
for reclaiming the political allegiance of the 'middle mass' of the
electorate. (Harloe 1995, 499)

The requisite "new set of principles and ideas" does not necessarily
imply a move away from the goal of providing decent housing to all
nor does it undercut a commitment to supplying housing on a non-
commodified basis, but it does open up the norm of equitable housing provision to vulnerabilities. Harloe asserts that the "middle mass"
of the post-Fordist epoch is seeking greater variety and more autonomy
in its housing accommodation and that bureaucratized social housing
programs were failing to respond to their wishes. Presumably a more
decentralized, flexible system could fulfill these criteria without resort
to full privatization. Nevertheless, encouraging home ownership for the
relatively well-off endangers the redistributional character of subsidized
housing.

Dilemmas arise when we consider criteria for evaluating claims to
housing assistance. Part of the reason for the shift to nongovernmental ownership of affordable housing is that private owners have greater
freedom to discriminate against problem tenants. From the viewpoint of
other residents, having criminal or psychologically disturbed neighbors
is undesirable, and most occupants probably support their exclusion.
Such people must live somewhere, however, and equity calls for providing everyone with a home. On the other hand, democracy would seem
to require that people have at least some control over their neighbors,
even while current sentiment among social-service providers in favor
of mainstreaming tends to deny it. Other issues involve how much rent
subsidy should be provided—should a subsidized household be able to
afford a better apartment than an unsubsidized one because of the supplement available? A further dilemma arises from the notches created by
any means-tested program—that is, the income level at which one no
longer qualifies for aid. The family that is one dollar or one euro above
the limit will typically feel unfairly treated.

Homeownership for the poor is a slogan that has been popular in the
United States but has recently proved disastrous in precipitating the sub-
prime mortgage crisis. Nevertheless, it reflects a generally held sentiment

promulgated by politicians but also assimilated by the affected public.[27] Increases in housing values during the postwar period make ownership seem advantageous, and title to one's domicile gives one greater freedom of use. Ownership frequently offers tax advantages. Although the United Kingdom and France have eliminated the tax deduction for home ownership, its continuation in the United States and most European countries has meant that owners in these countries receive a significant financial benefit—and the more affluent the owner, the greater the benefit (Haffner 2002). Reformers in the United States have long called for the elimination of the homeowners' tax deduction, which has a regressive effect, but politically this is a nonstarter. So the question for American policy makers who wish to create greater equity is how to even out the benefits to renters and owners in a way that makes housing more affordable for those in lower income ranges and allows them some of the privileges of ownership.

There is a tight link between policies for urban regeneration and for housing. Broadly speaking, the designation of uses for areas under redevelopment determines who will benefit from regeneration programs; to the extent that areas remain or become residential, who will live in them constitutes the core of redevelopment policy. The 1949 U.S. Housing Act incorporates urban renewal as well as public housing in its mandates and requires that land cleared under the urban renewal provisions be predominately residential. Its successor, the 1974 Housing and Community Development Act, likewise combines housing and neighborhood improvement programs. The Dutch control the form of urban redevelopment through decisions over where to locate housing. After the war, British, French, and German cities were reshaped through the development of social housing. Now mixed-use development that juxtaposes residential and commercial space has become the instrument for shaping urban areas.

The postwar history of urban regeneration programs has involved a repetitive group of conflicts. Generally they can be encapsulated in the phrase growth versus equity. They can take the form of downtown versus the neighborhoods; demolition versus preservation; community stability

---

27. See Goetz and Sidney (1994); Krueckeberg (1999). Krueckeberg cites a survey of Boston public housing tenants indicating that the majority shared the dream of home ownership. When, during a class lecture, I argued that individual ownership was not appropriate for people with unstable employment and low income, an African American student accused me of prejudice.

versus population change; institutional expansion and subsidized construction of sports facilities versus investments in social housing, education, or community facilities; expressway construction versus public transit; megaevents versus locally oriented festivities. The argument from equity normally takes the second position in each of these dichotomies, but, within capitalist cities that are competing with one another for investment, a reflexive opposition to inducements to investors may leave cities with very little to redistribute.

This conclusion underlies Paul Peterson's contention that only national governments have it in their power to be redistributive and city governments benefit everyone by fostering economic growth. His position, however, ignores the possibility of balancing goals. Further, it does not recognize that policies dismissed as merely redistributive might make a greater long-run contribution to economic viability than supposedly growth-inducing tactics such as subsidizing sports teams. Thus Clarence Stone, in contesting Peterson's argument, proposes that an emphasis on investment in human capital and a longer time frame would lead to policies that are both redistributive and growth producing. Moreover, he considers that neglect of such investment can ultimately prove harmful to a city's interests by producing an unemployable and belligerent population (Stone 2005, 247).

Politicians tend to favor "hard" expenditures in buildings and infrastructure over "soft" investments in human capital because their efforts become visible and are achievable in the short term. Even without direct pressure from business interests for commercial development, politicians feel the need to show something demonstrable to their constituents—democratic participation does not necessarily favor long-run strategies. In European cities, where most urban public expenditures are financed by the national government, local governments are much more inclined to engage in social expenditures than their American counterparts. But, increasingly, their leadership buys into competitiveness arguments that seemingly are supported by their constituencies.[28] Thus, we have seen electoral defeats of Left parties in municipal elections, along with a shift, even among social democratic governments, toward entrepreneurialism.

In summary, housing provision and urban regeneration, two key areas of local public policy since the Second World War, are arenas in which

---

28. See Judd and Parkinson (1990); Harvey (1989).

the values of diversity, democracy, and equity are in tension. Individual aspirations for privacy and control of one's surroundings; communal sentiments toward preservation and membership in a group of like-minded people; housing shortages and lack of affordability; economic restructuring and consequent obsolescence of land uses; environmental hazards; aging of housing and infrastructure—all these make up the conditions within which framers of housing and redevelopment programs must work. Defining each dispute in terms of what constitutes the most just solution means that the equity implications should always be spelled out and given priority, but depending on the context sometimes other values ought to prevail.

Regionalism: The Politics of Scale

An obvious criticism of any discussion of the just city is in the use of the term "city"; after all, the spatial boundaries of cities are essentially arbitrary, and virtually all cities are nested within metropolitan regions. Moreover, political jurisdictions have little meaning from the standpoint of economic production; production complexes and labor markets are regional in scope. Geographical scholarship has for some years been preoccupied with "the new regionalism," which focuses on the interdependence of firms across metropolitan territories and the movement of capital within and among regions. Political scientists, in the meanwhile, have revived earlier interests in the redrawing of boundaries so as to better reflect economic and social reality. Policy makers in both Europe and North America have promoted new policies for regional and metropolitan governance, based on arguments from efficiency, democracy, and equity.

The economic logic underlying a focus on the region is largely the same in both North America and Europe: synergies identified in areas such as Silicon Valley and Emilia Romagna imply that other regions could benefit from similar growth strategies. The political underpinnings, however, are different. In the United States, where municipalities are largely dependent on their own tax base to support services, proponents of metropolitan government such as David Rusk and Myron Orfield contend that consolidation is necessary for fair distribution.[29]

---

29. Rusk and Orfield have been active popularizers of metropolitan government in the United States. See Rusk (2003); Orfield (2002).

Business interests support greater regional coordination for different reasons: they usually are primarily concerned with the inefficiencies resulting from fragmented governance of service provision in such areas as transportation and water resources and with enhancing competitiveness (Kanter 2000). European governments and business interests are also concerned with coordination and competitiveness, but the move toward political regionalism results primarily from decentralization of national governmental functions rather than from consolidation (Brenner 1999). The justifying argument in Europe is that regional governments are more responsive to the public and to local conditions than remote central bureaucracies (R. Putnam 1993).

American scholars concerned with the inequitable distribution of resources between wealthy suburbs and impoverished cities have strongly supported forms of governance that allow urban governments to have access to taxpayers outside their jurisdictions (Dreier, Mollenkopf, and Swanstrom 2004; Frug 1999). They have also seen fragmented government as causal in racial segregation, and urban sprawl as contributing to the isolation of the poor. Thus, Dreier, Mollenkopf, and Swanstrom (2004, chap. 7) make a strong argument for preventing bidding wars among municipalities and reining in peripheral growth.

The argument against bidding wars is the most unassailable. Their effect, whether intra-metropolitan or among metropolitan areas, is to intensify the race to the bottom, wherein American cities give away their tax bases in order to encourage growth. These wars are most intense in the United States because of greater municipal autonomy. Even in Europe, however, they go on, usually in the form of regulatory concessions and infrastructure provision rather than tax benefits. Although in theory one can make an equity argument in support of such programs—they could be used to attract firms to high-unemployment areas that they would otherwise avoid—empirical studies do not indicate this effect has occurred.[30] Especially counterproductive are the battles in the United States for major league sports teams, in which municipal governments provide infrastructure, underwrite loans, and give tax subsidies while the teams pocket the revenues from the facilities and from media franchises (Austrian and Rosentraub 2003).

---

30. See Fisher and Peters (1998); Peters and Fisher (2003).

More problematic is the antisprawl argument. Opposition to sprawl is a virtually reflexive stance for progressive planners, and support for it usually is associated with market-oriented, right-wing commentators.[31] Andrew Kirby, however, when reviewing one of Myron Orfield's books, mounts a challenge from the left to compact development: "Sprawl is actually good for the residents of a city if we assess it in class terms and not racial terms. Bringing new land into development on the urban fringe is likely to bring relatively affordable housing onto the market (just as it did when Levittown was built 50 years ago)" (Kirby 2004, 756). Even more unorthodoxly, Kirby goes on to defend the rigid rules of conduct associated with the homeowner associations that govern common interest developments (CIDs), the term for planned, often gated communities. He speculates that residents will be more willing to accept social diversity if everyone must conform to strict regulations. His argument thus parallels mine regarding behavior in public space—regulating behavior forestalls discrimination based on ascriptive characteristics.

Kirby's silver linings, however, are somewhat overstated. Low-density fringe development does produce cheaper housing, but at the cost of increased transportation expenses in both time and money. Limits on behavior may make people feel safer, but at a price in personal freedom and, if they are simply imposed by the developer, in democracy as well. Environmental costs of sprawl have by now been well documented, although they have possibly been exaggerated (Krieger 2005). Nevertheless, Kirby does demonstrate that the impacts of sprawl on equity and diversity are not as clear-cut as is often supposed. Like many of the issues discussed here, the extent to which a particular pattern of development maximizes equity, diversity, and democracy simultaneously has to be evaluated within a specific context.

Also problematic is the issue of metropolitan or regional governance. Iris Marion Young (2000, 234) calls for a multitiered organization of government, in which regional government frames the relations among subsidiary units. She admits, however, that "everything depends on the institutional design and the political pressures of organized citizens to use regional institutions for undermining exclusion and promoting more equality" (Young 2000, 235). Young cites the examples of Minneapolis–Saint Paul and Johannesburg, which use tax base sharing

---

31. For example, Garreau (1992); Bruegmann (2005).

to promote equity and which have the power to locate affordable housing throughout their jurisdictions. The impacts of these redistributive measures, however, are at most moderate. In the Twin Cities the Metropolitan Council that governs the region has retreated from earlier activism; Minneapolis, although housing the area's poorest population, is a net contributor of revenue, and the Council has ignored fair housing mandates (Goetz 2003, 89). In South Africa firms and well-to-do citizens have moved beyond the boundaries of the metropolitan district so as to escape its strictures.

All of this indicates that there is nothing about regional bodies that automatically makes them vehicles for greater equity. Moreover, as measures for improving democratic participation they lack both the intimacy of smaller-scale communities and the capabilities and familiarity of higher levels of government, where citizens at least are likely to know who is representing them. Also, in regions where there is substantial income disparity the affluent tend to dominate regional entities. Regionalism can remove from low-income minorities the power they gained through dominating small political units, whether American inner cities or European working-class suburbs. Thus, while metropolitan governing institutions potentially can redistribute income, disperse affordable housing, encompass a diverse public, and offer the possibility of popular control of a level of government with greater capacity than small municipalities, the likelihood that they will produce these results is slim.

Implications

This chapter has shown that in relation to the broad issue areas of urban policy, values of democracy, diversity, and equity may pull in different ways. Within crucial urban policy arenas, context and historical moment make the choice of the most just policy indeterminate in the abstract. Does this mean that we can make no decision rules concerning policies that will further justice in the city? My argument in the concluding chapter of this book is that we can list criteria by which to formulate and evaluate policy comparable to Martha Nussbaum's listing of capabilities even if we cannot go as far as specifying programs. The particular policies that best satisfy the criteria will vary according to time and place, but the fact that we cannot specify *ex ante* the most progressive policies does not mean that we cannot establish bases of judgment.

The next three chapters examine the redevelopment histories of New York, London, and Amsterdam in relation to the issues discussed in this chapter. The purpose is to apply the criteria of justice—democracy, diversity, and equity—to policies adopted and, where they have been found wanting, indicate alternatives that would more closely conform to these values.

3

NEW YORK

New York City's history of urban redevelopment programs has been highly influential within the United States. Although New York, as a consequence of both its size and global importance, is not typical of American cities, the particular policies it has adopted have been widely replicated and raise clearly many of the issues discussed in the preceding chapter. In this chapter I present a brief history of redevelopment policy in the city and then examine some recent efforts in order to evaluate their impacts and to indicate alternatives that would contribute to more just outcomes.[1] I conclude with an evaluation of New York's performance in relation to the criteria of equity, democracy, and diversity.

From Robert Moses to Fiscal Crisis (1945–1975)

Between the end of the Second World War and 1960, when he resigned his various administrative positions in New York City and New York State, Robert Moses dominated planning and redevelopment in the city.[2]

---

1. Much of the historical information in this chapter is drawn from Fainstein and Fainstein (1988).

2. There is a substantial literature about Robert Moses. Robert Caro's (1974) magisterial biography is extremely critical. Ballon and Jackson (2007) have edited a book emphasizing his achievements.

Stuyvesant Town/Peter Cooper Village, an early postwar project, which Moses conceived before the federal government had established its urban renewal program, set the pattern for later endeavors in both New York and elsewhere. The city condemned eighteen blocks of tenements in Manhattan, housing twelve thousand people, then sold the land to the Metropolitan Life Insurance Company (Met Life), which assumed complete responsibility for planning and tenant selection (Simon 1970). The hallmarks of this endeavor were the total demolition of existing structures; the displacement of residents; private-sector control of design; a Manhattan location that reflected the centrality of that borough; the absence of citizen involvement; and restriction of the new housing to a white tenantry. Evaluated according to the three criteria of justice, planning for it most obviously was undemocratic and initially the complex was not diverse. Its impact on equity is somewhat more complicated to establish: income restrictions and rent regulation made decent apartments in nicely landscaped surroundings available to working- and lower-middle-class families, many of them including returning veterans—but at the cost of displacing the original residents. Eventually, as a consequence of court decisions, over several decades the complex became a model of diversity, housing a mixed ethnic and racial population encompassing a fairly substantial income range.[3] In 2006, however, Met Life, which had already moved about a quarter of the units out of the rent stabilization system, sold the project to real estate giant Tishman Speyer at a price indicating that the new owners had to push tenants out of the rent regulation system in order to make their purchase profitable (Bagli 2006). If they succeeded, the equity and diversity eventually achieved within the structures would diminish in the future. The impact of the 2008–9 recession, however, was to make the owners default on their debt service and go into foreclosure. Their already perilous financial situation had been further undermined by a court decision requiring them to refund rents they had already received. If bankruptcy forced the sale of the buildings at a heavily discounted price, it is possible that the future landlord could sustain the current, affordable rent structure (Bagli 2009). The sixty-year history of this project thus points to one of the difficulties of evaluation—over the course of time the same project can have quite varying outcomes in relation to principles of justice.

---

3. Because of rent regulation, as time passed the price levels of the apartments increasingly dropped below market rents.

Moses often declared his opposition to planning, but he nevertheless had a defined vision of a dense city, centered on Manhattan, efficiently connected internally and externally by a network of superhighways. He proceeded opportunistically, project by project, but implicit in his various schemes was the intention to create an efficient, modern metropolis that served the middle class. He notoriously ran expressways through closely knit neighborhoods, destroyed housing to allow expansion of institutions, and, as director of the city's Committee on Slum Clearance (CSC), displaced low-income communities in order to construct apartments for middle- and upper-income households.[4] At the same time, in his role as head of the New York City Housing Authority he oversaw the building of 135,000 new public housing units.[5] Although, as a consequence of demolition, he did not expand the supply of the lower-income housing stock, he nevertheless did produce social housing on a much larger scale than his counterparts in other American cities.[6] Together, the public housing program, middle-income construction subsidies, and rent regulation, which had been installed as an emergency measure during the war and retained thereafter, made New York unique among American cities in the extent to which its government promoted housing for lower-income groups. It did not, however, encourage racial diversity, and the city became increasingly segregated over the postwar period as urban renewal eliminated scattered sites of black residency, while the ghettos of Harlem, Bedford-Stuyvesant, Brownsville, and Jamaica enlarged and consolidated.

By 1960 the massive urban renewal program of the Moses years had halted in the face of community opposition. The emphasis changed to neighborhood preservation and rehabilitation, and Mayor Robert Wagner's administration committed itself to involving neighborhood residents in planning as well as to increasing the number of low- and middle-income units. Nevertheless, despite this commitment public housing construction dwindled. By the mid-1960s New York's public housing had become mostly black and Hispanic; consequently, it lost popular support, and referenda for public housing bonds were defeated in statewide

---

4. Middle-income housing was primarily built under the New York State sponsored Mitchell-Lama program, which subsidized private and nonprofit developers, who built both rental and cooperatively owned buildings. See McClelland and Magdowitz (1981, 156–60.)

5. In the initial years of public housing its occupants were predominately white and employed.

6. See Abu-Lughod (1999, 208); Friedland (1983).

votes in 1964 and 1965.[7] In the meanwhile, though, subsidized moderate-income housing had expanded substantially, resulting in desirable buildings throughout the city that for decades offered decent accommodation to large numbers of people and which, eventually, became increasingly racially and ethnically integrated. Thus, even though the developments were not originally intended to foster diversity, they ended up doing so. And, as housing prices escalated while the costs associated with living in these complexes remained relatively stable, their reach extended to lower levels of the income distribution than their original targets. The catch was that these projects all had sunset provisions that allowed them to revert to market rate after a period of years; thus, tens of thousands of units began to be withdrawn from the affordable housing pool around the start of the new millennium.

During the latter part of the 1960s and into the 1970s, New York became increasingly beset by conflict between urban bureaucracies, still strongly white dominated, and their black and Hispanic clients. The 1966 election of John V. Lindsay as mayor resulted in a move toward greater incorporation of minority groups into governance. The mayor, utilizing both city funds and federal Model Cities money, funneled more resources into the poorest neighborhoods.[8] Co-op City, a development sponsored by organized labor and subsidized by the State of New York, added over fifteen thousand units for moderate-income households in the Bronx.[9] Overall the Lindsay era was marked by redistributional programs, racial integration of the city's bureaucracies, decentralization of the administration along with new avenues for citizen participation, and symbolic recognition of minority groups. It was also, however, plagued by arson, housing abandonment, rising crime rates, and deteriorating public transit covered by graffiti.[10] Many considered the city to have become ungovernable (Yates 1977).

---

7. See Jackson (1976); Clapp (1976); Abrams (1965).

8. Lindsay is credited with averting the riots that occurred in other cities during these tumultuous times (Shefter 1985; Abu-Lughod 2007).

9. Between 1965 and 1975 total housing units increased by only 1.6 percent as a consequence of massive abandonment, despite the extremely low vacancy rate of 1.5 percent in 1965 (Kristof 1976).

10. Although an artistic avant-garde defended the graffiti—and indeed some of the graffiti writers became important artists—most people regarded the decorated subway cars as symbolic of the breakdown of order.

Mayor Lindsay's administration, despite its commitment to low-income groups, cannot be simply characterized by the expansion of programs serving poor and minority groups. Lindsay also encouraged commercial development in Manhattan through tax incentive programs. Zoning bonuses nominally rewarded developers for creating spaces open to the public, but they were frequently misused or hidden, allowing developers to build at scales greatly exceeding what was permissible under the zoning code while providing no public benefit (Kayden 2000). Moreover, a state-level agency, the Urban Development Corporation (UDC),[11] simultaneously sponsored large commercial projects as well as middle- and upper-income housing, including the development of Roosevelt Island in the East River. Meanwhile the Port Authority of New York and New Jersey, which likewise operated independently of the city government, built the World Trade Center; it opened in the early 1970s and resulted in the displacement of a thriving district of small electronics stores known as Radio Row (Goldberger 2004). The state agencies were able to operate with minimal public consultation and with little concern for the low-income population.

Lindsay's administration was thus rife with contradictions. In some ways the mayor was having his cake and eating it too. Even while addressing inner-city problems and speaking of the need to assist poor people, he was simultaneously looking to other levels of government to assist him in the creation of a restructured city, with an economy based in finance, fashion, the media, and advanced services. This strategy did not prevent his rhetorical support for poor minorities from fomenting a backlash among white working-class ethnic groups, who regarded him as coddling the undeserving poor at their expense. In truth this stratum was largely left out by his policies, which primarily served elite and minority interests and provided little for the port and manufacturing workers who were witnessing the disappearance of their jobs and community life. The widespread perception of Lindsay as out of touch with the white working class led directly to the backlash resulting in, first, the mayoralty of Abraham Beame, then the very long tenure of Edward I. Koch.

Lindsay was mayor during a period when the American economy was undergoing a massive shift out of traditional manufacturing. No urban government in the United States could do much to affect this, and it set

---

11. This agency was subsequently renamed the Empire State Development Corporation.

the context in which an intensified competition among cities for investment began. Thus, the blame that Lindsay incurred from white, working- and middle-class New Yorkers was largely for events beyond his control. His concern with minorities and the poor, however, alienated groups that were losing their once secure economic niches, either because of the shrinkage of industrial work or the integration of the civil service bureaucracies. In fact, one of the notable achievements of the Lindsay mayoralty in terms of increasing equity and diversity was to transform the public services (with the exception of police and fire) to more accurately reflect the composition of the larger population.[12] The effect of these policies, particularly within the area of education, was to exacerbate tensions between civil servants and their clients.[13]

The period commencing in 1974 marked a backtracking from the egalitarian goals of the Lindsay era. At the national level the Housing and Community Development Act of 1974 terminated the Model Cities program, which had been the principal source of funds used by Lindsay to assist impoverished communities. The Community Development Block Grant (CDBG), which replaced the federal urban renewal program as well as Model Cities, gave city governments wide latitude in how they used the funds they received. For New York the CDBG funding formula represented a reduction in resources available for redevelopment programs, and they were employed in a less targeted manner than Model Cities monies.[14] Abraham Beame, who succeeded Lindsay as mayor in 1974, began a trend away from a focus on poor areas of the city that largely continued for the rest of the century. An indication of his approach was his appointment of Roger Starr as head of his Housing and Development Administration. Starr proposed a "triage strategy" of "planned shrinkage" (Starr 1976) that would direct funds away from the neediest areas and

---

12. During the Lindsay years (1966–73) black public employment in New York increased by nearly two-thirds, although as a share of total employment it only grew from 21 to 25 percent since a substantial number of white public-sector jobs were also added. Between 1971 and 1990 the black share of government employment increased from 20.9 percent to 35.4 percent. (Fainstein and Fainstein 1994, table 1).

13. One of the formative battles of the period was the conflict over community control of the schools, which pitted minority parents against the predominately white, Jewish teachers union (Fainstein and Fainstein 1974).

14. New York uniquely used its CDBG funds to maintain in rem housing, the stock of housing acquired by the city on account of tax delinquency, with the result that the in rem program for a while became a second large public housing program. Eventually these properties were taken over either by community development corporations or private owners.

toward those "where they can accomplish something for the people who are living there" (Starr 1975, 262).[15]

In 1975 New York entered a fiscal crisis that resulted in the suspension of capital spending and a severe curtailment of services. It was only saved from bankruptcy by turning over the management of its finances to two unelected bodies, the Municipal Assistance Corporation (MAC), an autonomous city agency, and the Emergency Financial Control Board (EFCB), an agency of the State of New York. These two entities, which were controlled by business-dominated boards, salvaged the city's credit through allocation of public-service-union pension funds and designated tax revenues to debt retirement. Although New York eventually regained solvency and emerged from the dictates of the two oversight agencies, the government's previous commitments to welfare and impoverished neighborhoods diminished and economic growth became the lodestar of its endeavors.[16] Edward I. Koch, Beame's successor, claimed "I speak for the middle class" (Koch 1984) and brought together an electoral coalition of white Catholics and Jews (Reichl 2007). During his twelve-year reign he strongly promoted the use of tax subsidies to stimulate speculative office development and to keep firms from leaving the city.

Resurgence (1976–2001)

During the 1980s New York's fortunes revived. Immigration fueled population growth, resulting in the revitalization of moribund neighborhoods. The economic boom ensuing from deregulation, globalization, and innovation within financial institutions set off accompanying growth in the real estate sector and in business services such as advertising, architecture, and law. Even when New York was the country's largest manufacturing center, it was also its financial capital. Now, the increased importance of the financial sector meant that, despite the continued departure of headquarters of manufacturing firms and a precipitous drop in factory

---

15. Starr predicted that the city's population would shrink by millions and argued that the South Bronx, which had suffered serious abandonment at the time he was writing, should be vacated altogether. By 2008, however, New York's population had increased to its all-time peak, and the South Bronx was fully rebuilt and reinhabited.

16. See Mollenkopf (1988) and Brecher and Horton (1984). Marcuse (1981) argued that the crisis was deliberately created to force the city government to contract its social welfare expenses.

FIGURE 2. Diverse New York: Jackson Heights, Queens. Photo by John Powers.

jobs, the city retained its hold on an extraordinarily wealthy stratum of firms and individuals, who in turn patronized its cultural industries and purchased services and amenities of all kinds. During the latter part of his term of office, in response to political pressure, Koch inaugurated a ten-year housing program in which the city's own capital budget supplemented other sources of funds to support nonprofit community development corporations and for-profit builders in the construction of affordable units (Schill et al. 2002).[17]

The city suffered from a severe recession at the beginning of the 1990s, which caused many observers to fear that its upward economic trajectory had halted. David Dinkins, New York's first African American mayor, took office when the recession had pushed the city into its second fiscal crisis and severely limited his capacity to redirect resources toward his minority constituencies. By mid-decade Rudolf Giuliani had become mayor, and the trends of the 1980s reasserted themselves as a new stock

---

17. Most American cities restrict their housing subsidies to funds available from inadequate federal programs and do not provide money from own-source revenues.

NEW YORK

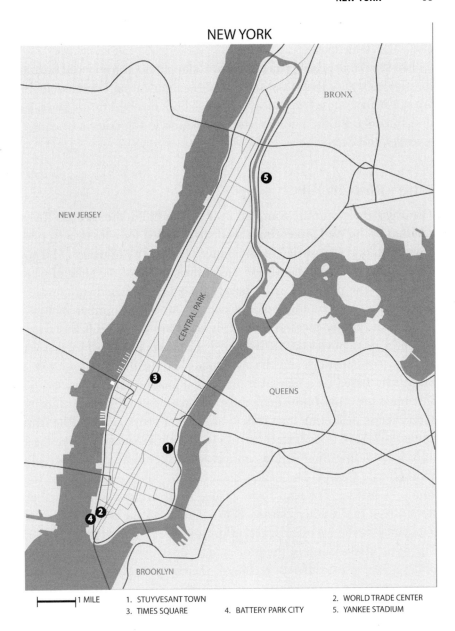

BRONX

NEW JERSEY

CENTRAL PARK

❺

❸

QUEENS

❶

❹❷

BROOKLYN

| ⊢——⊣1 MILE | 1. STUYVESANT TOWN | | 2. WORLD TRADE CENTER |
| | 3. TIMES SQUARE | 4. BATTERY PARK CITY | 5. YANKEE STADIUM |

market boom got under way. Despite the aggregate growth of the 1990s, however, median income declined (NYC Dept. of City Planning, n.d.) and only increased again during the mayoralty of Michael Bloomberg in the new century. The Giuliani administration was widely perceived as unsympathetic to racial minorities, and, as the housing market tightened, the city's contribution to mitigating its housing problems declined (Schill et al. 2002, table 1).

Two very large urban projects, both in Manhattan, commenced during the 1980s: Battery Park City and the redevelopment of Times Square.[18] We can analyze these two endeavors, which both involved major financial investments from the public sector, in relation to the criteria of equity, diversity, and democracy.

Battery Park City (BPC)

The original plan for the complex, built on landfill in the Hudson River adjacent to the Wall Street financial district, called for a modernist new town. The land was owned by the Battery Park City Authority (BPCA), a quasi-governmental institution under the control of the State of New York, with the power to issue bonds. To be constructed on elevated superblocks, each building would contain an equal number of low-, middle-, and upper-income units.[19] By the time the landfill was completed in 1976, however, the fiscal crisis had dampened enthusiasm for any new construction, and the site languished for the next four years. Eventually, based on a new plan that called for normal city blocks and jettisoned the aim of housing a range of income groups, the Authority succeeded in attracting investors. It accepted a proposal from the firm Olympia & York (O&Y) to construct the World Financial Center, a set of office buildings that would connect, via a skyway, to the decade-old World Trade Center. The offices succeeded in attracting some of the country's leading financial firms in luxurious accommodations; they were linked to a Winter Garden that was open to the public and were flanked by attractive open space, affording views of New York Harbor. The residential section of the project was constructed by a multiplicity of developers using different architects, thereby providing more physical variety than envisioned in the original plan. In terms of who could live in the dwellings, however, their price structure at first restricted occupancy to those able to afford the market rate. Later four "80–20" buildings, in which 20 percent of the units were reserved for families with incomes below 50 percent of the city median, slightly altered the

---

18. These two cases are described in greater detail in my book *The City Builders* (2001a).

19. One middle-income complex was built according to the original plan. See Ponte (1982), Gill (1990) and Gordon (1997) for discussions of the development of BPC.

FIGURE 3. Battery Park City Winter Garden. Photo by Susan S. Fainstein.

population mix. Shopping was rather limited, but in addition to luxury stores and a number of restaurants, there was a street of basic service establishments.

The BPCA continued to own the land and leased it to the developers. It received ground rent and a civic facilities payment to cover upkeep of the sumptuous outdoor common spaces that ornamented the development. In addition, the city received a payment in lieu of taxes (PILOT) based on the value of the commercial and residential properties, although tax abatements initially limited the amounts received. Sponsors justified the exclusion of low-income households from the residential buildings and the granting of tax subsidies for the office towers and luxury apartments by indicating that the proceeds would support construction of greater amounts of low-income housing elsewhere in the city where land was cheaper. In 1986 the BPCA issued $400 million of revenue bonds for low-income housing and promised to provide more. The city government, however, chose to place the money received after 1986 in the general fund rather than committing it to housing.

The contribution then of this project to equity and diversity is dubious but not nonexistent. It does add substantially to the city's tax base, and the retention of the land in government ownership means that the public fisc can gain from increases in its value. Its gorgeous parks, Winter Garden, playgrounds, and waterfront views offer a valuable amenity to all New Yorkers. Although its location and relative isolation mean that usage tends to be disproportionately by the well-to-do who live in or near the development, on sunny weekends one can see a considerable variety of users. In one instance the BPCA overrode residents' preferences in order to foster greater access by the wider public. Residents, out of a desire to maintain exclusivity, had opposed linking the south end of the development to Battery Park, a heavily used public space at the tip of Manhattan. Nevertheless, the Authority went ahead and built the connecting walkway, thus supporting equity and diversity over the preferences of residents. Whether this should be construed as overriding democratic decision making depends on how one defines the constituent public. Construction of a cinema multiplex, a hotel, a memorial to the Irish famine, and two museums have added to the mixture of uses and visitors. The scorecard on equity and diversity, then, is not wholly negative.

In terms of democracy, Battery Park City comes up short. No citizen participation was involved in the planning of the complex. Once the complex became inhabited, residents did acquire a voice in further recreation planning, causing changes in the uses of space, but there was no popular input into the composition of further construction. Given the evident desire of the residents to maintain the area as an upper-class enclave, if democratic participation were to produce greater equity, it would have had to include a much broader segment of the public than BPC residents and the local community board.[20] Even then, it is difficult to imagine how such a group would be constituted.

Was there an alternative that could have been more just? Critics of BPC see it as only a citadel of the wealthy and a simulacrum of design diversity rather than a real place (Kohn 2004). Yet many New Yorkers regard it as a welcome haven, one of the few locations where they can get unobstructed views of the water in attractive surroundings. The weekend crowd does not consist of those who have summer homes in the country but of ordinary people who welcome the chance to retreat to a pleasing environment,

---

20. New York's community boards are appointed by the city council members for their district and by the borough president. They exercise advisory power over land use and capital budget matters. See Marcuse (1987) on their role and limitations.

easily accessible on foot from the Lower East Side and by subway from Brooklyn and northern Manhattan. Its inaccessibility is exaggerated by its critics—Battery Park City does create a public space used by many.

On equity grounds the major issue is the exclusivity of the residential buildings. The argument that, by reserving space for upper-income people, the project generates substantial funds that can be used for housing and social services elsewhere is somewhat sophistical. There is no guarantee that the revenues will be used for redistributional purposes—and little evidence that they have been so used. Furthermore, even if the apartment prices are to be primarily set by the market, a far larger proportion could be retained for lower-income households. Also, although some affordable units have been added, the three buildings in the original complex, initially reserved for moderate-income households, are reverting to market rate as the time limit for restrictions on rent levels has passed.

A practical alternative program for the development could have used revenue bonds derived from the project's future earnings not just to fund housing elsewhere in the city but to supplement developers' cross-subsidies within the buildings so as to provide below-market units in every structure. Further, the subsidized units should never be allowed to become market rate, as has been the general case for privately owned subsidized structures. Provisions that would have required rent regulation to persist in the existing moderate-income complex also would have furthered equity. The result would have been both more equity and more diversity.

Producing a more democratic process, however, raises thorny issues. The exclusion of the city council from deliberation and placing governance of the project within an insulated public authority removed it entirely from public scrutiny. As well as New York City, the State of New Jersey, immediately across the Hudson River and only a five-minute train ride away, was affected by the development yet not included in any way.[21] Like the regeneration of London's Docklands (to be discussed in the next chapter) such a large project influenced not only its immediate district but a much larger region. Yet there was no forum in which regional deliberation could take place. At the micro level, since the complex was built

---

21. Because the World Trade Center was a project of the Port Authority of New York and New Jersey, New Jersey's governor had a voice in its creation. He insisted that the Port Authority take over and improve the PATH trains that ran between the two states as the quid pro quo for his assent to the project.

on vacant land, there was no existing community to be consulted, and the local community board represented a disproportionately affluent district, much of which was occupied by office buildings. Proponents of deliberative democracy offer few clues as to the mechanisms for a democratic process that would encompass multiple jurisdictions and involve more than just an interested few.

Battery Park City thus is not a clear-cut example of an unjust policy. It did not displace people, it generated substantial tax revenues by attracting major firms, and it provided ample public spaces that were open to the general public.[22] Nevertheless, it could have gone much farther toward accommodating a broader range of residents and, most important, used the revenues generated for the construction of affordable housing.

Times Square Redevelopment

Located in the center of Manhattan, Times Square after the Second World War became the home of increasingly seedy enterprises. Pornography purveyors acted as magnets for loiterers, hustlers, drug dealers, and prostitutes, who dominated the streetscape. The city government came up with a plan for the area that would transform it into a sober office district.[23] In addition to including massive tax forgiveness, the project involved the transfer of air rights over the theaters on 42nd Street, which allowed the buildings to achieve a height and bulk that greatly exceeded what was permitted under the zoning code.[24] Although initially developers were supposed to pay for renovation of the subway station beneath it—the city's largest and busiest—commitments to remodel the station were dropped. A public-private partnership, the 42nd Street Redevelopment Corporation, coordinated the project; as a subsidiary of the state's Urban Development Corporation, it held the power of eminent domain and the ability to override the city's zoning laws. Relocation of 240 businesses resulted in substantial hardship for many of them, particularly

---

22. In 2008 the investment bank Goldman Sachs constructed a 2.1 million square foot headquarters building on one of the remaining sites in BPC. It had earlier constructed a new building in Jersey City, but this proved unpopular with its employees.

23. The definitive work describing the transformation of Times Square is Sagalyn (2001). See also Fainstein (2001a).

24. Air rights become available when buildings do not reach the height allowed under the zoning code. Rights to the space not used can be transferred to adjacent buildings that then can be built higher than would otherwise be permitted.

FIGURE 4.   Times Square. Photo accessed http://flickr.com/photos/click-see/25803644/.

small firms. The adjacent Clinton residential neighborhood resisted the plan, fearing that it would produce gentrification of Manhattan's last centrally located working-class community.

The plan went through a number of permutations, and its implementation was subject to long delays, first as a consequence of lawsuits brought by businesses resisting eminent domain, then as a result of the economic recession of the early 1990s. The ultimate project encompassed office buildings just as large as originally projected, but clad in lively facades covered with illuminated advertising. Requirements that the new buildings include entertainment uses resulted in a more diverse district than originally anticipated. The completed project contained publishers, entertainment companies, prestigious corporate law firms, and major financial institutions as well as numerous clubs, restaurants, movie and legitimate theaters, hotels, and shops. It was an undeniable economic success, but it represented a plan that strongly reflected the desires of corporate capital and offered no direct benefits to nonelite groups, with the exception of $25 million awarded to the Clinton neighborhood in response to its protests.

Most of the criticism that has been levied against the new Times Square focuses on its "Disneyfication" and exclusion of the rougher elements that formerly defined the vicinity. According to Alexander Reichl:

> Forty-second Street has come to embody the Disney model of public space as an orderly, controlled, and themed environment. Private security and sanitation teams of the Times Square Business Improvement District (BID) supplement city services to create an enhanced sense of cleanliness, safety, and order. Public officials of the 42nd Street Development Project, in close cooperation with powerful developers and corporate investors—including Disney—determine which commercial and cultural products will have access to the street, and how they may present themselves visually....More and more, Forty-second Street and Times Square are Disneyspace. (Reichl, 1999, 175)

Although assessment of the authenticity of a place is necessarily subjective, I would still take issue with Reichl's fear that Times Square has become too orderly and controlled. It remains a place where extraordinarily diverse crowds clog the sidewalks to gawk at the signage on the buildings and at the productions under way at the MTV studios visible overhead (Sassen and Roost 1999). What has changed is that, while the former denizens of the area are still around, they are overwhelmed by the numbers of middle-class men and women who formerly shunned its streets or hastened through them on the way to other places. Times Square does not fail on the metric of diversity. In fact, the design of the redevelopment made the ground level into a place intended to draw in multitudes. In 2009 the Square was partially pedestrianized, and seating that attracted intense use was made available in what had been a roadway. The contemporary streetscape contrasts sharply with the area around the Times Square Marriott Hotel, built in 1985, which presents blank walls, has an upper-floor lobby, and gives the general appearance of a fortified bastion. Whereas the Marriott represents the prevalent view of its time that visitors would only come to a central-city location if it was clearly defensible and isolated, the renovated Times Square adheres to the concept that lively streets are desirable. Furthermore, at the beginning of the twenty-first century, as was true one hundred years earlier, the amusements on offer, which include video game arcades, cinema multiplexes, and themed restaurants, are aimed at popular taste.

Reichl better captures the real issues raised by this development project when he states that

> the desire to redevelop Times Square was ultimately driven by the recognition of the enormous profits that could be made from real-estate development on West Forty-second Street....It is this economic potential...that explains the persistence of redevelopment efforts. It also explains why owners had to be forced, through eminent domain, to part with property on the worst block in town; they saw the price of their holdings in terms of their potential for office development rather than in terms of their present uses. (Reichl 1999, 173)

Although it is difficult to calculate the total public subsidy, which includes land acquisition costs, infrastructure improvements, and tax forgiveness, it is substantial and certainly exceeds $1 billion.[25]

Times Square redevelopment contributed to economic growth in late twentieth-century New York and assisted in the conversion of the city's economy toward a stronger entertainment and tourism orientation. Because leisure industries are labor intensive, probably the new uses offered employment opportunities to workers competing for jobs in the low-wage sector.[26] At the same time, however, the development greatly increased pressure on the Clinton neighborhood, where many of the restaurant workers lived and frequently returned home from work in the early hours of the morning. Thus, their employment gains were balanced by their likely housing and transportation losses.

A more equitable development plan would have included affordable housing on the western part of 42nd Street, where two towers for

---

25. Problems of calculation result from the difficulty of estimating future tax receipts foregone over the course of many years and what the city's share will be of gains in value in which it participates (to some extent the two are inversely proportional). John Mollenkopf (1985, 13) estimated city tax expenditure would amount to a present value of $400 million at a time when its total expense budget was $20 billion. His was probably an underestimate due to the lengthy hiatus that occurred between the emptying of the existing buildings and occupancy of the new, resulting in a period when no taxes were collected in the area.

26. Large hotels and restaurants are unionized in New York. Thus, although most of the low-end jobs created as a result of expanded tourism pay less than the median wage, their returns are still relatively good compared to what service workers receive in other industries. They are, however, much lower than what factory workers in unionized industries get. See Gladstone and Fainstein (2003).

low- and moderate-income residents already existed.[27] It would have provided more public open space. The office buildings need not have been so massive as to result in constant extreme sidewalk congestion. The development agreement between the city and the developers of the office structures could have required that a portion of the profits be earmarked to benefit Clinton residents who were the citizens most immediately affected by the project.

From the standpoint of the city as a whole, the Times Square area had been underdeveloped relative to its central location and accessibility. Upgrading it was desirable, but the sacrifice of so much public money to make it happen is not justifiable on equity grounds. The claim was that without taxpayer support firms would not have been willing to develop office towers in such an undesirable part of town. The subsidies were intended to reduce development costs, resulting in lower rent levels to attract occupants otherwise unwilling to go there. As it turned out, however, the office buildings captured prestigious tenants paying very high rents. The developers kept the profits nonetheless—although the city to some extent shared in them, as it retained ownership of the land acquired through eminent domain and received lease payments from the building owners that reflected increased values. As in the case of Battery Park City (and the World Trade Center), public ownership of land meant that profits were not wholly privatized—an extremely unusual outcome of redevelopment activities in New York, and the United States more broadly.

Reichl (1999, 177) argues that the entire renewal area was under the control of one insulated authority, the 42nd Street Redevelopment Corporation, which "was created to implement the agenda of public and private elites." Although this entity did have operational control of the development, the plan required approval by the city's Board of Estimate.[28] Intense lobbying efforts accompanied the hearings before this body, and many opponents spoke against the project, arguing that it was too big, gave away too much to the developers, and would be a force for gentrification. Supporters contended that it would restore the area to its former

---

27. The buildings were mainly restricted to people in the entertainment business. Originally intended as upper-income residences, the city took them over when the original plan failed and used federal Section 8 subsidies to finance their use as low-income residences.

28. This is a now defunct body, which was declared unconstitutional because it did not conform to the one person–one vote principle. Its membership consisted of the mayor, the five borough presidents (who represented constituencies of quite different sizes), the president of the city council, and the city controller.

glory, provide needed space for the expansion of the midtown business district, and be key to the city's future economic development. There was extensive discussion and coverage in the press. In fact, during the past forty years there may well have been more deliberation over the future of Times Square than over any other project except the rebuilding of the World Trade Center after 9/11. It was, however, a clear case where deliberation failed to persuade those in power to change their views. In the words of Bent Flyvbjerg (2003), "*Power defines reality.* Power concerns itself with defining reality rather than with discovering what reality 'really' is."

New York after 2001

The aftereffects of the World Trade Center attack of September 11, 2001, and the national recession of that year comprised a surprisingly short-lived setback to the city's economy (Chernick 2005). Quick economic recovery emboldened the new administration of Mayor Michael Bloomberg to embark on an ambitious redevelopment program, harkening back to the early days of urban renewal (Fainstein 2005c). Under his hard-driving deputy mayor for economic development, Daniel Doctoroff, Bloomberg launched a number of megaprojects and framed a plan labeled PlaNYC 2030, which focused on environmental sustainability.[29]

The individual projects differed from Moses's urban renewal efforts in being rationalized in the name of economic development and environmental improvement rather than the elimination of blight and slum clearance. In their physical manifestations, which in many cases incorporated mixed uses and retention of the street grid, they constituted an absorption of Jane Jacobs's invective against the dullness created by city planning under urban renewal. But, even though they were not modernist in their physical forms, they were in their functional aims.[30] As in the first stage of urban renewal, they represented the imprint of a master builder rather than community-based planning. Participation by citizens was restricted to their testimony at public hearings, listening to presentations by the plans' progenitors, and the provision of advice by the community board for the affected area. Beyond these minimal requirements

29. See Angotti (2008) for a critique of the plan. The plan is on line at http://www.nyc.gov/html/planyc2030/html/plan/plan.shtml.

30. See Scott (1998) on authoritarian high modernism.

under the Uniform Land Use Review Process (ULURP),[31] no legislation imposed community input. Among the largest projects in terms of public expenditure was the construction of four sports facilities: new stadiums for the Yankees and Mets baseball teams; a football stadium for the Jets; and a basketball arena for the Nets.[32] The development of the new Yankee Stadium provided a particularly egregious example of the use of economic growth as a rationalization to disguise injustice.

Yankee Stadium

Yankee Stadium was a privately owned structure until 1972, when New York City condemned it and took over ownership. The city purchased the stadium in response to threats by the Yankees' owners that they would move the team elsewhere if it were not renovated (Blumenthal 1972). The city agreed to refurbish the structure and ended up spending more than $125 million, six times the initial estimate. At that time the city gave two reasons for its investment in the stadium: retaining the team would contribute to economic development and would stimulate the physical improvement of the West Bronx. Due to cost overruns, however, the promised community investment was cut from the budget (Bai 1994). More than thirty years later, these two arguments continue to be the justifications given for another, much larger city investment in Yankee Stadium.

In the 1990s under the Giuliani administration the team had again threatened to leave New York and demanded that it be permitted to move to a site on the Hudson River in midtown Manhattan. The city government countered with an offer of $650 million for improvements to the existing building along with construction of an adjacent "Yankee Village" and transit station. Bronx residents called instead for an alternate revitalization plan that would include a new police academy, which it was believed would serve the dual purpose of making the area safer and contributing year-round to economic development.[33] The city, however, claimed that,

---

31. The Uniform Land Use Review Process requires a series of approvals and includes scrutiny by the district's community board.

32. At the time of this writing, the three stadiums had been completed, but the Nets arena was being delayed due to the problems of the developer, Forest City Ratner, in gaining financing.

33. This would have meant moving the existing police academy from an affluent part of Manhattan to the Bronx. The proposal to relocate the academy drew strong opposition from

although it could afford to subsidize the stadium, it had no money for such a development. Discussion of the stadium went into hiatus, as the owner and the city remained in disagreement over the location.

In 2006 the city council finally approved plans for a new Yankee Stadium in the Bronx, adjacent to the existing one, and construction began shortly thereafter. The team's successes on the field along with improved perceptions of the South Bronx had contributed to sold-out games, causing the withdrawal of the Yankees' objections to keeping the stadium in the same location. The team, however, wanted a brand-new facility that would accommodate profitable skyboxes and incorporate shops and restaurants. Originally conceived as part of New York's (failed) bid for the 2012 Olympics, the new venue opened in 2009. Its cost was first estimated at $800 million but later escalated to $1.3 billion. The team was theoretically paying for the new structure itself, but it raised financing through tax-free state bonds, and its future payments in lieu of taxes (PILOT) to the city were to be used to service the bonds.[34] In addition, the city and state governments were directly assuming the costs for the construction of a new transit stop, two new parks to replace the park being taken for the replacement facility, and parking garages to accommodate fans.[35]

Many Bronx residents strongly opposed the plan, since the park on which the new stadium would sit had been intensely used. Although substitute space was to be provided, it was less conveniently located and would consist of two smaller parks rather than one big one. Moreover, the new stadium was unlikely to produce economic benefits for the small businesses around it, as the goods and services provided by the shops and eating and drinking establishments nearby would now be available within the

---

its Manhattan neighborhood, which welcomed the presence of large numbers of police trainees circulating within the area.

34. Since the baseball league allows teams to deduct capital expenditures from its fees to the league and the Yankees will be exempt from property taxes until the bonds are paid off, the net cost to the team is minimal. The use of $1.3 billion in tax-free bonds means that the state and federal governments are further subsidizing it through their loss of tax revenues on the interest bondholders receive.

35. In 2008 the cost to the city for infrastructure—parks, garages, and transportation improvements—supporting Yankee and Met stadiums was estimated at about $458 million, up from $281 million in 2005. New York State was contributing an additional $201 million. Those totals do not include an estimated $480 million in city, state, and federal tax breaks granted to both teams. In addition, neither team has to pay rent, though they are playing on city-owned land (Bagli 2008). See also Sandomir (2008); Hu (2006); and the testimony of Ronnie Lowenstein before the City Council Finance Committee (NYC Independent Budget Office 2006).

FIGURE 5.   New Yankee Stadium. Photo by Susan S. Fainstein.

stadium (Lee 2007).[36] Protests, however, failed to achieve much response. The Yankees agreed to a community benefits agreement whereby a quarter of the construction and stadium jobs would be reserved for Bronx residents and businesses, there would be a $1 million job training program, and half a million dollars would go to community outreach during the years of construction. The community board, which had rejected the plan, was punished by the borough president, who refused to reappoint members voting against it:[37]

> "He [Adolfo Carrión, the Bronx borough president] means we should have carried out his dictates," replied stadium opponent Mary Blassingame...who...lost her spot as chair of the land-use

---

36. It was reported that business, in fact, was down for establishments around the new stadium in its first summer (McGeehan 2009). Furthermore, the replacements for the park that the community lost in 2006 were not scheduled to be completed until 2011 (Dwyer 2009).

37. The board's powers were only advisory and thus its rejection did not constitute a veto. The Bronx borough president at that time, Adolfo Carrión, was subsequently appointed by President Obama to head his White House Urban Affairs Council.

committee. "You know, that stadium plan is a nightmare when you look at it. We have only a sliver of a park, and he wants to give it up, cut down 300 old-growth trees when we already have a high asthma rate. Plus it's a sweetheart deal—he's giving away the store." (Arden 2006)

Of the three cases discussed in this chapter, this one shows the most disregard for principles of justice. In terms of equity, the community loses a valued park, and few of its members are likely ever to be able to afford a ticket to a game.[38] The community benefits agreement, which has now become the standard way through which communities receive compensation for developments they do not want, offers little. The jobs reserved for local residents will be low paid and seasonal and will not really represent an increment to what already existed. On the other hand, the richest team in baseball attains enormous benefits from the city, state, and federal governments and keeps all the revenues from the lucrative skyboxes and ancillary commercial establishments. None of the huge sums from media coverage of the team go to the city, even though the population of the New York metro area provides the largest media market in the country. The well-paid players and wealthy owners largely live outside the city, so even their personal taxes go elsewhere. The *New York Times,* which generally supports Mayor Bloomberg's economic development initiatives, commented in an editorial:

> The Yankees have the richest franchise in the league, and they have played the better part of a century in a depressed area of the South Bronx without adding much to the neighborhood.... Economic development is a good thing, when the target is right. Mayor Michael Bloomberg's administration has delivered some worthy investments....But major professional sports teams just don't need the assistance. Government officials should be negotiating from positions of power, instead of standing ready to give away the store when professional teams bat an eye in New York's direction. (*New York Times,* March 27, 2005)

---

38. Most of the seats go to season ticket holders (Sandomir 2008). Individual purchases of single premium seats are $500, reduced from a larger amount after tickets did not sell at the expected rate. Ordinary field-level seats go for $375 (http://www.mlb.com/nyy/ballpark/seating_pricing.jsp). The Yankees did pledge a limited number of seats to community organizations as part of the community benefits agreement.

What makes this project particularly objectionable is that, even from the perspective of stimulating economic development, public spending on stadiums is unproductive (Rosentraub 1997). As is typical for such investments, proponents exaggerate the contribution the teams are making to cover costs and fail to account fully for the amount underwritten by the public (Long 2005). Since even stadium advocates are now aware of the research showing the minimal contribution to development of these projects, they are generally left arguing that the benefits come from enhancing a city's image. Although such a contention might have some validity for second-tier cities, it does not apply to New York. And, given the significance of New York's media market, threats to leave the area cannot be taken seriously. Thus, the equity contribution of the stadium is nil; it obviously does not increase diversity, since it creates a space that is wholly closed to any member of the public insufficiently wealthy to afford a ticket; and, as far as democracy goes, the local community was ignored in the decision-making process. The general public was represented only to the extent that elected officials were cheerleaders for the new stadium, but most likely, if the bonds had been subject to a public referendum, they would have been defeated.[39]

Could there have been a more just approach to getting the Yankees an up-to-date facility? Certainly. The Yankees could have used their own resources to pay for the new structure, borrowing on the normal capital market rather than taking advantage of tax-free bonds (which under new federal regulations will no longer be available for sports teams). They could have rebuilt on the site of the old stadium rather than in the park. While the stadium was under construction, the team could have played in Queens in the old Shea Stadium, which was being vacated by the Mets for their new facility. The local community board could have been involved in planning the new venue. Ancillary businesses within the stadium confines could be local purveyors rather than national chains. Since the city owns the land on which the stadium sits, it should receive rent, and the team ought to pay taxes rather than dedicating the PILOT to paying off its bonds. More tickets could be allocated to community organizations. The complicated deal combining tax forgiveness, tax-free bonds, and capital expenditures by different levels of government including the Metropolitan

---

39. General obligation bonds in New York must be submitted to the voters, but bonds tied to a specific revenue stream are not. In this case repayment was tied to the payments the team made in lieu of taxes.

Transit Authority, which will be building a new station for the stadium, makes it difficult to accurately estimate the total public costs of the project. Evidently it encompasses hundreds of millions and probably billions of public dollars, money which otherwise could be expended on schools and more urgent mass transit needs. Moreover, unlike the Battery Park City and Times Square cases, the city despite its substantial investment will not be participating in the revenues from the project.

Justice and Injustice in New York

Before the fiscal crisis of the mid-1970s, New York was possibly the most egalitarian of any American city. Trade unions had a strong voice in city politics; the free city university system was unique; the extensive network of public hospitals made health care widely available; social service programs were well developed; the size of the public housing program dwarfed that of other U.S. municipalities; the city's public transit system was unequalled; and hundreds of thousands of moderate income families were able to take advantage of the Mitchell-Lama housing program. The fiscal crisis was precipitated by, on the one hand, the withdrawal of the taxpaying middle class to the suburbs, and the continuing growth of the public sector, on the other. The requirement of a balanced budget combined with stringent limits on federal aid made retrenchment inevitable. Two business-dominated boards were given responsibility for restoring budgetary solvency; the cutbacks fell heavily on redistributional programs (Fainstein and Fainstein 1976).

In the ensuing decades the emphasis of mayoral policy was on fostering growth and shrinking the welfare rolls. The encouragement of citizen participation that occurred during the Lindsay years waned. Although inequality increased along with continued outmigration of the white middle class, immigration caused the city's population to grow and become more diverse. The Giuliani administration, widely perceived as hostile to African Americans, was welcoming to the newcomers and refused to seek out the undocumented.

After Michael Bloomberg became mayor in 2002, black-white tension diminished. Not all the projects developed under his aegis were as counter to claims of justice as Yankee Stadium. To its credit the administration was continuing Mayor Koch's commitment to constructing affordable housing and using its own capital budget for this purpose. At the same time, however, more units were being withdrawn from the low-cost housing pool than were going up, as a consequence of the expiration of the mandates placed on subsidized housing built in previous decades. When these complexes are owned either by a private firm or cooperatively by the occupants, the motive for moving to market rate as soon as the opportunity is available is irresistible. One clear finding from the three cases presented here is that public retention of land ownership potentially lets government receive a portion of the profits in public-private partnerships and can prevent the loss of affordable housing. As Yankee Stadium demonstrates, however, the theoretical possibility does not mean that it will be exercised in actuality.

Overall, the thirty-five years from 1975 to 2010 marked the transformation of New York into a global city characterized by greater inequality and diminished democracy. Still, as a result of the replenishment of desolate neighborhoods by the arrival of over two million people from all parts of the globe, it retained an extraordinary vitality. At the moment of this writing, it is too soon to tell what will be the lasting effects of the recession of 2008–9. So far the upper stratum of investment bankers has done extraordinarily well and the real estate market, while suffering, has not sustained the kinds of losses seen elsewhere in the country. In relation to the criteria of equity, democracy, and diversity, New York comes up strongest on the last, while showing a decline in the first two with little indication that the trend will change in the near future.

4

LONDON

Within the history of redevelopment policy London represents an inter-mediate case between the New York model and that of the continental cities of northern Europe. It has had a more activist and redistributional public sector than New York, and its institutional structure differs quite strongly from that of its American counterpart, allowing for party-based programs. It is increasingly looking to infrastructure improvements rather than wooing firms as the basis for promoting development. On the other hand, London's governing bodies have resembled New York's in using privatization, public subsidies, and deregulation to promote property speculation and entrepreneurship, and as in New York during the 1980s it moved away from earlier commitments to social welfare policies.

Planning and Urban Development (1945–1979)

After the Second World War, London, like New York, entered a period of active rebuilding on cleared sites. New York, of course, had not suffered bombing; demolition was obviously more of a necessity where buildings had been severely damaged by German attacks. Both cities, however, had substantial numbers of substandard buildings, and in London as in New York slum clearance was the preferred approach to housing improvement even for buildings untouched by the war. Social housing, financed by the national government but constructed and owned by local authorities, accounted for 30 percent of the stock in Inner London by 1970 and continued to rise during the next decade (Buck and N. Fainstein 1992).[1] Primarily located on large tracts, many of these housing estates ("council housing") were concrete high-rises, a form of construction at odds with traditional London buildings and increasingly unpopular. Nevertheless, a fairly broad cross section of the working and middle class lived in council housing, in contrast to New York where public housing was restricted to the poor (Hamnett 2003, chap. 6).

Britain was slow to recover from the effects of the war and experienced sluggish economic growth for many years. London's economy likewise struggled, and Greater London lost population, while the Outer Metropolitan Area was gaining residents. Even though total population was declining, large flows of immigration from Commonwealth areas were coming into Inner London, contributing to an "inner city problem" (Buck et al. 2002, chap. 4). Programs directed at alleviating distress (the Urban Programme, Comprehensive Community Programmes, Community Development Projects) imitated the Model Cities and War on Poverty efforts of the United States but similarly were short-lived and underfunded (Lawless and Brown 1986, chap. 16).[2] Despite the creation of the Greater London Council (GLC), which replaced the London County Council and had a remit to build social housing, develop highways, and provide planning guidance within the metropolitan area, most planning responsibility remained within the thirty-three borough councils, resulting in quite different approaches.

Until the 1970s British policy aimed at moving population and economic activity out of London into new towns. When outmigration began to occur at an alarming rate, this policy was reversed. A speculative office building boom in the 1970s was spurred initially by the national Conservative government's loosening of credit, and the succeeding

---

1. By 1981 the combination of council-owned and housing association–owned stock amounted to about half the Inner London total and about 30 percent of Outer London units (Hamnett 2003, figures 6.1 and 6.2). Inner London refers to the area that formed the original London County Council, while Outer London includes the area between Inner London and the greenbelt. Together Inner and Outer London formed the jurisdiction of the Greater London Council and its successor, the Greater London Authority. The area beyond the greenbelt that now constitutes part of the city region is referred to as the Outer Metropolitan Area.

2. Successor programs in the United Kingdom included City Challenge, the Single Regeneration Budget, and the New Deal for Communities.

Labour government further encouraged the recentralization of economic activity.[3] Nobody comparable to Robert Moses directed growth, and, although part of the impetus for creating the GLC had been to form a body with the power to build modern expressways within the metropolis, fierce opposition to the planned roads succeeded in stopping them (Fainstein and Young 1992, 214). Thus, London, for better or worse, never acquired anything comparable to Moses's highway system. Many neighborhoods were saved from destruction and some new tube (subway) lines were built, but traffic congestion and difficulties in using public transport became severe in subsequent years. In contrast to New York, regulation for the purposes of environmental protection was quite rigorous.

London, like New York, had seen its commercial property market crash during the mid-1970s as a consequence of rising interest rates and slackening demand. Service delivery suffered as the local authorities increasingly endured fiscal stringency brought on by the departure of middle-class ratepayers and the needs of service-dependent low-income households (Newton and Karran 1985). The results resembled those in New York. Accommodation for low-income groups was in large institutional housing estates, clustered in areas of generally low-income habitation. Upper-income groups in both the West End (roughly comparable to New York's Upper East Side in social composition) and in the suburban boroughs successfully battled efforts to build affordable housing in their midst.

Within the highly centralized governmental system of the United Kingdom, major allocative decisions rested with the national government. Substantial funding went into housing, the National Health Service, and income support. Thus, despite difficulties in financing services, London's local governments mostly did not have to rely on their own resources to cope with the burden of deprivation in their midst in a way comparable to New York. Furthermore, the agenda of a still avowedly socialist Labour Party supported social and housing programs and put pressure on the government when it was controlled by the Conservatives to support redistributive policies.[4] Thus, until the end of the 1970s policy was fairly consistent regardless of which party was in power.

---

3. Labour's emphasis was on reviving manufacturing and improving low-income areas (Lawless 1989). See Buck, Gordon, and Young (1986), chap. 2; Ambrose (1986); Ambrose and Colenutt (1975) for descriptions of urban policy and property development at that time.

4. During the postwar period control of the government oscillated between Labour and the Tories. Labour was in control during the periods 1945–51, 1964–70, 1974–79, 1997–present.

Transformation (1980–2009)

The election of the government of Margaret Thatcher in 1979 marked a sharp change of direction in U.K. urban policy. Its policies of deregulation and market incentives set in motion an engine of strong economic growth within London but also of increasing inequality. By the 1980s property developers, relying on borrowed money, responded to the increasing importance of the financial industry in the global economy by building new structures to accommodate the growth in demand for office space. The 1986 "Big Bang" of financial deregulation further sparked expansion of financial firms.

The government established enterprise zones and urban development corporations (UDCs) to attract capital investment to disadvantaged areas (Fainstein 2001a). Within the enterprise zones taxes were abated and regulations loosened. The UDCs became the planning bodies for areas under their jurisdiction, overriding local control. East London, the most deprived part of the metropolis, was partially placed under the aegis of a UDC, the London Docklands Development Corporation (LDDC) in 1981, and the Isle of Dogs within it became an enterprise zone. The emphasis in planning shifted markedly away from eliminating destitution through social welfare measures and toward providing incentives for entrepreneurship, especially within the property development industry. As stated in a document issued by Prime Minister Thatcher's secretary of state for the environment:[5]

> London's future depends on the initiative and energy of the private sector and individual citizens and effective co-operation between the public and private sectors, not on the imposition of a master plan. The role of the land-use planning process is to facilitate development while protecting the local environment. (UK Department of the Environment 1989, 5)

The longest stretch of one-party domination was during the Thatcher-Major regime, when the Conservatives held office for eighteen years.

5. Under the Thatcher government, authority for planning the London region became centered in the national Department of the Environment, which previously had limited itself to veto power. Until then preparation of the Greater London Development Plan was made at the metropolitan level, but under Thatcher it was prepared at the cabinet level. The cabinet department in charge of town planning has changed names frequently; in 2008 it was called the Department of Communities and Local Government (DCLG). Responsibility for transport planning moved to a new Department for Transport (DfT), whereas formerly the two were in the same ministry.

LONDON

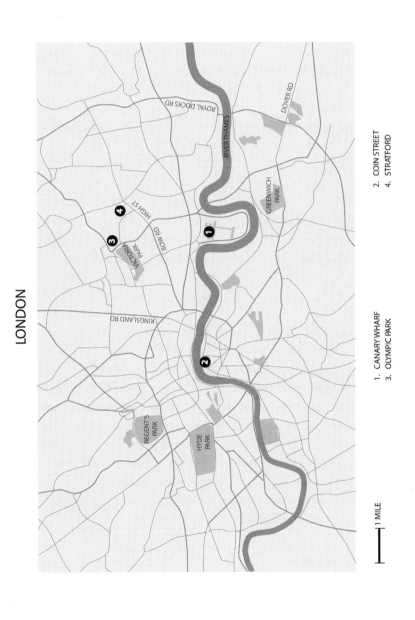

1 MILE

1. CANARY WHARF   2. COIN STREET
3. OLYMPIC PARK   4. STRATFORD

Reacting against the GLC's Labour-led espousal of social programs, Thatcher eliminated that body, thereby getting rid of the principal coordinating institution for the region. Under the leadership of Ken Livingstone the GLC had opposed Thatcherite policy in planning, transport, social welfare, and revenue raising (Fainstein and Young 1992, 213). Its termination had a similar effect on London as the imposition of external financial controls on New York after the fiscal crisis: it reoriented policy away from direct assistance to lower-income groups and toward a trickle-down strategy. As in New York, ensuring global city status with the financial industry as its cornerstone became the principal developmental goal of those in charge of governing London. Physical regeneration through incentives to the property industry became the means.

The growth in the number of the well-to-do put increasing pressure on residential property markets. Some of the demand was accommodated through new construction, especially in formerly shunned areas of East London, but much of it was absorbed in conversions of working-class habitation as gentrification spread throughout the inner city (Hamnett 2003, chap. 7). The "right-to-buy" program made home ownership available on desirable terms to council tenants, and the more attractive publicly owned housing stock was quickly bought up. The effect of the program was to increase the assets of many lower-middle class households, at the same time diminishing the availability of affordable rental housing and leading to the residualization of the remaining social housing.

The Thatcher years transformed London, making it a more glamorous, wealthier, but less egalitarian city than formerly. Increasing prosperity, job growth, the end of government clearance activities, and immigration combined to cause the population to expand once again. Two very different projects of the 1980s, Docklands redevelopment and Coin Street, indicate the varying thrusts of planning during those years, reflecting both the ambitions of the Thatcher government and the countervailing forces that still existed within London.

Docklands Redevelopment

The LDDC used the incentives of cheap land, tax forgiveness, and relaxation of regulations to promote investment within the mainly vacant Docklands of East London.[6] The docks had been abandoned as

---

6. This section summarizes the case study presented in Fainstein (2001a, chap. 9).

shipping had moved away to modern containerized port facilities, and vast areas along the river lay disused. Residential occupation of the river boroughs was almost entirely within council flats, where unemployment was high due to the departure of shipping and manufacturing jobs. While the preceding Labour government had envisioned construction of additional council housing and light industrial facilities along the river, the Conservatives were hoping for offices, hotels, exhibition space, and market-rate residences. The LDDC, however, had no fixed idea of what should go where but mainly simply responded to initiatives from developers.

At the peak of the 1980s boom, investment poured into the area. Between 1981 and 1992 over sixteen thousand housing units were added, of which nearly 80 percent were constructed for owner occupation at market rates (LDDC 1992). Nevertheless, the area retained thirteen thousand units in council and housing association–owned buildings, and many of them were upgraded during this period. Consequently the riverside switched from being homogeneously lower and working class to mixed income, making it much more diverse than formerly. Most of the middle and upper class in-migration was to newly constructed apartment buildings, so there was not gentrification in the sense of direct displacement, while the retention and renovation of the existing social housing produced physical improvements and more attractive public spaces for the residents. This transition highlighted the ambiguity of increasing diversity, since the newly mixed character of their neighborhoods was resented by many of the original inhabitants. The negative emotions expressed were not a response to any objective deterioration in the residents' situation but instead were a reaction to loss of cultural domination by the long-established community of dockers and factory workers (Foster 1999). Diversity as one of the defining characteristics of a just city is tricky, because, while it might be a desirable end state, the path toward achieving it is fraught with pitfalls.

The LDDC program changed the economic base as well as the population composition of the Docklands. Although it had originally been anticipated that only a secondary office sector would develop in the area, interest first by an American consortium then, when it withdrew, by Olympia & York (O&Y), the Canadian builder of the World Financial Center in New York's Battery Park City, upped the development potential. O&Y committed itself to building 4.6 million square feet of floor space by 1992 and an additional 7 million square feet thereafter at Canary Wharf

FIGURE 6.   Canary Wharf. Photo by Susan S. Fainstein.

(National Audit Office 1988, 19).[7] In addition, it pledged to hire local construction workers, finance the running of a construction training college, establish a trust fund for local schools and colleges, and contribute toward the Docklands Light Railway and the Jubilee Line Extension (JLE). The investment was an expensive gamble, since it was an attempt to plant Class A office space (i.e., space built to the highest standard) in a location generally regarded as lower class and distant from the central London business core. Indeed the gamble did not pay off for O&Y, which went bankrupt on account of it. Only after the recovery of the property market following the recession of the early 1990s did the Canary Wharf complex begin to thrive. In 2009 the perilous state of the financial firms that were

---

7. As of September 2008 approximately 14.1 million square feet of office and retail space on ninety-seven acres had been constructed. The development comprised over thirty completed buildings and more than two hundred shops, bars, and restaurants within four retail malls. It also had a conference and banqueting center, two Docklands Light Railway stations, a Jubilee Line station, car parks, and approximately twenty acres of landscaped open spaces. About ninety thousand people worked there. (Canary Wharf Group 2008).

its major occupants made its future somewhat less certain, although its continuation as a major office center was not in doubt.

The initial failure of Canary Wharf resulted from the bad luck of coming on the market in the midst of a recession and the riskiness of O&Y's method of financing the construction.[8] Although the government had paid a substantial sum to provide a road connection to the development, its refusal to assume the front-end costs of putting mass transit in place before the complex opened meant that there was no reliable way by which people could get to work.[9] The consequence was that firms were reluctant to occupy the development. Critics of the endeavor argued that even if it had averted bankruptcy, the office complex would not have provided jobs suitable for the unemployed residents of the eastern part of London.

In addressing the question of whether or not Docklands development enhanced equity, diversity, and democracy, one has to take into account the time span over which the judgment is made, the geographical area to be considered in making the evaluation, and the constraints of the London economy. Initially the megaproject provided relatively little direct benefit to low-income residents of the area. The government-funded Docklands Consultative Committee, however, made up of representatives from the affected boroughs, put pressure on the LDDC for social expenditures, and eventually the development corporation spent £110 million on social and community development, representing about 7 percent of net expenditure (Cambridge Research Associates 1998).[10] This was in addition to the expenditures by the developers on employment training and public space and by housing associations and councils in improvements to the existing social housing. Although the extent to which the original local residents benefited from the increases in employment directly attributable to the

---

8. O&Y, instead of relying on loans from financial institutions, issued its own short-term commercial paper. Although this method of raising capital reduced its costs, it meant that, when the company appeared in difficulty, it could not roll over the notes.

9. The only transit connection that existed when the complex opened was the Docklands Light Railway, an inadequate trolley system. O&Y had pledged itself to defray much of the cost of an extension of the Jubilee tube line to the site but was unable to meet this obligation. Eventually the government did extend the line, the development attracted major tenants, and the Canary Wharf Group, which had taken possession of the complex for a price well below the cost of building it, repaid the government its share of the tube line's construction costs.

10. About half the expenditure was in education and training, amounting to £1,350 per head of the 1997 population; it was spent on improvements for all the schools and health centers within the urban development area. About 44 percent was devoted to new construction and upgrading of social housing (Rhodes and Tyler 1998, 38–39).

new developments was difficult to estimate, it was clear that the link to jobs in the rest of London provided by the JLE was significant.[11] Moreover, the JLE was a clear benefit to Docklands residents by increasing their access to the city center for all purposes, not just employment.

The primary beneficiaries of public investment in Docklands were property developers, employees in the corporations that settled there, and owner occupants of the new, relatively inexpensive market-rate housing. Docklands development also provided benefits for Greater London as a whole by establishing a third central business district, relieving congestion in the West End and the City and bolstering London's role as a global financial center. Assessing the impact on equity of transforming such a large area as the London Docklands raises the question of how much weight should be placed on the interests of residents in the immediate locality as against those of the entire metropolis. Even focusing on local residents, however, over the long term (1980–2008), one cannot find that they were particularly harmed by the development and indeed they were able to extract specific benefits in terms of housing, health, and education. Greater equity was attributable to the increasingly stringent requirements for developer contributions to community benefits that transpired during the unfolding of the project and the enactment of such requirements into law under the Labour government that took office in 1997.

The LDDC went out of existence in 1998, and planning powers over the development area reverted to the local borough authorities. In its early days the LDDC had no mechanisms for community consultation and was perceived to be a high-handed, undemocratic body that took no interest in the welfare of local residents. After 1987, however, it began to consult the borough authorities and entered into agreements with them regarding social programs. In its final years, despite never establishing formal consultative bodies, it increased its efforts to work with

---

11. The concept behind the tube extension was that it would bring workers out to Docklands from central London. It turned out that the inbound trains carried passengers well above the initial estimates, indicating that they were bringing the once isolated East Enders to work in other parts of the metropolis. There was no way of estimating the extent to which original residents were now working in the office complexes, as Census measures of the numbers of local residents working nearby could not distinguish between new and old occupants. Furthermore, even though those losing employment from the departure of shipping and manufacturing were unlikely to be still in the workforce a quarter century after the start of Docklands construction, many of their sons and daughters might have acquired sufficient training to work in the new offices.

the boroughs, setting a model that was later adopted in the proliferation of community-business-government "partnerships" subsequently established throughout London. Brownill, Razzaque, and Kochan (1998, 61), who evaluated the role of community participation in Docklands development, concluded:

> In terms of [community] power and influence there has been a general movement up the ladder, but this trend has been variable....We have also seen that influence over operational issues and community spend increased *while that over strategic decisions did not.* (Emphasis added.)

The authors furthermore expressed doubt as to whether partnership models really gave power to community organizations or simply co-opted them (65–67).

In terms of both democracy and equity, the issue here—one that affects all development plans modified by community benefits agreements—is highlighted by the doubt Brownill, Razzaque, and Kochan express over whether community groups affected strategic decisions. The overall direction of Docklands development (and likewise of the New York projects discussed in the previous chapter) came from high-level, authoritative officials—in the case of the United Kingdom, the prime minister herself. These were leaders committed to a free-market ideology. Whether or not the politicians were directly influenced by business groups, such an ideology necessarily implied priority to investor interests. Brownill, Razzaque, and Kochan describe how the hostility between Labour-led borough councils and the LDDC diminished over the course of time, in part due to concessions by the LDDC but also as a consequence of more entrepreneurial thinking on the part of the councils. Their depiction points to both the potential and limits of local action. Through mobilization and political response lower-income communities can gain concessions from developers and their governmental sponsors, but they rarely can, within a competitive global system and a national ideological framework of privatization, change the *strategic* emphasis on offering incentives to business interests in return for investment in property development. In other words, they can achieve positive results from specific projects, but they rarely can define the types of projects developed. Thus, when establishing evaluative criteria for local policies, we look minimally to the extent that developments cause no harm to the relatively disadvantaged and more positively at the extent to which they receive benefits. By these criteria Docklands development can be judged to have been reasonably equitable, somewhat democratic, and contributory to diversity. The development was not, however, designed to specifically favor low-income people and therefore was not redistributive.

Coin Street

Coin Street represents the unusual instance where local action changed strategic decision making.[12] This centrally located site, on the south side of the Thames facing Westminster and the edge of the City of London, had been largely vacant for many years before 1980, when the new Conservative central government called for proposals for a mixed-use development.[13] Two competing proposals were presented: one, designed by Sir Richard Rogers and sponsored by Greycoats, a major speculative developer, called for a million square feet of offices, as well as housing, shopping, and some light industrial workshops; the other, proposed by a community coalition, consisted of low-rent housing, managed workshops, and a supermarket. While the proposals were under consideration, the GLC switched from Tory to Labour-led, and in 1982 it decided to back the community scheme. In the end Greycoats sold its land interests to the GLC:

> The developers were defeated by the combination of an extraordinarily effective local campaign and the considerable muscle of the GLC. In addition to failing to obtain all the necessary permissions [to carry out its scheme], Greycoats realized that it would face community opposition all the way. (Brindley, Rydin, and Stoker 1996, 85)

Once the alternative scheme prevailed, a community-based nonprofit development company, Coin Street Community Builders (CSCB), was established, which purchased the land from the GLC for the low amount of £750,000.[14] In turn the CSCB sold the sites for a nominal value to

---

12. This has also been the case where middle-class preservationist movements have succeeded in blocking demolition of historic structures, as, for instance, in the case of Covent Garden. Although this kind of successful community mobilization does not typically change the distribution of benefits, it can be regarded as enhancing democracy.

13. The information for this case is mainly drawn from Brindley, Rydin, and Stoker 1996.

14. The GLC had imposed restrictive covenants on the land, some of which it had itself owned originally, and the rest of which it had acquired from Greycoats. These covenants greatly reduced the value of what could be built on the land, thus lowering its price. CSCB

FIGURE 7. Coin Street: Oxo Tower. Photo by Susan S. Fainstein.

the Society for Co-operative Dwellings, which was to act as the housing developer. Management of the housing would rest with co-operative housing associations, which were exempt from "right-to-buy," thus ensuring the retention of the units in the affordable housing pool. An issue, however, arose in regard to who should have priority in obtaining housing, with the Lambeth borough council insisting on nominating tenants from its housing waiting list while the CSCB wanted to give preference to residents of the immediate area who had been involved in the long fight for the program. Racial tensions might also have been involved, as the immediate area was mainly white, while Lambeth had a policy of racial integration. Ultimately Lambeth prevailed.

As well as building new structures, the CSCB sponsored the rehabilitation of the Oxo Tower building, a well-known South Bank landmark, to accommodate craft workshops, a small museum, flats, and a high-end

---

obtained mortgages from the GLC and from the Greater London Enterprise Board, an economic development corporation that the GLC had previously established to assist local business. Repayment of the mortgages would be from temporary income from parking facilities and advertising signs.

restaurant, the proceeds of which would be reinvested in CSCB projects. It also developed Gabriel's Wharf, a supposedly temporary but now long-lived retail and restaurant area occupied by independent local businesses, and offered support services to small firms. It contributed to beautification of the riverfront and retained part of the area as a public park, the site of an annual, multiethnic festival. A neighborhood center provided daycare, preschool, and after-school activities. In 2008 CSCB won approval of its proposal to replace a parking facility with a public swimming pool and leisure center, the studios of a modern dance company, and 329 new flats for purchase in a slender high-rise structure (CSCB press release, August 20, 2008). The proceeds from the flats were to pay for the construction and operations of the leisure center, but at the cost of providing no affordable housing: "With regards to not providing affordable housing it was concluded [by the Labour secretary of state for communities and local government] that the inclusion of a sports centre and swimming pool at no public cost negated this necessity and that the increase in resident population would assist in local regeneration" (*World Architecture News.com,* 2008).

Thus, reflecting, and contributing further to, the changed demographics of the South Bank, CSCB was constructing the kind of high-end building that it had once opposed. Ironically, the CSCB's activities, which had hugely enlivened the area, fostered the greater appeal of the once forlorn South Bank. As Brindley, Rydin, and Stoker (1996, 208–9) note:

> There has been a marked shift in the style of planning at Coin Street, as the popular plan of the mid-1980s has been gradually implemented and new development pressures have emerged on the South Bank.... By the mid-1990s the South Bank was the site of a host of new projects and improvement schemes, involving the public and private sectors, separately and together, and Coin Street had been redefined as both a model development and a catalyst for wider change. This seems to reflect a shift from a modernist concept of regeneration, based on planning provision for measurable local need...to the essentially postmodernist concept of 'cultural regeneration,' where arts and culture provide a focus for change and renewal.

Although the leisure center would provide for the recreational needs of the low-income community, it was also an amenity for the new, middle-class residents of the South Bank.

FIGURE 8.   Coin Street: Gabriel's Wharf. Photo by Susan S. Fainstein.

The success of the most recent housing plan of the CSCB seems to represent the views of New Labour, which under the Blair/Brown leadership embraced much of the market-led approach of its Conservative predecessor. The earlier plans of the CSCB constituted an equity-oriented strategic direction whereby the principal beneficiaries of any project were low-income households. The more recent approach to development is one in which relatively poor communities are conceded a piece of profit-making enterprises, and where greater income diversity means that community pressures will be less in the direction of redistributional programs and more in favor of market-rate owner-occupied housing and public amenities.

In discussing the fruition of the original co-operative housing plan, Brindley, Rydin, and Stoker (1996, 93) comment that it was "uniquely due to the support and intervention of Ken Livingstone's administration at the GLC." This argument points to the crucial underpinning of participatory planning through the support of elected officials. In comparing New York and London in terms of equity and democracy, we can see that greater equity was achieved through the actions of public officials chosen on a party program that evinced a commitment to redistribution. Changes in the character of the British Labour Party, however, reveal a diminution of this commitment and acquiescence to the definition of urban policy in terms of competitiveness. The reestablishment of a Greater London Authority in 2000, and the return of Ken Livingstone, who was elected as mayor over the opposition of the national party, did not restore the radicalism that had once characterized his leadership. As he put it after his time in office: "The modern mayor is basically a huckster for the city....If you couldn't show that your policies produced growth, you wouldn't get anywhere."[15] In an interview conducted while he was still mayor, he justified his support for a finance-led strategy that produced high levels of inequality by saying: "I can't see an alternative. There's no way this [national Labour-led] government is going to give me the power to redistribute wealth in London....What else could it [mayoral strategy] be focused on [besides finance]? Am I going to rebuild manufacturing? This is not the world you create, it's the world you're in" (Massey 2007, 21).

Brindley, Rydin, and Stoker (1996, 210) conclude that "popular planning has lost its radical edge [in London] at the same time as popular opinion has been drawn into the planning of urban regeneration." They note that as the planning process became more open and pluralistic, the "community" became less unified, less committed to redistributional policies, and more amenable to fashionable regeneration strategies based on design and consumption. Thus, while Coin Street's original development resulted in the reinforcement of democracy, diversity, and equity, after a quarter century democracy and diversity still prevailed, but equity diminished. Nowhere was this shift more evident than in planning for the 2012 Olympics, for which London's successful bid was considered one of the triumphs of Ken Livingstone's tenure as mayor of London.

Planning for the 2012 Olympics

London's winning bid for the 2012 Olympics reflected the emphasis on sport and spectacle widely prevalent among cities around the world. Unlike New York, where plans to build the Olympic Stadium on Manhattan's West Side had provoked strong opposition to its competing bid, London's populace apparently strongly supported bringing the Games there. While the International Olympic Committee (IOC) was still considering

---

15. Interview with the author, July 26, 2008.

the various proposals for 2012, a public relations campaign plastered the city with advertisements to "Back the Bid!" Its success was evidenced in opinion polls that showed 70 percent support, an online petition to "Back the Bid" signed by 1.2 million Londoners, and the willingness expressed by ten thousand volunteers to be helpers at the Games. A multitude estimated at eleven thousand people gathered in Trafalgar Square in July 2005 to watch the awarding of the Games on giant television screens (Newman 2007).

The city's strong push for the Games derived from Mayor Livingstone's view that pouring public money into these kinds of endeavors could be justified by their contribution to economic competitiveness and their potential to revive derelict urban areas: "In London's bid, the greatest emphasis is placed on the legacy and after-affects [sic]…rather than the event, its content and purpose" (Evans 2007, 299). However, in the words of Gold and Gold (2007, 6):

> The main problem is that there is no guarantee that these alluring longer-term gains will materialize, as the experience of many host cities readily testifies. The Olympics in Sydney 2000 and Athens 2004 provided festivals that were highly praised at the time but saw both cities saddled with the legacy of underused stadia and supporting facilities.

Further justification, allegedly impressing the IOC selection committee, was that the Games would support London's social diversity. According to Prime Minister Tony Blair:

> When I talk to people about why we won the 2012 bid, the thing that comes out most strongly from everything they say is that there was a picture of London, a story told about London that day when we made the presentation that was a story of a city that was comfortable with the future, open, actually believed its diversity was a source of richness and strength, and was kind of confident and unafraid. (UK, Prime Minister's Office 2006)

Since the direct impact of the Games would be short-lived, the main emphasis on selling the public on the huge expenditures involved was on the Olympic legacy. This involved five "promises":

- We will make the UK a world-leading sporting nation.
- We will transform the heart of East London.

- We will inspire a new generation of young people to take part in volunteering and physical activity.
- We will make the Olympic Park a blueprint for sustainable living.
- We will demonstrate the UK is a creative, inclusive and welcoming place to live in, visit, and for business. (UK, DCMS 2007)

Three years after the award the promises look tenuous. The impact on participation in athletics so far has been almost nonexistent, and the expenditures on Olympic venues have diverted public funds from the construction of recreational facilities throughout the country.[16] Transformation of East London was increasingly problematic in the face of fiscal difficulties. Plans called for the construction of thirty-five hundred housing units in the Olympic Village, which, after the Olympics, was to consist of both market rate and affordable housing. Intended as a component of a massive redevelopment scheme for Stratford City within the East London borough of Newham, the Village was to be the principal contribution of the Games to regeneration. Its realization, however, was jeopardized by the crisis in the credit markets that began in 2008. The huge Australian property firm Lend Lease had been selected as the developer of the complex. In the summer of 2008, Lend Lease revealed that it was unable to raise financing for the venture, and its European managing director resigned. Newspaper reports indicated that the Village had a £250 million funding shortfall that would have to be met from public money and that its size was being reduced by around a third.[17] The other principal contribution of the Games to the future of East London was to be the media center for journalists covering the event. This £450 million project was ultimately intended to accommodate five thousand permanent office

---

16. Byrnes (2008); Locum Consulting (2006); London Assembly (2008). The Olympic legacy goals included "inspiring young people through sport" by offering "for all 5 to 16 year-olds in England five hours of high-quality sport a week and all 16 to 19 year-olds three hours a week by 2012" and helping "at least two million more people in England [to] be more active by 2012" (UK DCMS 2008). According to an article in the *Guardian* (Byrnes 2008): "Progress thus far has been so miniscule ('statistics are edging up but it is less than 1%,' says Sport England's chief executive, Jennie Price) that it seems there's no chance of us achieving the aim of 2 million more people breaking into the odd trot, still less of their darkening the doors of their local gym." A later article in the *Independent* (Merrick 2009) notes that, although the commitment to a sports legacy was crucial to London's winning the Games, progress toward getting more participation by 2012 had stalled, there was a significant decline in participation in a number of sports, and the drop in participation was especially noticeable among target groups including women, the disabled, and seniors.

17. Property Wire (2008); Hipwell (2008); GamesBid.com (2008); William (2008).

FIGURE 9.   Stratford Station, linking the Jubilee Underground line and the Channel Tunnel Railroad. Photo by Susan S. Fainstein.

or industrial jobs, but no developer appeared interested in converting the facility for some other use (Gibson 2009). Furthermore, no future probable demand was evident for the £525 million Olympic stadium, and it would either have to be demolished or maintained as a much smaller facility for very occasional use.[18]

Along with its failures to obtain planned private sector funding, thereby forcing an increase in public expenditure, the government was accused of deliberately underestimating predictable costs in order to win support for the bid. The head of a parliamentary committee claimed that the original budget had been "entirely unrealistic" (quoted in Kelso 2008). Initially set at £4 billion, the cost estimate had jumped to £9.3 billion by 2008.

18. Drury (2008). Because the British Olympic Committee was committed to keeping the venue suitable for track and field events, it could not accommodate a premier football (soccer) team, the only potential user for a very large stadium. (Placing a running track around the circumference of the field would create too great a distance between spectators and the playing field). As of this writing the plans were to shrink the facility to accommodate twenty-five thousand spectators.

The committee criticized the Olympic Development Agency for failing to provide a detailed assessment of the Olympics legacy and for the decision to use an additional £675 million of National Lottery funds, on top of £1.5 billion initially committed, to finance the increased budget. The National Lottery, established under Prime Minister John Major, had funded the construction of cultural facilities throughout the United Kingdom. The effect of the diversion to the Olympics meant that other parts of the nation would lose out substantially. Additionally the original revenue commitment, which had required Londoners to pay a £20 per annum tax on each household up to £240 to cover the costs of the Games, even with the diversion of lottery funds, would not be sufficient. As of this writing, it was not clear how the remaining funding gap would be met.[19]

An evaluation of the Olympic bid would give it poor marks on grounds of equity. Although its effect was to direct resources to one of the poorest parts of London, there was little probability that it would better the lot of the people living there beyond some transportation, infrastructure, and park improvements. Although some affordable housing would be created as part of the Olympic Village, the amount would not be great and, since it would be subsidized by housing associations rather than by a cross-subsidy from the private developer, the Olympics was not a prerequisite for housing construction in Stratford. At the same time, land takings for the Olympic Park were allegedly displacing close to five hundred people and over three hundred businesses (Centre on Housing Rights and Evictions 2007). Moreover, the huge expenditure involved took away resources from other parts of London and the country more widely without providing them any benefits beyond the glory of hosting the Games. The construction jobs created would have resulted from any major public works project, while, given London's already high numbers of tourists, travelers to the city drawn by the Olympics would likely substitute for other visitors. Many of the displaced businesses ended up in locations far distant from their original sites (Centre on Housing Rights and Evictions 2007). Those who rejected buyouts or relocation were labeled a "handful of greedy businessmen" by the mayor (quoted in Newman 2007, 258). Thus, except for temporary jobs created during the two weeks of Olympic activity, the Games would probably not enlarge employment

---

19. Kelso (2008); Evans (2007); Dinwoodie (2008). Efforts were being made to reduce costs by downsizing venues or making them less elaborate. Cost reduction alone, however, would be insufficient to close the gap.

opportunities for East Londoners and could even cause them to shrink as a consequence of business relocation.

In relation to diversity, the claim of the Olympic movement has always been that the Games contributed to international understanding. London, in its bid, made particular reference to the diversity of the city and its welcoming nature. Newman (2007, 263) comments that, when the London delegation took a group of children from the East End to present the London bid to the IOC and got Nelson Mandela to endorse the bid, they were tying in to "a wider ideology identified in the government of a multicultural city." While the claim is difficult to dispute, neither is there any strong evidence to demonstrate that these kinds of international events contribute to tolerance.

There was undeniable widespread popular support for bringing the Games to London, and the borough of Newham, where most of the activities were to take place, strongly favored the bid. The framing of the proposal took place under a joint planning committee including the London Development Authority and representatives of the affected boroughs, which organized extensive public consultation. Once the Games were awarded, the plan was revised to reduce land takings (Newman 2007). Thus, the original formulation of the proposal can be regarded as democratic. The management of the Games, however, under the auspices of the IOC and the host country's organizing body—in this case the Olympic Development Authority—was top-down and embedded in a powerful public relations machine. Moreover, decision making was not democratic in the sense of public input into resource allocation as opposed to physical planning of the Olympic site.

The popularity of sporting events raises difficult issues for critical analysis. According to Maurice Roche (2000, 168):

> Marx's legendary dictum that religion is 'the opium of the people' needs to be modified to apply to the ostensibly non-religious culture of late twentieth-century society.... In this context, perhaps it is more appropriate to observe that 'sport is the religion of the people'. That is to say, it provides apparently secular, but (from a sociological perspective) quasi-religious experiences, such as those of sacredness and transcendence, communal ritual and symbolism, and collective drama and emotionality.... Sports calendars and cycles of controlled contest provide rich experiences and forms of participation for mass audiences.

Roche's statement contains an essential ambiguity. By first quoting Marx on religion, then characterizing sport as religion, he implies that public absorption in sporting events is a form of false consciousness, distracting people from the issues that really matter in terms of their lives and livelihoods. But the argument that sport provides rich experiences and participatory opportunities indicates that genuine benefits are received from athletic displays. It takes a pure Marxian materialism to deny the psychic payoff of rooting for a team. Consequently a judgment as to whether the Olympic bid represented the outcome of a democratic process rates a qualified yes. Unlike the Yankee Stadium case, where the affected community protested strongly and the wider public was not consulted, London's winning of the Olympics rested on strong public approbation at both the metropolitan and local levels. Possibly people were sold a bill of goods in terms of the alleged Olympic legacy, but the general enthusiasm for getting the Games seems less a product of their regeneration potential and more a desire for the glory of playing host. For the immediate locale there was only gain, since financial support was coming from the national and Greater London governments.

Overall the Olympic bid was dubious on equity grounds, possibly contributory to London's aura of tolerance and cosmopolitanism, and responsive to democratic impulses. In a rather remarkable statement for a politician, Prime Minister Blair indicated his awareness of the typical Olympic saga:

> We all know we are going to encounter a few sceptics along the way. There is a very familiar Olympic story, if you look at what happens with every other city that has ever hosted this, and it runs something like this—the city wins the bid, against the odds, shortly afterwards the recriminations start, the preparations are in a poor state, it soon becomes apparent they are hopelessly behind schedule, the prices escalate as public money is held up for ransom, the various parties to the organisation squabble and fight, the stories creep into the press, the race against time begins: will it be ready, will there be a track for the 100 metres, will synchronised swimming have to be dropped because the Olympic pool won't be built in time?
>
> Miraculously then suddenly the mists clear, the chaos is abated, the athletes take over and the Games are declared an enormous success. Then a month later the recriminations start

FIGURE 10.   Vision of future Olympic Park. Courtesy of ACOM Design + Planning/OAKER.

up again—what has been the legacy of the project, what really has been purchased for all that investment, why do we have this uninhabited village on the edge of the city, does anybody have a use for a big stadium?

…But we, hopefully, are going to show there is another story to be told….One of the reasons why we won was because we were able to show that the benefits would not disappear with the close of the Games, that was a powerful part of our winning pitch, and I have got no doubt at all that we can do that. (UK, Prime Minister's Office 2006)

There is, in fact, ample reason to think that the benefits will mostly evaporate at the close of the Games and that London's will not be a different story from elsewhere, although the attention and infrastructural investment associated with the Games may serve to integrate East London more closely with the rest of the metropolis.[20]

---

20. Stratford, as well as being the site of the Olympic Village, will have the easternmost London station for the Eurostar rail link to France and will be a stop on Crossrail, a new commuter

How Should We Evaluate London?

London has become increasingly diverse as a consequence of ongoing flows of immigration. Even while legal immigration from former colonies has been largely cut off, there is continued movement from other EU member states, especially the recent accession states of Eastern Europe. Both Inner and Outer London continue to be ethnically diverse, although the Outer Metropolitan Area is substantially less so. Gentrification of much of the core and right-to-buy have made neighborhoods more homogeneous than formerly, but the continued existence of social housing throughout the metropolitan area ensures that some amount of mixing has continued, and segregation is not increasing (Buck et al. 2002, chap. 4). Butler and Robson (2003, 193) go so far as to say that "London is not only a global node, but also a metropolis arguably less racially segregated than any other city in the industrialized world...It is the diversity of London that enables such a flexible form of the metropolitan habitus to be constructed."

London's form of popular influence on government is radically different from New York's. The Coin Street Builders are an exception—the kinds of citizen participation that are widespread in New York are largely lacking in London, where popular pressure is far more likely to be channeled through the party system. Despite the creation of the Greater London Authority and Assembly the metropolis remains decentralized to the thirty-three local authorities, which are more accessible to residents than New York's centralized municipal government. The borough authorities continue to be the most important decision makers regarding services and the specific forms that development takes; although they must work within the guidelines stipulated by the mayor, they have substantial discretion. There is considerable variation among them regarding the extent to which they solicit community input; by and large, however, it tends to be subdued. There are no exact equivalents to New York's community development corporations with responsibility for developing and managing property. The housing associations perform a similar service function but they are not community-based. The proliferation of partnership arrangements requiring participation by government, business, and community members around development sites offers another avenue for

---

train line being constructed across London. These two transportation facilities, however, were planned independently of the Olympics and did not depend on the success of the bid.

FIGURE 11. Brick Lane: location for generations of immigrants, just adjacent to the City of London. Photo by Susan S. Fainstein.

citizen input, but the amount of influence possessed by local communities is questionable. Objectors to development schemes can appeal to the national ministry in a fashion somewhat parallel to the use of the courts in New York.

At the same time, the party organization of local government means that broad class interests are reasonably well represented, and the party organization is (unevenly) open to grassroots insurgencies. Governance in many Labour-controlled boroughs changed character as a result of the takeover of the local party machinery by citizens wishing to see government take a different direction. Thus, oligarchies directed by aging male trade unionists gave way to councils under the control of younger, more highly educated, ethnically and gender-diverse members.

In regard to equity, the strengthening of the National Health Services, supplemental benefits available to all people meeting income requirements, a still large stock of social housing, and requirements that new developments contain affordable units indicate that over a decade of Labour government at both national and local levels caused London to follow a trajectory different from New York's. Nevertheless, the governments that direct London have been no less anxious than New York's to capture global city functions and to provide the infrastructure and regulatory lenience to encourage them. The Olympics offer a prime example of this bias, in which billions of pounds, including a tax on all Londoners, are devoted to a two-week-long spectacle with a doubtful legacy.

The effect of global city status, in London as in New York, is to greatly sharpen income inequality, primarily as a consequence of growth at the top (see Fainstein 2001b). While there was a slight increase in the number of people at the bottom, the principal cause of heightened inequality was not just the increase in size of the group of high earners but the enormous jump in incomes of those in elite professions:

> London has become a far more unequal city, and at the top end the double-earner professional and managerial households form a core group of the well-off and pose a sharp contrast to the large group of no earner households at the bottom.
>
> It is important to make one further point. The growth of inequality in London and in other world cities...is not an inadvertent or accidental by-product of their leading global role in financial, business and creative services or their peculiar industrial structure. It is a direct consequence of this role. Earnings inequality is an inscribed characteristic which is inevitably associated with their role and occupational structure. To a very significant extent, the economy of the City of London and the salaries which are paid there generate massive inequalities. (Hamnett 2003, 102)

London has a larger public sector than New York, which means that more income, housing, and services are available to people at the bottom and middle of the income distribution than in New York. At the same time, as a consequence of ever greater encouragement of the financial, business services, and cultural sectors, the trend is away from equity toward competitiveness as the force driving policy. Whether this will continue to be the case in conditions of economic downturn, when both the needs caused by rising unemployment and the demands for support by the financial industry press upon the government, remains to be seen.

5

AMSTERDAM: A JUST CITY?

Many observers regard Amsterdam as a city that embodies equality, diversity, and democracy. In the words of John Gilderbloom (2008, 18):

> Amsterdam shows that a capitalist city can meet the essential needs of the people, such as health, housing, safety, individual freedom, sustainable living, and transportation. Amsterdam shows how within the framework of capitalism, democracy, green thinking, and providing for basic human needs and opportunities can be met for nearly all of Amsterdam's residents. Amsterdam is a place of freedom, not repression.

Patsy Healey calls the city "the ideal of those for whom the heart of urban place quality is an open and diverse cosmopolitan ambience" (2007, 37). In earlier work I too used Amsterdam to demonstrate the potential for a just city within a capitalist political economy, a realistic utopia (Fainstein 1999). In recent years, however, the commitment to redistributive policies has been receding, and open friction among ethnic groups has manifested itself (Buruma 2006; van der Veer 2006). Nonetheless, compared to New York and London, Amsterdam remains a place of considerably greater equality; its culture continues to be defined in terms of tolerance; and it offers substantial public amenities, excellent, cheap transit, and extensive social services.[1] It did well economically during the last decade of the twentieth century and the first part of the new millennium. Like both New York and London the city recovered from population decline and houses a large immigrant population, although unlike them the immigrant flow has been largely curtailed. Although in relation to its past self Amsterdam may have become less equitable, it still, in 2009, presented a model of considerable justice and, in comparison to the policy orientation of most other cities in Europe and the United States, responded to global pressures for increased competitiveness and to changing demographics more constructively.

History of Planning and Urban Development (the Postwar Period)

Amsterdam has a very long history of planning.[2] Its topographical circumstances have meant that the government has always played a role in land clearance and allocation. Since construction requires drainage and landfill, which must be conducted on a larger scale and at greater cost than is feasible for individual developers, the government has for much of the city's history carried out land preparation and thereby determined which areas would be developed. By the end of the nineteenth century the municipal government obtained additional power over development by embarking on a policy of land acquisition: the municipality would own the land; private developers could only obtain leasehold rights to their property; and the public fisc would gain from increases in land values (Terhorst and van de Ven 1997). As more residential space was needed, extensions to the built-up portions of the city were mapped and carried out according to detailed plans. In 1917 the city council approved an elaborate scheme for a southern extension under the direction of the architect H. P. Berlage and in 1935 it endorsed the Algemeen Uitbreidingsplan (AUP) or General Expansion Plan. The AUP, which required that new developments include ample provision for public space and social housing, continued to guide development well into the 1950s. Although

---

1. See *Economist* (2005); Dias and Beaumont (2007).

2. The postwar history of Amsterdam does not fit well into the periodization that I used for New York and London. Therefore, in this introductory section I describe history up to the end of the twentieth century then follow it with specific case studies that overlap in time.

subsequently supplanted, its underlying precepts regarding comprehensive planning, environmental protection, public space, clearly demarcated boundaries to development, and low-cost housing remained in effect much longer.[3]

The initial emphasis of postwar planning was on housing provision. Although Amsterdam had not sustained extensive war damage, it suffered from a severe housing shortage and much of what existed was in poor shape. Its Socialist-dominated government enforced strict rent control and, using funds from the national government, embarked on a major program of housing production on newly annexed territory. Ninety percent of new residential construction between 1945 and 1985 was for publicly assisted rental dwellings. Because expansion of the city resulted directly from government investment in housing construction, it could be carried out strictly according to plan. The original planning model was of a city with clear edges, limited growth along corridors, functional segregation of uses, and congestion relieved through the building of new towns outside the city boundary.[4]

Speculative office construction affected Amsterdam's development during the last century less than New York's or London's. Until the mid-1980s the municipal government's emphasis was on social benefits not economic growth. Since Amsterdam was only a second- or third-tier city within the world financial system and its specialization in relation to the global economy was in transshipment rather than financial services, pressure for additional commercial space was not robust. No effort was made to create a single high-prestige location along the model of Paris's La Défense; consequently, several office nodes developed. The absence of a dominant business district led to a failure to exploit the city's potential for office-based development, as none of the existing office complexes seemed to offer the synergies of clusters like those at Canary Wharf in London or Wall Street/Battery Park City in New York (Dieleman and Musterd 1992, 9). Therefore, speculative construction of new space without a committed tenant seemed too risky, and the kind of demand for space stimulated by the post-1975 restructuring of the world economy and the enlarged role for finance within it did not shape Amsterdam as much as it did the global cities at the top of the world hierarchy.

---

3. Amsterdam Physical Planning Department (APPD) (2003); Faludi and van der Valk (1994), 110–111.

4. Van de Ven (2004), 181; Terhorst and van de Ven (1997), 298–99; APPD (2003).

Amsterdam was nonetheless the financial and commercial center of the Netherlands and housed two major banks with worldwide scope. Furthermore, it was the home of substantial accumulated wealth, the product of its colonial and trading history. Thus, it did have a fairly significant financial and advanced services sector, while its easy accessibility made it a desirable location for firms serving much of northern Europe. Traditionally business had operated within the historic center, but in response to increasing conversion of traditional canal houses to office uses, the city sharply restricted such transformations. In response to demand for offices requiring large floor plates, business centers developed on the periphery, but, in contrast to Amsterdam's residential extensions, little land-use planning was imposed on these complexes. They physically resemble anonymous business districts around the world, with high-rise, modernist architecture, large parking garages, and blank plazas discouraging to pedestrians (Claval 2000, 61, 65)

During the 1960s the Dutch economy expanded, and employers dealt with labor shortages by importing workers from Turkey and Morocco. Both groups had rural roots and low educational levels (Kramer 2006, 63). At the same time growth in household size and demand for more spacious dwellings precipitated a move to the suburbs by white middle-class households. Then, in 1975, the Dutch colony of Surinam became independent, and a wave of Surinamese immigrants migrated to the Netherlands, many settling in Amsterdam. A large number were housed in the newly developed Bijlmermeer (see below), producing an ethnic concentration there.

By the end of the 1970s the Netherlands faced serious problems caused by pressures on wages, high levels of government spending, inflation, and rising unemployment. Amsterdam was particularly affected: "The economic crisis of the late 1970s and early 1980s in the Netherlands was exceptionally severe by international standards....And the city of Amsterdam, a welfare state city par excellence, was in an even deeper crisis. It was a city in deep economic and demographic decline" (Terhorst 2004, 1). Then, as in New York and London, Amsterdam's history during the final two decades of the twentieth century involved recovery from severe fiscal crisis and a restructuring of welfare systems. However, a continuation of housing support policies, involving both construction of additional social housing and rent subsidies, mitigated cuts in other benefits, while increased labor market flexibility and tax reductions pushed up employment levels. Even though, as in New York and London, city government increasingly emphasized economic growth and entrepreneurship, it was less at the expense of working-class residents, and Amsterdam continued to be a city of relative equality when compared to these counterparts (Fainstein 1997, 2001b). Through the end of the century the majority of Amsterdam's residents still lived in social housing, and a further group enjoyed rent control in private rental housing (Vlist and Rietveld 2002). The municipality could afford generous benefit levels because it received almost all of its revenues from the national government rather than its own taxpayers (Terhorst 2004), placing the city in the enviable position of possessing both considerable policy autonomy and substantial funding from an outside source.[5]

The distribution of welfare payments and social services including education depended on a unique Dutch system entitled "pillarization." The result of the compromise that ended hostilities between Protestants and Catholics, pillarization allowed state money to be funneled through religiously based organizations as well as through secular philanthropic, cultural, or political groups:

> Since the beginning of this century and sometimes even longer, each 'pillar' in the Netherlands has had its own schools, hospitals, housing corporations, trade unions, social work agencies, political party, sports clubs, broadcasting association, and so on. Within each pillar there was a strong sense of solidarity that cut right across class lines. Inter-pillar contacts were virtually absent in the private sphere; in the public sphere they took place only between the elites; hence the metaphor of pillars jointly carrying their roof. The major function of the system was to guarantee each cultural or religious grouping a substantial degree of autonomy. At the same time their internal solidarity proved to be very effective in achieving better chances for the less privileged members of each group. (Cross and Entzinger 1988, 16)

One consequence of pillarization was a lessened pressure for spatial segregation by class since public services were delivered through the pillars rather than by neighborhood (Terhorst and van de Ven 1997, 273). Data presented by Musterd and Ostendorf (2008, 88) show that even in the

---

5. Terhorst (2004) shows that the proportion of municipal revenues provided by the central government between 1953 and 2000 ranged from 84 percent to 94 percent.

city's poorest neighborhood the lowest quintile of the population by income constituted only 34 percent of the population, as compared to nearly 60 percent in the middle three quintiles and 7 percent in the highest 20 percent.

Urban Renewal

The urban renewal program begun in the late 1960s proved even more contentious in Amsterdam than in New York, but, although the design content of Amsterdam's redevelopment planning resembled Robert Moses's, its sponsors had a strikingly different ideology and constituency. Schemes were promulgated to tear down broad swaths of the inner city so as to move automobile traffic more readily and to destroy existing housing with the intent of constructing modern dwellings. The principles underpinning these efforts were not ones of stimulating private market investment but rather of producing a city conforming to social ideals of modernity and equity. Working-class families, not business and the middle class, were the intended beneficiaries. Indeed, the designs resembled those being implemented in the countries of socialist Eastern Europe: a subway system, big roads, and large apartment blocks for the relatively disadvantaged. Resistance to the developments, on the other hand, was based in collectivities similar to those protesting in New York and London: community activists, students, and disaffected elements on the social fringe. In contrast to New York, the Amsterdam groups confronted the intransigence of an "Old Left" committed to mass production of housing for an undifferentiated public rather than an urban growth machine aiming at a more profitable, more middle-class city.

Geert Mak (1999), a well-known Dutch journalist, termed the period from the mid-1960s until the mid-eighties the "Twenty-Year Civil War." Inspired by dreams of a more democratic, freer, more expressive society, urban social movements aimed at transforming Amsterdam in accordance with their libertarian goals. The epoch was one in which two distinguishable branches of the left fought each other, sometimes violently in the streets, at other times symbolically or around conference tables. Urban renewal became a focal point of the struggle. According to Mak (1999, 307), the city council, which was dominated by a Left coalition of traditional socialists, "assumed that Amsterdam could be renewed by demolishing most of its older districts, by building motorways everywhere, by replacing the Nieuwmarkt [a historic, centrally located square]

AMSTERDAM

RINGWEG NOORD

IJ TUNNEL

RINGWEG ZUID

1 MILE

1. SOUTHERN EXTENSION BERLAGE PLAN
3. NIEUMARKT

2. BIJLMERMEER
4. ZUIDAS SOUTH AXIS

with an office complex, and the Jordaan [a working-class residential and industrial area] with a sort of modern garden city."

The official history of planning in Amsterdam acknowledges the victory of urban renewal's opponents and comments:

> The planned 'engineering of the city' was condemned to the annals of history, along with the planned office construction and cuttings for transport infrastructure in the historic quarters. Small-scale, affordable housing and 'building for the community' became the new catchphrases in urban renewal. After the victory of the activists…in the mid-1970s, the most important aspect of modern urban design, the large-scale intervention in the layout of the existing city has hardly ever arisen again. (Amsterdam Physical Planning Department 2003)

The battle over Nieuwmarkt represented the most significant of the various skirmishes surrounding urban renewal planning. The site of an old market building, the square was the location of a stop on the new subway line that was originally expected to reach the outskirts of the city. Subway construction had already involved the demolition of many old houses. Further destruction was to result from the cutting of a major road through the square, which would take with it the landmark building at its center. The riots against the proposed demolitions succeeded in stopping them and are now memorialized in large murals in the subway station beneath it. The once derelict area became a lively center of restaurants and cafés; the central open space accommodates a market during the day and throngs of young people in the evening. As in many other examples of the success of preservation movements, however, the location of former working-class houses and productive enterprises has largely been given over to consumption activities, and the area as a whole has a theme park aspect.

As well as sparking protest, the urban renewal schemes gave rise to a squatters' movement. Plans called for the demolition of much of the nineteenth-century ring that surrounded the historic center. Although the old canal houses of the center had been identified as "monuments" and their owners could receive subsidies for renovating them, the structures of the later period were deemed not worth saving. Like all of Amsterdam's buildings, they were created atop pilings sunk into the marshy soil of the city. Replacement of the rotting foundations was costly, and the buildings themselves, while typifying a period, were not of outstanding

FIGURE 12.   Nieuwmarkt with floating police station in foreground. Photo by Susan S. Fainstein.

architectural merit. As the buildings were emptied, preparatory to razing them, squatters moved in and managed to beat back attempts at removal. They also occupied some of the monument buildings in the center that had been acquired and vacated by property speculators. The squatters resisted eviction, sometimes with force. Ultimately many of the squats throughout the city were legalized and turned over to their occupants, including some very valuable canal houses.[6]

The municipal government eventually rescinded the plan for the nineteenth-century ring, which would have destroyed its texture and raised the height of the streetscape. Since the battles of the 1970s and 1980s, there has been infill construction and some demolition in that part of the city, with new structures designed to fit into their context. Initially the squatters associated themselves only with the protests against urban renewal; later, however, they focused on the absolute shortage of housing

---

6. The Amsterdam city government purchased two hundred squatted buildings and turned them over to housing associations, which leased them to individual squatters (Pruijt 2003, 139).

FIGURE 13.   Houseboats moored on Amstel River. Photo by Susan S. Fainstein.

and thus their demands were not satisfied simply by the change in regeneration strategies (Uitermark 2004a). Also, by the end of the 1980s one element within the movement had seized the opportunity presented by toleration of the presence of squatted buildings around the city to use them as the basis for an alternative way of life: "The relative autonomy they enjoyed in squats enabled them to put into practice anarchistic ideas about self-management.... Squats were hotbeds for struggles against authoritarianism, apartheid, environmental degradation and—more recently—neoliberal globalization" (Uitermark 2004b, 690).

In comparison to London's Coin Street rebellion, the protest against urban renewal in Amsterdam had much greater scope. Rather than simply turning around a single project, it succeeded in reversing the entire approach to planning for a quarter of a century. The method for redeveloping inhabited areas ceased to be top-down and modernist but instead involved soliciting community input, emphasizing preservation, and operating on a small scale. At the same time, the egalitarian aims of the original strategy, as embodied in a commitment to social housing,

FIGURE 14.   Diverse Amsterdam. Photo by Susan S. Fainstein.

remained. Diversity in the sense of class mixing was upheld, as expensive canal house conversions occupied sites next to squatted premises, and houseboats moored in front of mansions. Class segregation was minimal, although ethnic isolation, while declining, existed. Demographically, Amsterdam became more unlike its suburban environs, as it lost middle-class families desiring greater space and home ownership and became increasingly inhabited by seekers of alternative lifestyles, along with immigrants and youthful sophisticates (Terhorst, van de Ven, and Deben 2003). As will be discussed later in this chapter, this demographic shift, combined with continued pressure for owner occupation, underlay more recent moves toward a lowered emphasis on social housing (Van Ham, van Kempen, and van Weesep 2006).

Social Housing

Social housing constituted the great proportion of new residential construction during the postwar twentieth century. By the 1990s, however, the requirement for social housing as a proportion of new development had declined from 90 to 70 percent,[7] and in the next decade it dropped further. In 1992 the national government, in order to bring its budget in line with European Union rules about the relationship between revenues and expenditures, ceased to provide a direct subsidy to the housing associations responsible for most housing construction and management in Dutch cities.[8] At the same time the associations were freed of their debt obligations to the state, permitted to sell housing units, and allowed to raise rents in line with costs. Low-income tenants were protected from rising rents by the continuation of rent subsidies for those meeting income qualifications, but higher income households that had remained in buildings owned by housing associations saw their out-of-pocket expenditures increase. In the context of rising real estate values, the associations found themselves very prosperous.[9] They did not respond, however, by engaging in massive new construction; between 2003 and 2008 the total housing stock of Amsterdam increased by only 9,371 units (Amsterdam Research and Statistics 2008). One of the causes of the small net increase was the ongoing demolition of structures as part of neighborhood regeneration programs directed at removing relatively low-quality postwar social housing.

The response of the Amsterdam government to the demand for home ownership combined with policies of demolition has been leading to the gradual residualization of the social housing stock:

> Indeed, since the end of the 1980s, Dutch housing-policy memorandums stated repeatedly that it was unwise to continue building inexpensive social rented dwellings in massive numbers. Because of the rising building costs and the related rise in (supply- and demand-side) subsidies, and because many social rented dwellings were inhabited by households that did not have low incomes, it was advocated that the owner-occupied sector should be expanded. While the owner-occupied sector was deemed to play a more prominent role on the Dutch housing market, at the same time state subsidies for social rented housing were supposed to

---

7. Information provided by J. F. W. Smit, Physical Planning Department of Amsterdam (interview, March 10, 1996).

8. In 2003 the fourteen housing associations of Amsterdam owned 55 percent of the total stock.

9. Information provided by Léon Deben and Willem Salet (written communications, September 2, 2007). See also Priemus (1995, 2006).

be diminished. The direct effect was a growing stock of owner-occupied dwellings. A subsequent effect was the increasing concentration of low-income households in the social rented sector, especially because higher-income households could find a home in the newly built owner-occupied dwellings. (van Ham et al. 2006, 333)

The move to develop housing for owner occupation was a component of a policy to create more socially integrated neighborhoods (Musterd and Ostendorf 2008). Of particular concern was the concentration of immigrants in specific neighborhoods and the worry that social exclusion was increasing. There was a general belief that earlier policies of multiculturalism had undermined social cohesion: "Even though the debate is incredibly complex and large, it is not difficult to see that one view is shared by most participants: different ethnic groups have been living too far apart from each other and should now integrate" (Uitermark and Duyvendak 2008, 6). In order to maintain a social mix in each neighborhood, it was necessary to respond to the demand for home purchase from more affluent groups.[10] Without the availability of ownership opportunities in the city, the municipality as a whole, and especially those neighborhoods with high concentrations of social housing, would lose their middle and upper class residents, resulting in the isolation of lower-income groups.

Critics of the policy, however, argue that it is at the expense of low-income people. Although advocates for the new policies claim that they are intended to reduce social exclusion, their effect is to displace a substantial proportion of the low-income residents of the affected neighborhoods and, for those seeking to acquire housing for the first time, to place it entirely out of reach. According to Stan Majoor:

> Extreme low income groups have difficulties with the extensive renewals, while people with more chances are generally satisfied about the better quality housing that is being built, and the opportunity to become an owner. Amsterdam is still a city with a very large social housing stock.... [but] the whole distribution system for social housing is jammed, meaning you have to wait at

---

10. Although there is a correlation between income and ethnicity, those buying property were by no means exclusively drawn from the native Dutch.

least 7 years to be eligible even when you are on a list. (Personal communication, July 12, 2008)

Another critic remarked:

> When I studied the urban renewal projects in Amsterdam New West of the last 10 years…I found a discrepancy between the houses which were demolished and those that were newly built. First of all there was a transition from 80 percent social housing and 20 percent owner-occupied houses into a 50–50 balance. Secondly these newly built owner-occupied houses are so expensive that it is hard to imagine how the original residents of the demolished houses are ever going to be able to buy a new house in Amsterdam New West…The original inhabitants are relocated to unknown destinations.…I came to the conclusion that the renewal of Amsterdam West is very good for the city of Amsterdam but not necessarily for the people who lived in Amsterdam West. (Jelle Adamse, personal communication, March 14, 2007)

Since the displaced renters would continue to receive a housing subsidy enabling them to live in decent housing somewhere, the issue for them was more one of location than of housing poverty. As the proportion of the centrally located stock available for rental diminished, the choices of the displaced became more restricted. Because displacees were given priority in social housing elsewhere, the time spent on waiting lists by others lengthened, and newly formed, low-income households could only look for housing within the private rental sector. The basic issue in Amsterdam was that more people of all economic levels wished to live there than could find housing. The withdrawal of government from housing construction, the reluctance of housing associations to build once that they were dependent on their own resources, and the small amount of undeveloped land available for housing resulted in extreme competition for space among different classes of users. The increase in housing for purchase meant that relatively affluent households no longer needed to languish on a waiting list until social housing units became available; as Justus Uitermark characterizes it, "they could jump the queue" (interview, November 8, 2008). Thus, a form of inequality measured by access to opportunity rather than distribution per se grew in the years after the shift away from social housing construction. At the same time Dutch housing reform, because it did not promote large-scale individual purchase of publicly owned units, as had been the case in the United Kingdom under the Thatcher right-to-buy program, did not result in the total marginalization of the social housing stock, which continued to be attractive to middle-income households if they did not have to wait too long for it (Brandsen and Helderman 2006).

Post-1975 Planning

The three prongs of post-1975 planning policy—social housing, then, later, peripheral business development and owner occupation—were epitomized in three developments: the Bijlmermeer, Amsterdam South Axis, and the harbor islands. This chapter describes the first two, which changed from their initial conception as single-use projects to mixed-use developments. The harbor projects differed from these in that they were on mostly vacant land. Including KNSM, Java, Borneo, and Sporenburg, they consisted predominantly of low- and mid-rise, dense complexes of single-family and multifamily dwellings with a variety of architectural designs, of which many were owner occupied. Containing eight thousand dwelling units on the sites of what were mainly transport facilities, they have been successful in attracting middle-class residents (Amsterdam Physical Planning Department n.d.).

The Bijlmermeer

Constructed on drained land at the southeastern edge of the city, the Bijlmermeer incorporates two strikingly different concepts of urban development and redevelopment. Originally constructed in the 1960s and 1970s, the complex was intended to house one hundred thousand people in forty thousand dwelling units (Luijten 2002). Occupants were to be working- and middle-class families seeking more spacious accommodation than could be acquired in the center. Although the development never reached its planned capacity, many immense structures were built according to high modernist concepts of urban design. The original architects of the Bijlmermeer were strongly influenced by Le Corbusier and were active participants in the conferences of the Congrès Internationaux d'Architecture Moderne (CIAM): "In their [the Dutch designers'] new, modernist ideals the cities were hygienic, green, spacious and light with efficient traffic systems. Urban planning was ordering collective life in a rational manner by making a clear spatial distinction between functions. The chaotic city would become the functional city" (Luijten 2002, 11). Enormous buildings stretched out uniformly; their concentrated densities left ample space for landscaping. Auto and pedestrian functions were segregated; shopping, consolidated into a small, obscurely located mall, was meant only to serve the daily needs of residents. Residence and work were strictly separated by a railroad embankment that cut off the residential district from the nearby office center.

Even while the Bijlmermeer was still under construction, planning wisdom had moved away from the principles on which it was designed. Influenced by critiques of the inflexibility and coldness of modernism, planners were prescribing more vernacular designs, heterogeneous groupings, street walls, and malleability. Subsequently plans were made to transform the development from being exclusively composed of social-rented housing to a more diverse mix with adjacent shopping and office schemes, according to design concepts decreeing varied uses and street life. Thus, both its ostensible beneficiaries and the planning establishment eventually rejected what the original planners had regarded as a physical design embodying the egalitarian ideal of a decent home for everyone.

Signs of failure appeared early on, and in 1985 the complex had a vacancy rate of 25 percent (Luijten 2002, 17). Only about half the intended number of buildings was completed, and calls for rethinking the scheme arose soon after construction began. The project provoked distaste among the Dutch middle class for whom its large, airy apartments were intended; consequently it became the home mainly, though not entirely, of ethnic minorities, especially Surinamers.[11] The apartments proved suitable for large families, who could afford their rents thanks to the housing allowances provided by the Dutch national government.[12] Thus, in addition to the architecture being generally regarded as unattractive, the area was

11. Surinam gained its independence in 1975, sparking the emigration of many of the former colonial subjects to the Netherlands. At that time there were numerous vacant units available in the Bijlmermeer. By 1996 the population was 25 percent native Dutch, 35 percent Surinamese, 10 percent Ghanaian, 7 percent from the Dutch Antilles, and 25 percent other, primarily African and South Asian (Kwekkeboom 2002, 84).

12. Although the project had been constructed by a group of nonprofit housing corporations, the rents reflected the cost of construction and thus would have exceeded the ability to pay of the families moving in without the assistance of the government. For families that could have afforded the rent without assistance, units in the surrounding new towns were more appealing.

perceived as dominated by immigrants. Furthermore, cleaning up of the drug marketplace in the city center near the railroad station had caused this commerce to move to the open spaces and garages of the Bijlmermeer, reinforcing its reputation for being dangerous housing of last resort.[13]

The gargantuan structures were very far from Dutch ideals of urbanity. In order to understand the original motivations for building the Bijlmermeer, it is worth quoting from an interview with one of its remaining defenders, a white Dutchman who continued to live there:

> It was the first time something was built on this magnitude and scale in the Netherlands. And yet keeping classical social-democratic ideals in mind, that it wasn't for the flashy elite but for the masses....I think the concept of the Bijlmermeer is very good, and I think its execution was also pretty successful. And it's a shame that the renewal didn't opt for taking out the teething problems and adding a little extra.[14]

In other words the early conception of the Bijlmermeer conformed to socialist ideals of equality and collectivism within the framework of a uniform landscape rather than to a consumerist individualism.

In the late 1980s the Amsterdam authorities began to reconstruct the entire area of Amsterdam Southeast, of which the Bijlmermeer formed part. In 1987 they opened a large shopping center and office building directly adjacent to the housing complex. As well as serving the residential district, the retail complex acted as a portal to the office structures on the other side of the railroad that bordered the Bijlmermeer, creating a link to this center of employment. Residences above stores were added, office space for small business made available, and artists' live-work space constructed. In 1992, under the auspices of a public-private partnership, demolition of many of the Bijlmermeer buildings commenced. The razed properties were replaced with low-rise housing intended for owner occupancy, the remaining large buildings were brightly painted so as to mask their drab concrete facades, and new elevators were added. Residents displaced from the original buildings were either relocated to other rental properties in the area or purchased residences among the newly constructed homes. The high vacancy rate that preceded demolition meant that ample space

---

13. Bruijne et al. (2002); Terhorst and van de Ven (1997), 299–301; Baart (2003).

14. Dirk Frieling, professor of urban planning at the TU Delft University. Quoted in Baart (2003), unpaginated.

FIGURE 15. Bijlmermeer with new owner-occupied building in foreground. Original building in back. Photo by Susan S. Fainstein.

existed for those who wished to stay as renters. Although black residents initially resisted the plans as coming from the top down and aimed at making the area white, they became supporters of the redevelopment when the planning process became more inclusive. The local council increased its number of minority members, and ethnic organizations were given a more prominent role in framing plans (Bodaar 2006, 182). Interestingly many of the Surinamese residents, who by the twenty-first century had risen up the economic ladder, welcomed the opportunity to stay in the development by purchasing houses and flats in the new low-rise structures.

What is particularly striking about the redesigned project is that it retained its ethnic mix. In fact, the promotional strategy for the area targeted middle-class cosmopolitans by playing up the strengths of existing diversity, and its multicultural character was one of its attractions to home buyers:[15] skepticism about the appeal of relatively expensive

---

15. Bodaar (2006), 181. According to Léon Deben, in 2006 the population was approximately 33 percent Surinamese, 30 percent Dutch, 21 percent "non-Western," 8 percent Western non-Dutch, 6 percent Antillean, and 2 percent Turkish/Moroccan.

housing in an area that remained dominated by social housing turned out to be unwarranted. Interviews with owner-occupiers, captured in the book *Territorium,* pointed to the reasons why the new townhouses and apartments had proved popular:

> Now many people from [the original buildings of] the Bijlmermeer are buying and renting in renewed areas. A bigger middle class has emerged.... Surinam's independence changed the Bijlmermeer enormously. Now you're seeing that a middle class has emerged from the group that came after independence....They think it's sensible and responsible to buy. (Interview with Inder Mataw, sociologist and resident)
>
> I feel at home in Bijlmermeer. The renewal plans are good, and you can really see progress. Maybe I feel at home because so many Surinamers live here. (Interview with Jerry Drakenstein, switchboard coordinator)
>
> It was beautiful in the Bijlmermeer, actually, and it still is....I wouldn't want to live anywhere else. It's to do with the area but also with the different races that live here. (Interview with Jules Fränkel, house painter)
>
> People [in the new owner-occupied buildings] view one another as equals. If you didn't have a decent income, you wouldn't have been able to buy this flat. Everyone who lives here makes a certain income and has a place somewhere on the societal ladder. We don't have to care whether you come from Ghana or from the Antilles. (Ingrid Perk, teacher)[16]

The story of the Bijlmermeer embodies a particularly Dutch approach to urban development: if a problem exists, a rational solution must be found. Its initial construction was based on an ambitious, coherent plan. Once its realization proved not to match the hopes of its progenitors, it was restudied and rethought. In contrast to its beginnings, development now is proceeding more organically, district by district, as the planners are refraining from imposing a single model on the entire project and allowing for participation by residents.[17] Four partners participated in

---

16. Interviews are recorded in Baart (2003, unpaginated).

17. Critics argue that participation has co-opted potential dissidents and that there are now long waiting lists for the remaining social housing (Justus Uitermark, interview, November 8, 2008).

FIGURE 16. Ajax Stadium—Amsterdam Southeast, adjacent to the Bijlmermeer. Photo by Susan S. Fainstein.

the program: the City of Amsterdam, the Southeast District Council, the Nieuw Amsterdam Housing Corporation, and the Patrimonium Housing Foundation, which took over administration of the project (Kwekkeboom 2002, 93). Total investment was more than €1.6 billion in 2002. Total housing stock in 2002 was 21,500 units, an increase of two thousand over the amount when demolition began, and more housing continued to be constructed. A stadium for Ajax, Amsterdam's premier football team, was built adjacent to a new railroad station, and other entertainment venues were added to the area, including a multiplex theater. The aim was to create greater vibrancy for the district, which until then consisted exclusively of residences, shops, and offices.

Concern with high levels of unemployment and at-risk youth caused physical planning to be combined with social policy. Efforts were made to provide work space for very small businesses. A cultural and education center was established to house various outreach services. In the 1996–2000 period, €36.3 million was invested in over one hundred socioeconomic projects; for 2000 to 2004 an additional €63.5 million was budgeted. Community and ethnic organizations participated in allocating funds; a multicultural advisory group to the district council was set up; and hiring for top management of the district aimed at creating ethnic balance (Kwekkeboom 2002, 84–85).

In 2008 it was still not clear whether the revitalization was a complete success. Despite densification, mixed-use development around the shopping center, a greater variety of housing, and the introduction of enhanced social programs, parts of the area still looked rather dreary, especially at a distance from the train station and retail mall. Although the project as a whole was mixed use, much of it remained exclusively residential and far from activity centers. The entertainment precinct around the Ajax stadium was very lively when games were being played, but otherwise was dead. Unsurprisingly, given that most housing remained in the social rented category, crime and unemployment continued to be problems, and young people complained of boredom (Shakur and Halsall 2007). Furthermore, very low income occupants were not able to afford the higher rents after renovation, even with a rental subsidy (Stan Majoor, personal communication, July 12, 2008). Still, the area was substantially improved over its former self, and the revitalization was predicated on a commitment to multiculturalism, egalitarianism, and community participation.

Amsterdam South Axis (Zuidas)

Of Amsterdam's recent developments, Zuidas most closely resembles the large office projects of New York and London such as the World Financial Center and Canary Wharf. Before the latest plans for the area, a number of large office structures already existed. They had gone up in a fashion whereby there was little relation of one to another. Many were bold architectural statements, but the area as a whole was incoherent, cold, and unfriendly to pedestrians. As in the Bijlmermeer the ambitions of the planners were to retrofit an existing single-use area so as to create an urbane, multifunctional space. The challenge was particularly daunting because a multilane expressway and railroad tracks divided the district, blocking pedestrian traffic and preventing design coherence. The proposed solution was extremely costly—a 1.2 kilometer tunnel to accommodate the road and railroad tracks as well as a level for parking.[18]

---

18. This discussion is based on Majoor (2007, 2008) and interviews in August 2007 with Willem Salet, professor of urban and regional planning at the University of Amsterdam; Pieter

FIGURE 17.   Rendering of future Amsterdam South Axis (Zuidas). Used by permission of Bewondersplatform Zuidas.

Amsterdam Zuidas was already the largest office complex in the Netherlands with 248,600 square meters (2.7 million square feet) built or under construction in 2007. The national government envisioned it as becoming an area that would allow Amsterdam to compete with Paris, Frankfurt, and Milan for global city functions. It has excellent access to both Schipol Airport and the city center. In the early 1990s the two large Dutch banks ABN-AMRO and ING were seeking modern office space; they wanted easy auto access and wished to evade the inevitable community controversy if they built high-rises in the central city.[19] The municipality responded with a plan for the area due south of the center that

---

Terhorst, associate professor of geography at the University of Amsterdam; and A. J. Jolles, a senior planner of the municipal government of Amsterdam.

19. The headquarters building of the bank ABN-AMRO has been the largest structure in the Zuidas. During the 2008 financial crisis the Dutch government nationalized the divisions of the bank formerly owned by Fortis, a Belgian-Dutch bank, while the UK government gained control over sections that had been acquired by the Royal Bank of Scotland in a 2007 buy-out.

included housing, retail, educational, and cultural facilities. Only the office structures were built, however. Over a decade later the municipal government, with financial participation by the central government, sought to realize the vision of a multifunctional scheme. The proposal incorporated a larger role for the private sector in providing infrastructure than had previously characterized Dutch projects.[20] The plan was to use the vehicle of a public-private partnership with the very expensive burying of the rail and highway right-of-ways mainly financed by the private sector. Sixty percent of the costs would be borne by the private participants, who in return would receive development rights for one million square meters (10 million square feet) on the newly created space. The public portion involved the city, provincial, and national governments.

In 2008 the master plan called for the creation of 1.1 million square meters (11.8 million square feet) of office space, 1.1 million square meters of apartments (11.8 million square feet), and half a million square meters (5.3 million square feet) of public facilities, to be built over thirty years (Majoor 2007, 53). It would also include a campus for the Free University of Amsterdam. Seventy percent of the housing would be market rate, an unusually large proportion for Amsterdam, although the target of 30 percent social housing would be considered high elsewhere.

The commitment to this type of office center on the urban periphery follows the trend pioneered in the development of La Défense on the outskirts of Paris. Old European cities could not offer modern office accommodation within their cores without extreme injury to the historic fabric and strong citizen opposition. The decision to move the economic center out of the core changed the character of the inner city of Amsterdam, causing it to shift toward entertainment, tourism, and small business functions and away from being the main center of production, finance, and business services.

The proposal was out for bid at the time of this writing, and whether it would actually be financed remained a question. Amsterdam suffers from an oversupply of office space, and banking consolidation could jeopardize occupation by financial institutions. Requirements imposed on the private sector included contributions to public space and facilities that would not

---

The threat that a foreign owner might move the headquarters had apparently passed, but the future of the bank and its space needs under straitened circumstances remained hazy.

20. A plan for the city's waterfront that was formulated in the 1980s foundered because its requirements for private-sector financing of public benefits were deemed overdemanding.

produce any financial return and might be more onerous than developers were willing to risk. As at Stratford City, the site was expected to offer the principal station outside the city center for high-speed rail (see chapter 4); but also, as at Stratford City, its actual arrival lay somewhere in the future. In its initial phases the project showed few signs of fulfilling the planners' ambitions of creating a "new urbanity": "[So far] the Zuidas has failed to create a strong urban feel. Neither have important (public) investments been made that could underline its urban ambition. At the moment people do not regard Zuidas as either an urban place, or a *potential* urban place…It [is] questionable if this perception can change" (Majoor 2008, 118).

Like Stratford City, Amsterdam Zuidas did not provoke much opposition (Majoor 2007). A number of open public meetings were held to discuss the plan, and its mixed-use conception reflected popular sentiment. The project, however, did not attract much attention for the same reason as was the case in Stratford—nobody lived there. Here the land was a greenfield site occupied mainly by sports clubs, which were awarded alternative locations. Both Stratford and Amsterdam Zuidas pointed to the difficulty of gaining citizen involvement in planning when the project did not impinge directly on people's lives and when the future occupants of the site were as yet unknown.

Is Amsterdam a Just City?

Amsterdam remains the strongest of the three cities evaluated in this book in terms of diversity, democracy, and equity. In relation to diversity, there has been considerable debate within the Netherlands concerning policy toward minority groups—whether tolerance of difference within the general principle of pillarization or an active effort toward assimilation is the better approach. Two assassinations—of the filmmaker Theo Van Gogh by a Muslim and of the right-wing politician Pim Fortuyn—caused previously suppressed ethnic hostility to rise to the surface.[21] Nevertheless, despite fears of increasing separatism, recent analysis by Sako Musterd and colleagues indicates that Amsterdam has been succeeding

---

21. Van Gogh had made a film, *Submission,* that accused Muslims of oppressing women. Fortuyn, an openly gay, iconoclastic figure, had opposed immigration on the grounds that religious Muslims were intolerant of Dutch liberal social mores. Both van Gogh and Fortuyn represented, within the Dutch context, a conservative populism that counterposed Islamic tradition to Dutch culture. See Van der Veer (2006).

in achieving inclusion of immigrant groups. They find increasing spatial integration of the two largest such groups, Moroccans and Turks, along with improved educational performance and labor market participation (Musterd and de Vos 2007, 351). Musterd and Ostendorf (2008, 87–88) conclude that

> between 1998 and 2004 ethnic segregation levels dropped in Rotterdam (Turks, from 50 to 44; Moroccans, from 45 to 40; Surinamese, from 25 to 21 [as measured by the index of dissimilarity, where 100 would indicate total segregation]) and [were] ... slightly lower [in Amsterdam] compared to Rotterdam.... So, academic research does not produce evidence that supports the political debate. This indicates that the main aim of [national urban] policy, creating a social mix, is to a large extent not necessary, because in the welfare state of The Netherlands social mix in neighbourhoods is already a reality. The Minister ... fears a problem ... that does not exist.

As regards democracy, decentralization of governance to the district level and encouragement of participation in planning indicate substantial commitment. Districts are much smaller than either New York's community districts or London's boroughs.[22] The districts have responsibilities for planning, zoning, public services, and cultural activities, possess substantial budgetary authority, and are governed by elected councilors. According to Léon Deben, they have sufficient financial means to develop policies and "certainly represent neighborhood interests," causing conflict between "what is good for the neighborhood and what concerns the central city."[23] On the other hand, the subsidence of protest movements might imply that forces for transformation have weakened or been co-opted.

The principal cause of injustice—the absolute shortage of available housing—affects all population groups, albeit not equally. Social housing continues to shelter the majority of residents, and rent subsidies ensure that everyone has access to shelter somewhere. The fact that rent levels are fairly low (although increasing) for most of the population mitigates class differentiation and, along with pillarization, contributes to income

---

22. There are fifteen districts with populations ranging in size (except for one very small outlier) from about thirty thousand to eighty-three thousand; the median size is 48,673 (Amsterdam Office of Research and Statistics 2009).

23. Personal communication, February 5, 2009. Professor Deben, as well as being a distinguished scholar of the city and former head of the University of Amsterdam Sociology Department, served for some years as a district councilor.

heterogeneity within neighborhoods. The (slow) decline in the proportion of units kept as social housing and continued in-migration of affluent owners, however, may ultimately cause gentrification to become a more serious threat.

Figures are not available for income distribution in Amsterdam. Data for the Netherlands as a whole show a Gini coefficient of .27, compared to .23 for Denmark, .32 for all OECD countries, .33 for the United Kingdom, and .38 for the United States (OECD 2008, 25).[24] Although by this measure the Netherlands ranks ninth among the thirty OECD countries, only Luxembourg and Norway exceed it in the amount of income flowing to the bottom decile of the population, and Norway's figure is greater by only a tiny amount (OECD 2008, 37). The contribution of low housing costs to general welfare is usually missed in comparisons of inequality, since these studies measure individual income flows rather than cost structures. Thus, the fact that the majority of Amsterdam's households still live in social housing implies that their disposable income minus housing costs may well be greater than would be indicated by the Gini coefficient.[25] The continuing rise in rents, however, will diminish this factor.

Overall, in relation to the three criteria of diversity, democracy, and equity Amsterdam remains exemplary. Social policy establishes a floor beneath which people may not sink; and while there is a numerous well-to-do class, there are few signs of the excesses of wealth evident in New York and London. Democratic participation is encouraged, and both decision-making authority and resources are sufficiently decentralized to make it influential. The population of the city is diverse, and this diversity is evident in most neighborhoods and public spaces. Amsterdam may not be the ideal city, and it is less egalitarian than in the past, but it still represents a model to which others might aspire.

---

24. The Gini coefficient is defined as the area between the Lorenz curve (which plots cumulative shares of the population, from the poorest to the richest, against the cumulative share of income that they receive) and the 45 degree line, taken as a ratio of the whole triangle. The values of the Gini coefficient range between 0, in the case of "perfect equality" (i.e., each share of the population gets the same share of income), and 1, in the case of "perfect inequality" (i.e., all income goes to the individual with the highest income). The figures given are for "disposable household income"—that is, income after taxes and transfers. The Amsterdam metro area comprises about 8 percent of the total population of the Netherlands.

25. I am assuming here that the Amsterdam metro area conforms generally to the calculations for the Netherlands as a whole.

6

CONCLUSION: TOWARD THE JUST CITY

At the beginning of this book I listed the following questions as the basis of my discussion:

1. What are the qualities comprising a just city within the wealthy Western world?
2. To what extent have the qualities of a just city been realized in the recent history of Western cities, as represented by New York, London, and Amsterdam?
3. What are the economic and social forces, politics, planning, and policies that have shaped this history?
4. What strategies can be followed at the subnational level to improve social justice and what are the institutions/social movements that might bring them about?

In regard to the first question, I have argued earlier that equity, democracy, and diversity are the three primary qualities constituting urban justice; however, these standards may sometimes be in conflict, both internally and with each other. In chapters 3, 4, and 5, I presented an evaluation of New York, London, and Amsterdam in relation to these three criteria and partially addressed the third question. In this chapter I discuss the forces that have shaped the history of these cities. Then I attempt to distill from these various experiences a set of broadly applicable policy norms. My assumption is that each situation may lead to a different interpretation of the broad principles of equity, diversity, and participation, but nevertheless some general guidelines, intermediate between the three governing values and specific actions, still apply. My approach conforms to the argument presented by Rainer Forst (2002, 238) in *Contexts of Justice:* "The principle of general justification is context-transcending not in the sense that it violates contexts of individual and collective self-determination but insofar as it designates minimal standards within which self-determination is 'reiterated.'"

Forst's assertion echoes Nussbaum's (2000, 6) contention that there is a threshold level of capabilities (i.e., the potential to "live as a dignified free human being who shapes his or her own life" [72]); below this level justice is sacrificed, and it is incumbent on government to provide the social basis for its availability although not for its actual realization. In a somewhat similar vein, Young (1990, chap. 2) lists forms of oppression and deduces justice as being free from those kinds of oppression; in other words, although she does not specify particular policies, she posits a minimum level of freedom from oppression as constituting justice. Both Nussbaum's and Young's stipulations point to criteria for policy evaluation, but they do not go as far as identifying what sorts of policies would bring about the outcomes they desire. My argument, rather than stating minimum standards, presses for the maximization of the three values of equity, diversity, and democracy, as expressed in a set of norms by which to direct and evaluate policy. These criteria by themselves do not indicate how much of a value need be present to meet the standard of justice nor indicate what trade-offs are acceptable. Thus, I go further and seek to identify the kinds of policies available to local decision makers that are likely to increase justice as measured by the three criteria. The intent is to specify programs that would benefit relatively disadvantaged social groups and to call on policy makers to make a kind of justice impact statement when choosing particular strategies.

The Context of Policy

Demands for justice in the three cities can be traced back to nineteenth-century radicalism and the crisis measures adopted during the Great Depression. Efforts at building social housing and urban institutions responsive to the needs of low-income families intensified after World War II. The period between the end of the war and 1975 is often characterized by the shorthand term Fordist, referring to a time in which the urban economies of the West were dominated by factory production.[1] Although dating of the onset of the Fordist period is inexact and variable from country to country, there is general agreement that the postwar era constitutes its full flowering, along with the height of the Keynesian welfare state. The urban politics of the epoch functioned within a context of relative social homogeneity and powerful unions.[2] In Western Europe and even the United States, national governments played an important role in financing and guiding local welfare and development programs.

The specific forces underlying program adoption varied from place to place and involved both national and local factors. A combination of pressure from below and political-bureaucratic receptiveness led to broad-based programs providing benefits to putative majorities. Cities were not especially the focus of national policies; nonetheless, many social programs, particularly for housing but also health and welfare, had their primary impacts on urban populations. In explaining the adoption of redistributive policies in the postwar period, Theda Skocpol (2003) cites the example of the American Legion's push for veterans' programs. She sees them as exemplifying policies wherein greater social justice is achieved as a consequence of majoritarian support, even though the American Legion is generally associated with right-wing viewpoints. Although Skocpol's attention is to the United States, we can identify similarly broad-based movements in Europe that pressed for social welfare programs after the war. Although left-wing parties and unions were certainly key components of such movements, conservative Christian Democratic parties also supported social programs, and bureaucratic commissions often were the source of policy ideas.

Despite—or in part because of—the majoritarian character of social programs, the postwar era also encompassed urban redevelopment policies that rode roughshod over low-income communities and, in the case of the United States, drove suburbanization and consequent hyper-segregation. In other words, the coalitions that underlay redistributive measures led to

---

1. The usefulness and generalizability of the terms Fordist and post-Fordist have been much debated (see Amin 1994). I am using them here as labels of convenience to designate the periods rather than necessarily accepting the theory underlying them.

2. There is huge variation among countries in the extent to which there is an autonomous sphere of urban politics. During the Fordist period, before considerable decentralization within Europe, urban autonomy was much greater in the United States than in Western Europe. See Pickvance and Preteceille (1990).

regressive as well as progressive changes. The GI Bill, cited as exemplary by Skocpol, while redistributive in allowing access to housing and education for large segments of the population, excluded African Americans from many of its housing and educational benefits, either implicitly or explicitly. The 1949 Housing Act, sponsored by conservative Republican Senator Robert Taft, established the U.S. public housing program but was part of the compromise that produced urban renewal to the benefit of downtown business interests and the detriment of working-class communities. Skocpol (2003) complains that increasingly fragmented publics with advocates voicing the concerns of particularistic interests have precluded the development of redistributive programs with wide benefits during the present, post-Fordist period. Such programs, however, frequently proved indifferent or withholding in their administration and were staffed by "street-level bureaucrats" who intruded into the lives of working-class and poor people in ways for which they were deeply resented (Lipsky 1980). Despite their egalitarian aims, public bureaucracies administering the programs of the welfare state generated oppositional movements on the left in the 1960s and '70s in both the United States and Western Europe. As Castells (1977) has argued, urban bureaucracies rather than capitalist employers became the target of movements aiming at equity and recognition.

Because both social welfare programs and affected populations were concentrated within metropolitan areas, protests over the quality of public programs and perceived discrimination in their execution occurred primarily within cities. Cities became the arena in which conflict among racial and ethnic groups took place and were the birthplace of movements for sexual freedom.[3] The uprisings of the '60s and early '70s derived from interests that often cut across class and had their basis in group identity (blacks, gays) or ideology (feminists, environmentalists) or both. Their success was in obtaining specific benefits, particularly in terms of hiring practices or access to funds for housing construction, but their relatively narrow bases meant that the concessions they sought lacked universal applicability and thus did not attain much support from political majorities. The rise of neoliberalism and the end of the perceived communist threat lessened the pressure on governments to pursue both the broad

---

3. Castells (1983); Fainstein and Fainstein (1974); Piven and Cloward (1971).

redistributive goals of the pre-1975 era and the more limited programs demanded by the protesters of the epoch's end. Then, contrary to the expectations of theorists who foresaw the withdrawal of social welfare programs as producing a crisis of legitimacy, a conservative, market-oriented approach to policy triumphed in the face of relative acquiescence.[4]

There is by now a vast literature analyzing the period bracketed by the fiscal crises and profit plunges of 1975 and the global financial crisis of 2007–9. A multitude of factors ultimately destabilized the Fordist system as it had been operating.[5] Within the economic structure reduced labor needs resulting from both increased capitalization of industry and the rise of non-Western manufacturing locations broke up the working-class unity that had developed within mass-production industries.[6] Migration of blacks from the American South to northern cities and of economic and political refugees from all over the world to the wealthy countries intensified competition for jobs. Unions lost membership, the political clout of union-based political parties diminished, and the aims and social composition of adherents to European Left parties and the U.S. Democratic Party changed.[7] Technological breakthroughs in communications and computerization allowed both the rapid mobility of capital and globalization of economic sectors, making every locality increasingly vulnerable to sudden withdrawals of investment. Heightened individualism and consumerism among the middle classes along with rebellion against seemingly unresponsive governmental bureaucracies made portions of the public receptive to an ideology favoring deregulation and

---

4. James O'Connor's book, *The Fiscal Crisis of the State* (1973), had as its thesis that concessions to the disadvantaged combined with antitax sentiment among the well-off inevitably led to fiscal crisis. He did not expect that the ensuing retrenchment would meet with so little resistance. Alcaly and Mermelstein (1977) developed his argument within the urban context. See also Block (1981).

5. Castells in a 1980 book showed great prescience in identifying the systemic problems that would force a restructuring of the global economic system, at that time still in gestation.

6. Within the newly industrializing countries of Latin America and Asia, production was based in branches and subsidiaries of international corporations as well as in homegrown competitors. See Glickman and Woodward (1989).

7. The U.K. Labour Party transformed into New Labour, having given up its socialist aspirations. The U.S. Democratic Party moved toward the center, continental communist parties vanished, and social democratic parties on the European continent moderated their demands, were often outflanked by green parties with radical but not necessarily redistributive programs, or joined with them in Red-Green coalitions.

reliance on market processes. The urban political movements that had grown during the latter part of the 1960s and into the 1970s faded with the conservative onslaught.[8]

Within this set of forces urban planning and policy became increasingly oriented toward a single-minded focus on encouraging growth through the vehicle of public-private partnerships, as chronicled in the three case studies presented here. Although these are not "ordinary cities" in the sense described by Jennifer Robinson (2006)—that is, they are certainly different from cities in the developing world and even from most in their own countries in their economic importance and global connectedness— the kinds of projects formulated and the conflicts around them are quite typical. The extent of variation among the three cases points to the extent that, within the existing structure of global forces and national politics, we can hope for a more just city.

Principles to Guide Planning and Policy

The assertion that meaningful justice is attainable in cities caught within the contemporary system of global capitalism provokes two possible responses: (1) It is impossible to work within this system and achieve a modicum of justice. (2) The pressure for nonreformist reforms can lead to incremental changes in the system that place it on a path toward justice. Harvey (2009, 46), who takes the first position, contends that "acting within the existing capitalist regime of rights and freedoms...[can only result in] mitigating the worst outcomes at the margins of an unjust system." My own view is that sufficient leeway exists that reform backed by political mobilization can produce significant change. The two views are not totally irreconcilable—demands expressed by groups such as the Right to the City Alliance and the Los Angeles Alliance for a New Economy and in antiglobalization demonstrations do represent efforts to reconstitute the system of global capitalism in ways that are less than totally revolutionary. Harvey (2009, 48–49) himself names participatory

---

8. For an overview of the factors at work post-1975, see Castells's (2000a, 2000b, 2004) magisterial trilogy, *The Information Age: Society, Economy, Culture.* It is possible to list hundreds, if not thousands, of books and articles addressing the themes briefly recapitulated in this section. I do not elaborate on them here, since I can add little that is new and the causes of present injustice are not the principal concern of this book.

budgeting as a collective form of governance that has, in fact, emerged within the context of capitalism. At the same time he argues that "a Just City has to be about fierce conflict all of the time" (2009, 47). One wonders, though, whether democratic participation is compatible with fierce conflict, and whether most people wish to live in a state of constant battle. Harvey (2009, 45) quotes the sociologist Robert Park as calling the city humanity's most successful attempt to model the world "after his heart's desire." But is unending fierce conflict truly the heart's desire of most people? My objective has been to lay out principles that can move cities closer to justice, which will undoubtedly involve their proponents in conflicts not easily settled, but which do not depend on revolutionary change for their realization.

An analysis of the development of universal health provision in Western Europe contends that the varying forms it has taken are the consequence of path dependency: "Each [national system] has taken a drastically different form, and the reason has rarely been ideology. Rather each country has built on its own history, however imperfect, unusual, and untidy" (Gawande 2009, 30). We could expect that the form of governmental intervention and nonprofit activity in the provision of housing and local economic development would similarly vary according to city and country and their historic path of development. Nonetheless, we can imagine a movement toward a common goal of increasing equity in relation to housing, economic development, and access to public space. The following section enumerates types of policies that are conducive to social justice in cities without spelling out the particular institutional forms or legislative mandates by which they would be accomplished.

Naming specific policies derived from the general criteria defining urban justice undoubtedly goes beyond what would be acceptable to rigorous deontological philosophers.[9] The list is more context-dependent and much more detailed than Nussbaum's presentation of capabilities.[10] It assumes societies with a preexisting commitment to democratic-egalitarian norms as well as a history of applying such norms, albeit through practice that may fall well short of the ideal. The contents of my list apply only

---

9. Nussbaum (2000, 78) does specify certain requisites in her list of capabilities that involve public policy, including adequate shelter, adequate education, and protection against discrimination.

10. Fincher and Iveson (2008, 214) provide a similar, but much shorter list under the categories "planning for redistribution"; "planning for recognition"; and "planning for encounter."

to planning and policies conducted at the local level; although national policy severely constrains or enables local efforts to achieve justice, localities still have it within their power to make decisions that are more or less favorable to justice.[11] The list is as follows:

In furtherance of equity:

1. All new housing development should provide units for households with incomes below the median, either on-site or elsewhere, with the goal of providing a decent home and suitable living environment for everyone. (One of the most vexing issues in relation to housing, however, is the extent to which tenant selection should limit access to people likely to be good neighbors. It is an area where the criteria of equity and democracy as well as different ways of calculating equity are at odds with each other, and no general rule can apply. Another issue pitting democratic determination against both equity and diversity arises because crises of housing availability lead to pressure for building at higher densities. Proposals for densification, however, tend to be met by strong neighborhood opposition, even though, if requirements are in place for a substantial amount of affordable housing, as has been the case under Labour in London, they would enhance diversity as well as equity.)

2. Housing units developed to be affordable should remain in perpetuity in the affordable housing pool or be subject to one-for-one replacement. (Until recently U.S. law required one-to-one replacement of demolished public housing, but this rule was eliminated.)

3. Households or businesses should not be involuntarily relocated for the purpose of obtaining economic development or community balance except in exceptional circumstances. When relocation is needed for the construction of public facilities, to improve housing quality, or to increase densities so as to accommodate additional population, adequate compensation requires that the dislocated be given sufficient means to occupy an equivalent dwelling or business site, regardless of whether they are renters or owners and independent of the market value of the lost location. Reconstruction

---

11. The components of a just national urban policy are more complex and will not be discussed here. Markusen and Fainstein (1993) develop the elements of a national urban policy for the United States.

of neighborhoods should be conducted incrementally so that interim space is available in the vicinity for displaced households who wish to remain in the same location.

4. Economic development programs should give priority to the interests of employees and, where feasible, small businesses, which generally are more locally rooted than large corporations. All new commercial development should provide space for public use and when possible should facilitate the livelihood of independent and cooperatively owned businesses.

5. Megaprojects should be subject to heightened scrutiny, be required to provide direct benefits to low-income people in the form of employment provisions, public amenities, and a living wage, and, if public subsidy is involved, should include public participation in the profits. If at all possible, they should be developed incrementally and with multiple developers.

6. Fares for intracity transit (but not commuter rail) should be kept very low. Low-income people are disproportionately reliant on public transit. Local government thus has the power to affect income distribution through collecting tolls and taxes on automobiles and designating the proceeds for transit support. Low-income people with no choice but to commute by car should receive rebates.

7. Planners should take an active role in deliberative settings in pressing for egalitarian solutions and blocking ones that disproportionately benefit the already well-off.

The policy directives listed as furthering equity respond to the most pressing concerns arising from current urban programs in the three cities discussed here. Increasing the supply of affordable housing is the most urgent need, but all three, at least until the economic crisis of 2008–9, have been engaged instead in promoting megaprojects that provide only limited amounts of low-income housing (Fainstein 2008). Although many of these projects (e.g., Battery Park City in New York; Stratford City in London; Amsterdam's Western Garden Cities) aim to provide new, high-quality housing and include some proportion of low-cost units, they mainly involve transformation of the social composition of the affected areas and are aimed at higher income groups. Financing issues are, as of this writing, stalling the full realization of uncompleted projects for housing and commercial development; only sports facilities (the Yankee, Mets, and Jets stadiums in New York and the Olympics venues in London) have continued despite the contraction of credit markets. This is in the face of serious problems of housing availability and affordability in the three cities and an epidemic of mortgage foreclosures (repossessions in U.K. vocabulary) in the United States and the United Kingdom. In the United States the commitment to enlarging the stock of affordable housing is the lowest of the three countries, but even the Netherlands has increased reliance on demand-side subsidies rather than housing construction.

In furtherance of diversity:
1. Households should not be required to move for the purpose of obtaining diversity, but neither should new communities be built that further segregation.
2. Zoning should not be used for discriminatory ends but rather should foster inclusion.
3. Boundaries between districts should be porous.
4. Ample public space should be widely accessible and varied; where public spaces are provided by private entities, political speech should not be prohibited within the property. At the same time, groups with clashing lifestyles should not have to occupy the same location.
5. To the extent practical and desired by affected populations, land uses should be mixed.
6. Public authorities should assist groups who have historically suffered from discrimination in achieving access to opportunity in housing, education, and employment.

Kwame Anthony Appiah (2006, xv), who uses the term "cosmopolitanism" to express his view of what I have called diversity, identifies two strands to the concept: (1) we have obligations to others stretching beyond those to whom we are related by blood or nationality; (2) we take seriously the value of the lives of others, including taking an interest in the practices and beliefs that lend them significance (i.e., we give recognition, in the terminology of other philosophers).[12] Adherence to this set of guidelines in respect to diversity does not require that people who cannot get along live next door to each other. Indeed, people should have

---

12. Ulrich Beck (2006) argues that, in a globalized world, cosmopolitanism is a necessity, reflecting an irreversible process of intermingling.

the right to protect themselves from others who do not respect their way of life. What is important is that people are not differentiated and excluded according to ascriptive characteristics such as gender, ethnicity, or homelessness.

In furtherance of democracy:
1. Groups that are not able to participate directly in decision-making processes should be represented by advocates.
2. Plans should be developed in consultation with the target population if the area is already developed. The existing population, however, should not be the sole arbiter of the future of an area. Citywide considerations must also apply.
3. In planning for as yet uninhabited or sparsely occupied areas, there should be broad consultation that includes representatives of groups currently living outside the affected areas.

There need not be an expectation of high levels of participation by people who do not wish to take part. The purpose of inclusion in decision making should be to have interests fairly represented, not to value participation in and of itself. If justice is the goal, the requirement of democracy is mainly instrumental—without it, those with less power are likely to be treated badly. Democratic theory regards democracy as a good in itself—a means by which people educate themselves and reach an understanding of their own interests, as well as an expression of citizenship. My purpose is not to dispute these other aims but rather to limit my discussion to the achievement of the just rather than the good and thus to give less priority to democracy than to equity.

State and Market

The guidelines, as well as assuming the context of a liberal-democratic political tradition, reflect societies in which markets have historically played a dominant role in allocating resources. The policy specifications do not call for government takeover of functions such as housing or business premises. Nevertheless, they do require a considerable increase in government involvement through regulation and some increase in public ownership. Thus, development of affordable housing could occur via the governmental, for-profit, and nonprofit sectors, but would depend on generous public subsidy and intervention. Likewise, public space may be government or privately owned, but if the latter it should be subject to substantial constraint.

Can we, with these policy guidelines in mind, conceive of a framework that retains market coordination while giving the state a larger role? Andrew Sayer and Richard Walker propose one vision of a social market economy that offers more latitude than the standard capitalist model:

> The classic answer [to the problem of economic coordination] has been through firms and markets. The capitalist controls the internal organization of the firm by virtue of ownership and the power it confers, while the price mechanism coordinates relations among many firms.... But the matter of economic integration is not exhausted by a simple duality of firm and market. Many other modes of organization exist...and there are several means of integration at work in these various institutional frames, besides exchange and hierarchy, including persuasion, reciprocity, extortion, and indicative planning. (Sayer and Walker 1992, 6)

According to this reasoning it is necessary to recognize multiple forms of economic organization and "[no particular mode] of integration can be wholly endorsed or condemned irrespective of the context and the nature of the activities being coordinated, be they the provision of education, electricity, food, books, broadcasting, childcare, or holidays" (Sayer and Walker 1992, 269). Their argument points toward an incremental approach to increasing fairness of access to employment, public space, housing, and other socially produced goods and services, employing a variety of hortatory and market-based devices to make the system function. This means identifying opportunities as they arise and constantly pushing for a more just distribution.

In respect to the extent of public ownership, national context is crucial. Within the United States, national subsidies for urban programs have shifted decisively toward supporting private initiatives. Reversal would have to be at the national level and thus largely outside the power of local determination. Europe has also moved toward public-private partnerships and housing privatization, but government regulation and ownership remain more prominent than in the United States, and public ownership enjoys more popular support. As a principle, where public subsidy enables large projects to go forward, the public should share in the profits.

Equity participation of government in small business development is also a possibility. During the 1970s the Greater London Council, under the leadership of Ken Livingstone, established the Greater London Enterprise Board (GLEB), which sponsored small- and medium-sized businesses in deprived areas. It operated by acting as a lender, an intermediary between financial institutions and borrowers, a landlord providing business premises, and a consulting service (Fainstein 2001a, 91–92). It was sufficiently successful that it was able to continue without government support and belied the premise that state-created entities are incapable of efficient operations.[13]

In both Europe and the United States, local governments have the power to channel resources toward the nonprofit sector rather than depending wholly on deal-making with private developers who, in return for governmental largesse, offer a public benefit as a component of their projects. A move toward greater reliance on nonprofits, which would require both assured funding and guarantees of their longevity, would produce a public-private hybrid that was less bureaucratic than programs operated directly by government, although with some loss of accountability. European housing associations and American community development corporations (CDCs) both make use of a combination of philanthropy and public subsidy in order to produce housing, and in the case of CDCs, support business ventures as well. In all three of the cities described in this volume, autonomous nongovernmental organizations (NGOs) using public funds have substantial responsibility for implementing housing and social welfare policies. They tend, however, to be crowded out of the market during boom times. The use of land banking, as is done in Amsterdam, can alleviate the problem. The government's role is in planning its use and releasing the land; the private and nonprofit sectors carry out the actual development.

NGOs frequently face the problems of unpredictable funding and difficulties in gaining support for ongoing staff as opposed to specific projects. Ways of dealing with this issue include the establishment of housing trust funds, the use of loan pools, and the recycling of revenues from commercial enterprises in which they have equity shares. The GLEB model and the activities of some American community economic development corporations offer examples of the possibilities. The goal is to

---

13. After Margaret Thatcher's national victory, the GLEB was spun off as an independent entity. Now called Greater London Enterprise (GLE), it is owned by the thirty-three London local authorities, but it is responsible to a board of directors made up principally of private and nonprofit sector individuals.

move incrementally, as much as possible, to removing critical areas that impinge directly on the well-being of most of the population from the injustices caused by market distributions.[14]

Factors in the Development of Just Policies

Much of the response by groups opposed to neoliberalism has been to demand greater democracy. Realism, however, points to calling for better representation rather than broader participation. Mansbridge (2009) distinguishes between "sanctions" and "selection" models of representation. In the former, representatives are simply held accountable and can be deposed if they do not adequately represent their constituencies; in the latter a representative "already has self-motivated, exogenous reasons for doing what the...[constituency] wants" (Mansbridge 2009, 369). She argues that employing the selection model relieves communities of the need for continuous participation while at the same time allowing for input:

> If we view democratic political representation as a principal-agent problem, a constituent can reasonably want to adopt a selection model and save on monitoring and sanctioning whenever the representative's established direction and policies are largely those the constituent desires and the representative also has a verifiable reputation for being both competent and honest. In the selection model, the representative's accountability to the constituent will typically take the form of *narrative* and even *deliberative* accountability rather than accountability based on monitoring and sanctions. In *narrative* and *deliberative account-ability*, the representative explains the reasons for her actions and even (ideally) engages in two-way communication with constituents, particularly when deviating from the constituents' preferences. (Mansbridge 2009, 369–370)

Mansbridge's argument addresses only the problem of making elected representatives responsive to the needs of their constituents. Our concern here, however, encompasses unelected policy makers as well, both those

---

14. See DeFilippis (2004) for a discussion of the potential of community-based, nonprofit enterprise.

who work for state bureaucracies and those who advocate for community groups within civil society. In both cases there is a need for actors to promote just policies and to get them to do so without constant monitoring and activism by those on whose behalf they act.

In my description of recent policies toward development in the three cities, I showed that Amsterdam revealed a stronger, if diminishing, commitment to equity across a range of policies. In London, where a social-democratic ethos still to some extent prevails, more is being asked from developers than is the case in New York. In both London and Amsterdam the direct governmental contribution to housing also is greater than in New York, because the national governments play a much larger role in financing affordable housing development. Even in these cities, however, much depends on the profitability of the market-driven parts of projects. Only three forms of construction have the potential to generate big profits for private developers: luxury residences and hotels, large-footprint office towers, and shopping malls. The extent to which the gains from profit-driven property investment are spread throughout the society depends on the extent of governmental commitment to public benefits. This is greatest in the Netherlands, where the welfare state, albeit somewhat shrunken, lives on; it is least in the United States, where the small size of national expenditures on housing and social welfare means that low-income people must depend almost wholly on trickle-down effects to gain from new development.

On the other hand, American cities have been more flexible in their absorption of immigrants, who, despite some anti-immigrant sentiment, have been viewed by many city governments as invigorating their local economies. Generalizations concerning the extent to which majorities in different countries tolerate "the other" are difficult to make and attitudes vary within each country as well. Nevertheless, American cities have clearly become extraordinarily diverse, and multiculturalism, whether sincere or not, has become the official dogma promulgated in school systems and public gatherings across the country.

At the time of this writing the future of urban policy is highly uncertain. The past few decades have encompassed a significant shift in urban structure and the emphases of urban planning. Postwar policies reflected Fordist strategies of mass provision of housing, promotion of office and large-scale retail development, reliance on the automobile, and segregated land uses. The post-Fordist era has witnessed a move toward tourism promotion, the exploitation of cultural distinctiveness, gentrification, and commodification of urban space (Hoffman, Fainstein, and Judd 2003). The range of groups that participate in policy making has widened, although the extent to which nonbusiness interests have actually prevailed is questionable and highly variable from place to place. From the point of view of maximizing equity and diversity, these changes have been double-edged. On the one hand, uniformity has lost its valued position in the planning pantheon, and ethnic communities are seen as adding to the attractiveness of cities. Gentrification has made neighborhoods at least temporarily more diverse, and commodification of space has made cities more attractive. On the other hand, ethnic neighborhoods have become the object of the tourist gaze (Urry 2002), immigrant workers are often exploited, and differentiation of urban spaces is becoming increasingly artificial. Tourism and consumer services have replaced manufacturing in providing easy-entry employment, with the loss of the pay levels and benefits that accompanied unionized industrial work.

This whole transformation of urban functions depends on a consumer-oriented economy that, at the present moment, is in crisis. With the economic freefall of 2008–09, characterized by the collapse of credit markets, soaring unemployment, the shrinkage of discretionary income, and budgetary crises for local governments, the economic base of cities becomes highly problematic. The kinds of investments that have dominated the past decades were premised on the recentralization of certain services within urban centers and a growing demand for urban lifestyles among an affluent population. None of this can still be counted on. Thus, it is with trepidation that I conclude by presenting some general strategies for the achievement of the policy guidelines I outlined above.

Strategies

Planners and policy analysts work within public bureaucracies, private for-profit consulting firms, and nonprofit organizations. They lack the power to implement policy on their own, and they are restricted by their political masters and their clients regarding the objectives they can seek. Nevertheless, they have one significant advantage that can empower them to shape policy. Max Weber (1958, 232) comments that bureaucrats can use their control over information to bend their political superiors to their will: "Under normal conditions, the power position of a fully developed bureaucracy is always overtowering. The 'political master' finds himself in the position of the 'dilettante' who stands opposite the 'expert,' facing the trained official who stands within the management of administration." Much of planning and policy development involves the collection and aggregation of data and the choice of how to present it. To the extent that experts present analyses not just of benefit/cost ratios but of who gets the benefits and who bears the costs, they can shift the debate toward a concern with equity.

To do so, however, they require support from some political base. In this respect citizen activism is important, not because citizens in their deliberations always or even mostly place justice at the top of their hierarchy of values but rather because they have an interest in knowing who is getting what. In response to a lecture I gave on the just city, James Throgmorton wrote:

> My experience as an elected official leads me to think that the planners of any specific city cannot (and should not) simply declare by fiat that their purpose is to create the just city. In the context of representative democracy, they have to be authorized to imagine, articulate, pursue, and actualize the vision of a just city. This means that a mobilized constituency would have to be pressuring for change. (Personal communication, January 28, 2006)

In terms of practical politics Throgmorton is completely correct—without a mobilized constituency and supportive officials, no prescription for justice will be implemented. But regardless of authorization or not, justice is a goal to continually press for and to deploy when evaluating decisions. It is way too easy to follow the lead of developers and politicians who make economic competitiveness the highest priority and give little or no consideration to questions of justice.

Schemes for public participation in planning can, if well constructed, lead to desirable outcomes. One model is the Minneapolis Neighborhood Revitalization Program (NRP) (see chapter 2), in which every neighborhood in the city, including wealthy ones, was given a sum of money to spend on their communities. The amounts, however, were allocated according to the type of neighborhood, so that poor neighborhoods received considerably more than well-to-do ones. The fact that everyone got something made the program politically viable even while it was redistributional. The neighborhood organizations supervising the planning process were required to be inclusive in their planning efforts, thus fulfilling mandates for both diversity and democracy. Although the results were uneven, with homeowners dominating the process in many neighborhoods, the program nevertheless succeeded in diverting funds from downtown development to community betterment and, in several neighborhoods, contributing to improvements in housing, social services, and public facilities directed at low- and middle-income residents.[15] New York's system of community planning boards is less successful in mobilizing resources to effect community change in favor of disadvantaged groups since the boards' powers are wholly advisory, membership is appointed by borough presidents and the city council rather than community organizations, and they are not provided with financial resources to distribute (Marcuse 1987). Amsterdam's district governments administer areas substantially smaller than New York's community districts or London's boroughs but have planning and budgetary power similar to those of London's local authorities. Thus, while neither London nor Amsterdam has neighborhood planning bodies comparable to those of Minneapolis's experiment, their planning and allocative authorities are much more decentralized than New York's, have considerable power, and have the potential to bring nonelite interests to bear on the planning process.

Beyond sanctioned modes of participation the role of protest movements is crucial to more equitable policy. Without pressure from beneath, official participatory bodies are likely to become co-opted; when there is a threat from below, governments become more responsive to popular interests. As I am writing, the economies of the United States and Western Europe face their gravest crisis since the Great Depression. It has precipitated protest, and in some instances riots, in parts of the world, but so far these disturbances have been quite limited. It is impossible to foretell whether quiescence will continue; much depends on whether the situation worsens and the ideological framework through which the crisis is interpreted. A cursory examination of history indicates that crisis can mobilize both progressive and regressive movements. World War I and the Great Depression begot social reform in the United States and much of Europe, but they also gave rise to fascism, Nazism, Stalinism, and right-wing movements within the liberal democracies.

At the moment the emphasis on cultural identity that came to the fore during the latter part of the twentieth century and into the new millennium has been subsumed by a focus on economic division and the role

---

15. Fagotto and Fung (2006, 19); see also Fainstein and Hirst (1995).

of capitalist financial institutions in producing economic collapse. Even in the United States, where negative perceptions of outlandish incomes for the captains of industry and finance have long been muted, class resentment has become outspoken. As noted in the *New York Times,* there is "rising public fury about huge pay packages for executives at financial companies being propped up by federal tax dollars" (Andrews and Bajaj 2009). Greater consciousness by large publics of their class interests and, as a consequence of governmental acquisition of ownership stakes in financial institutions, the politicization of corporate decision making mean that economic differences are removed from the market-governed private realm.

Foglesong (1986) identifies the capitalist-democracy contradiction in regard to planning as occurring when

> the need [arises] to socialize the control of urban space to create the conditions for the maintenance of capitalism, on the one hand, and the danger to capital of truly socializing, that is, democratizing, the control of urban land on the other. For if the market system cannot produce a built environment that is capable of maintaining capitalism, reliance on the institutions of the state, especially a formally democratic state, creates a whole new set of problems, not the least of which is that the more populous body of nonowners will gain too much control over landed property. (Foglesong 1986, 23)

The involvement of the U.S. government with the financial institutions that own mortgages, as well as pressures at all levels of government to reduce the release of carbon dioxide, produces exactly the contradictory situation Foglesong describes. Because the private sector cannot coordinate responses to the mortgage crisis on its own nor limit the emission of greenhouse gases, it has been forced to turn to the state to carry out this role. With the involvement of the state, however, come the interests of nonowners of capital in limiting the discretion of investors and injecting concerns with justice into policy making.

In conclusion, there are obvious limits to what can be accomplished at the metropolitan level. At the very least, however, a concern with justice can prevent urban regimes from displacing residents involuntarily, destroying communities, and directing resources at costly megaprojects that offer few general benefits. More positively, it can lead to policies that foster equitable distribution of governmental revenues, produce a lively, diverse, and accessible public realm, and make local decision making more transparent and open to the viewpoints of currently excluded groups. If the discourse surrounding policy making focuses on the justice of the decision rather than simply its contribution to competitiveness, much will have been accomplished. Discourse and outcomes are surely connected, but it is the substantive content of the discourse, not simply the process by which it is conducted, that matters if justice is to be the outcome.

References

Abrams, Charles. 1965. *The City Is the Frontier.* New York: Harper and Row.

Abu-Lughod, Janet L. 1999. *New York, Chicago, Los Angeles: America's Global Cities.* Minneapolis: University of Minnesota Press.

———. 2007. *Race, Space, and Riots in Chicago, New York, and Los Angeles.* New York: Oxford University Press.

Ackerman, Bruce. 1980. *Social Justice in the Liberal State.* New Haven: Yale University Press.

Albrechts, Louis, and Seymour Mandelbaum. 2005. *The Network Society: A New Context for Planning.* New York: Routledge.

Alcaly, Roger E., and David Mermelstein, eds. 1977. *The Fiscal Crisis of American Cities.* New York: Vintage.

Altshuler, Alan. 1965. *The City Planning Process.* Ithaca: Cornell University Press.

———. 1970. *Community Control.* New York: Pegasus.

Altshuler, Alan, and David Luberoff. 2003. *Mega-Projects.* Washington, D.C.: Brookings Institution.

Ambrose, Peter. 1986. *Whatever Happened to Planning?* London: Methuen.

Ambrose, Peter, and Bob Colenutt. 1975. *The Property Machine.* Harmondsworth, U.K.: Penguin.

American Institute of Planners (AIP). 1959. "Urban Renewal: A Policy Statement of the American Institute of Planners." *Journal of the American Institute of Planners* 25, no. 4: 217–21.

Amin, Ash, ed. 1994. *Post-Fordism: A Reader.* Oxford: Blackwell.

Amsterdam Office of Research and Statistics. 2009. *Amsterdam in Cijfers* 2008. Bron:O+S. http://www.os.amsterdam.nl/publicaties/amsterdamincijfers/.

Amsterdam Physical Planning Department (APPD). 2003. *Planning Amsterdam, 1928–2003.* Rotterdam: NAI.

———. N.d. *Eastern Harbour District Amsterdam.* Rotterdam: NAI.

Amsterdam Research and Statistics. 2008. "Key Figures Amsterdam: Urban Development." http://www.os.amsterdam.nl/tabel/11324.

Andrews, Edmund L., and Vikas Bajaj. 2009. "Amid Fury U.S. Is Set to Curb Executives' Pay after Bailouts." *New York Times,* February 4.

Angotti, Tom. 2008. "Is the Long-term Sustainability Plan Sustainable?" *Gotham Gazette,* April 2008. http://www.gothamgazette.com/article/sustainability watch/20080421/210/2495.

Appiah, Kwame Anthony. 2006. *Cosmopolitanism.* New York: W. W. Norton.

Arden, Patrick. 2006. "Carrion: No Payback for Foes of Stadium: Claims of Revenge on Community Board 4 Greatly Exaggerated, Borough Pres. Says." *Metro New York,* June 15.

Arnstein, Sherry R. 1969. "A Ladder of Citizen Participation." *Journal of the American Planning Association* 35, no. 4: 216–24.

Austrian, Ziona, and Mark S. Rosentraub. 2003. "Urban Tourism and Financing Professional Sports Facilities." In *Financing Economic Development,* ed. Sammis B. White, Richard D. Bingham, and Ned W. Hill, 211–32. Armonk, N.Y.: M. E. Sharpe.

Baart, Theo. 2003. *Territorium.* Rotterdam: NAI.

Bagli, Charles V. 2006. "Megadeal: Inside a New York Real Estate Coup." *New York Times,* December 31.

——. 2008. "As Stadiums' Costs Swell, Benefits in Question." *New York Times,* November 3.

——. 2009. "Buyers of Huge Manhattan Complex Face Default Risk." *New York Times,* September 10.

Bai, Matt. 1994. "Yankee Imperialism." *New York Magazine,* July 25, 30–35.

Balbus, Issac D. 1971. "The Concept of Interest in Pluralist and Marxian Analysis." *Politics & Society* 1, no. 2: 151–77.

Ballon, Hilary, and Kenneth T. Jackson, eds. 2007. *Robert Moses and the Modern City: The Transformation of New York.* New York: W. W. Norton.

Barber, Benjamin. 1984. *Strong Democracy.* Berkeley: University of California Press.

Bartels, Larry M. 2008. *Unequal Democracy.* New York: Russell Sage Foundation.

Beauregard, Robert A. 1990. "Bringing the City Back." *Journal of the American Planning Association* 56, no. 2: 210–15.

Beck, Ulrich. 2006. *The Cosmopolitan Vision.* Translated by Ciaran Cronin. Cambridge, U.K.: Polity.

Benhabib, Seyla. 2002. *The Claims of Culture.* Princeton: Princeton University Press.

Bennett, Larry. 2006. "Downtown Restructuring and Public Housing in Contemporary Chicago: Fashioning a Better World-Class City." In *Where Are Poor People to Live?* edited by Larry Bennett, Janet L. Smith, and Patricia A. Wright, 282–300. Armonk, N.Y.: M. E. Sharpe.

Bennett, Larry, Janet L. Smith, and Patricia A. Wright, eds. 2006. *Where Are Poor People to Live?* Armonk, N.Y.: M. E. Sharpe.

Berman, Sheri. 2003. "The Roots and Rationale of Social Democracy." *Social Philosophy and Policy* 20: 113–44.

Berry, Brian. 2005. *Why Social Justice Matters.* Cambridge: Polity.

Blair, Tony. 2006. "Speech to Greater London Authority." April 4. http://www.number10.gov.uk/Page9281.

Blauner, Robert. 1969. "Internal Colonialism and Ghetto Revolt." *Social Problems* 16, no. 4: 393–408.

Block, Fred. 1981. "The Fiscal Crisis of the Capitalist State." *Annual Review of Sociology* 7: 1–27.

Blumenthal, Ralph. 1972. "Yankees to Stay 30 Years in Pact Approved by City." *New York Times,* March 24.

Bodaar, Annemarie. 2006. "Multicultural Urban Space and the Cosmopolitan Other: The Contested Revitalization of Amsterdam's Bijlmermeer." In *Cosmopolitan Urbanism,* edited by Jon Binnie, 171–86. London: Routledge.

Boyte, Harry C. 1980. *The Backyard Revolution.* Philadelphia: Temple University Press.

Brandsen, Taco, and Jan-Kees Helderman. 2006. "The Rewards of Policy Legacy: Why Dutch Social Housing Did Not Follow the British Path." In *Reform in Europe: Breaking the Barriers,* edited by Liesbet Heyse, Sandra Resodihardjo, Tineke Lantink, and Berber Lettinga, 37–57. Aldershot, U.K.: Ashgate.

Brecher, Charles, and Raymond Horton. 1984. "Expenditures." In *Setting Municipal Priorities, 1984,* edited by Charles Brecher and Raymond Horton, 68–96. New York: New York University Press.

Brenner, Neil. 1999. "Globalization as Reterritorialization: The Re-Scaling of Urban Governance in the European Union." *Urban Studies* 36, no. 3: 431–51.

Brindley, Tim, Yvonne Rydin, and Gerry Stoker. 1996. *Remaking Planning.* 2nd ed. London: Routledge.

Bronner, Stephen. 1999. *Ideas in Action.* Lanham, Md.: Rowman and Littlefield.

Brooks, Michael P. 2002. *Planning Theory for Practitioners.* Chicago: Planners Press.

Brown, Wendy. 2006. *Regulating Aversion: Tolerance in the Age of Identity and Empire.* Princeton: Princeton University Press.

Brownill, Sue, Konnie Razzaque, and Ben Kochan. 1998. "The LDDC and Community Consultation and Participation." *Rising East (Journal of East London Studies)* 2, no. 2: 42–72.

Brugemann, Robert. 2005. *Sprawl: A Compact History.* Chicago: University of Chicago Press.

Bruijne, Dick, Dorine van Hoogstraten, Willem Kwekkeboom, and Anne Luijten. 2002. *Amsterdam Southeast: Centre Area Southeast and Urban Renewal in the Bijlmermeer, 1992–2012.* Bussum, Netherlands: Thoth.

Buck, Nick, and Norman Fainstein. 1992. "A Comparative History, 1880–1973." In *Divided Cities,* edited by Susan S. Fainstein, Ian Gordon, and Michael Harloe, 29–67. Oxford: Blackwell.

Buck, Nick, Ian Gordon, Peter Hall, Michael Harloe, and Mark Kleinman. 2002. *Working Capital: Life and Labour in Contemporary London.* London: Routledge.

Buck, Nick, Ian Gordon, and Ken Young. 1986. *The London Employment Problem.* Oxford: Oxford University Press.

Buruma, Ian. 2006. *Murder in Amsterdam.* New York: Penguin.

Butler, Tim, with Garry Robson. 2003. *London Calling.* London: Berg.

Byrnes, Sholto. 2008. "This Sporting Strife." *Guardian,* October 26. http://www.guardian.co.uk/commentisfree/2008/oct/26/fitness-healthandwellbeing.

Cambridge Research Associates. 1998. "Regenerating London Docklands." *Report to the UK Department of the Environment, Transport and the Regions (DETR).* London: DETR.

Campbell, Heather. 2006. "Just Planning: The Art of Situated Ethical Judgment." *Journal of Planning Education and Research* 26: 92–106.

Campbell, Heather, and Robert Marshall. 2006. "Towards Justice in Planning." *European Planning Studies* 14, no. 2: 239–52.

Campbell, Scott. 2003. "Green Cities, Growing Cities, Just Cities? Urban Planning and the Contradictions of Sustainable Development." In *Readings in*

Planning Theory, edited by Scott Campbell and Susan S. Fainstein, 435–458. Oxford: Blackwell.

Canary Wharf Group. 2008. *Fact File.* http://www.canarywharf.com/mainFrm1.asp?strSelectedArea=Factfile.

Carens, Joseph H. 2003. "An Interpretation and Defense of the Socialist Principle of Distribution." *Social Philosophy and Policy* 20, no. 1: 145–77.

Caro, Robert. 1974. *The Power Broker.* New York: Knopf.

Castells, Manuel. 1977. *The Urban Question.* Cambridge: MIT Press.

——. 1980. *The Economic Crisis and American Society.* Princeton: Princeton University Press.

——. 1983. *City and the Grassroots: A Cross-Cultural Theory of Urban Social Movements.* London: Edward Arnold.

——. 2000a. *End of Millennium.* 2nd ed. Oxford: Blackwell.

——. 2000b. *The Rise of the Network Society.* 2nd ed. Oxford: Blackwell.

——. 2004. *The Power of Identity.* 2nd ed. Oxford: Blackwell.

Ceccarelli, Paolo. 1982. "Politics, Parties, and Urban Movements: Western Europe." In *Urban Policy under Capitalism,* edited by Norman Fainstein and Susan S. Fainstein, 261–76. Beverly Hills, CA: Sage.

Centre on Housing Rights and Evictions (COHRE). 2007. *Fact Sheet—Forced Evictions and Displacements in Future Olympic Cities.* Geneva: COHRE.

Chapple, Karen, and Edward G. Goetz. 2008. "Spatial Justice through Regionalism? The Inside Game, the Outside Game, and the Quest for the Spatial Fix in the U.S." Paper presented at the Spatial Justice International Conference, University of Paris X—Nanterre, March 13.

Chernick, Howard, ed. 2005. *Resilient City.* New York: Russell Sage Foundation.

Clapp, John. 1976. "The Formation of Housing Policy in New York City, 1960–1970." *Policy Sciences* 7, no. 1: 77–91.

Claval, Paul. 2000. "The Cultural Dimension in Restructuring Metropolises: The Amsterdam Example." In *Understanding Amsterdam,* 2nd ed., edited by Léon Deben, Willem Heinemeijer, and Dick van der Vaart, 59–92. Amsterdam: Het Spinhuis.

Clavel, Pierre. 1986. *The Progressive City.* New Brunswick, N.J.: Rutgers University Press.

Cohen, G. A. 2006. "Are Freedom and Equality Compatible?" In *Contemporary Political Philosophy,* edited by Robert E. Goodin and Philip Petit, 416–31. Oxford: Blackwell.

Cohen, Joshua. 1996. "Procedure and Substance in Deliberative Democracy." In *Democracy and Difference,* edited by Seyla Benhabib, 95–119. Princeton: Princeton University Press.

Cohen, Saul. 1964. *Progressives and Urban School Reform.* New York: Teachers College Press.

Cooke, Maeve. 2006. *Re-Presenting the Good Society.* Cambridge: MIT Press.

Corburn, Jason. 2005. *Street Science.* Cambridge: MIT Press.

Cross, Malcolm, and H. Entzinger. 1988. "Caribbean Minorities in Britain and the Netherlands: Comparative Questions." In *Lost Illusions: Caribbean Minorities in Britain and the Netherlands,* edited by Malcolm Cross and H. Entzinger. London: Routledge.

Crozier, Michel. 1964. *The Bureaucratic Phenomenon.* Chicago: University of Chicago Press.

Currid, Elizabeth. 2007. *The Warhol Economy: How Fashion, Art, and Music Drive New York City.* Princeton: Princeton University Press.

Dahl, Robert A. 1961. *Who Governs?* New Haven: Yale University Press.

——. 1963. *A Preface to Democratic Theory.* Chicago: University of Chicago Press.

——. 1967. "The City in the Future of Democracy." *American Political Science Review* 61: 953–70.

Dahrendorf, Ralf. 1959. *Class and Class Conflict in Industrial Society.* Stanford: Stanford University Press.

Davidoff, Paul. 2003. "Advocacy and Pluralism in Planning." *Journal of the American Institute of Planners* 31, no. 4: 331–38.

DeFilippis, James. 2004. *Unmaking Goliath.* New York: Routledge.

——. 2009. "On Globalization, Competition, and Economic Justice in Cities." In *Searching for the Just City,* edited by Peter Marcuse, James Connolly, Johannes Novy, Ingrid Olivo, Cuz Potter, and Justin Steil, 144–58. London: Routledge.

Dias, Candice, and Justin Beaumont. 2007. "Beyond the Egalitarian City." Paper presented at the Conference on Urban Justice and Sustainability, Research Committee 21 of the International Sociological Association, Vancouver, Canada, August 22–25.

Dieleman, F. M., and Sako Musterd. 1992. "The Restructuring of Randstat Holland." In *The Randstad: A Research and Policy Laboratory,* edited by F. M. Dieleman and Sako Musterd, 1–16. Dordrecht: Kluwer.

Dinwoodie, Robbie. 2008. "MSPs Back Motion for Lottery Cash Games Legacy." *Herald* (Scotland), September 26. http://www.theherald.co.uk/politics/news/display.var.2452951.0.MSPs_back_motion_for_lotterycash_Games_legacy.php.

Dreier, Peter, John Mollenkopf, and Todd Swanstrom. 2001. *Place Matters: Metropolitics for the Twenty-First Century.* Lawrence: University Press of Kansas.

Dror, Yehezkel. 1968. *Public Policymaking Reexamined.* San Francisco: Chandler.

Drury, Ian. 2008. "£525m Olympic Stadium Could Be Demolished to Make Way for Premiership Football Club." *MailOnline,* September 5. http://www.mailonsunday.co.uk/news/article-1052772/525m-Olympic-stadium-demolished-make-way-Premiership-football-club.html.

Dryzek, John. 1990. *Discursive Democracy.* Cambridge: Cambridge University Press.

Dwyer, Jim. 2009. "Yankees Claimed a Park; Children Got Bus Rides." *New York Times,* October 25.

Economist. 2005. "The New Dutch Model?" March 31. http://www.economist.com/world/displaystory.cfm?story_id=E1_PRDJRDN.

Eisenstein, Hester. 1983. *Contemporary Feminist Thought.* Boston: G. K. Hall.

Evans, Graeme. 2007. "London 2012." In *Olympic Cities,* edited by John R. Gold and Margaret M. Gold, 298–317. London: Routledge.

Evans, Peter B., Dietrich Rueschemeyer, and Theda Skocpol, eds. 1985. *Bringing the State Back In.* Cambridge: Cambridge University Press.

Fagotto, Elena, and Archon Fung. 2005. *The Minneapolis Neighborhood Revitalization Program: An Experiment in Empowered Participatory Governance.* Unpublished report, John F. Kennedy School of Government, Harvard University, February 15.

——. 2006. "Empowered Participation in Urban Governance: The Minneapolis Neighborhood Revitalization Program." *International Journal of Urban and Regional Research* 30, no. 3: 638–55.

Fainstein, Norman I., and Susan S. Fainstein. 1988. "Governing Regimes and the Political Economy of Development in New York City, 1946–1984." In *Power, Culture, and Place,* edited by John Hull Mollenkopf, 161–99. New York: Russell Sage Foundation.

Fainstein, Susan S. 1996. "Neighborhood Organizations and Community Power: The Minneapolis Experience." In *Revitalizing Urban Neighborhoods,* edited by Dennis Keating, Norman Krumholz, and Philip Star, 96–111. Lawrence: University Press of Kansas.

——. 1997. "The Egalitarian City: The Restructuring of Amsterdam." *International Planning Studies* 2, no. 3: 295–314.

——. 1999. "Can We Make the Cities We Want?" In *The Urban Moment,* edited by Sophie Body-Gendrot and Robert Beauregard, 249–72. Thousand Oaks: Sage.

——. 2000. "New Directions in Planning Theory." *Urban Affairs Review* 35, no. 4: 451–78.

——. 2001a. *The City Builders: Property Development in New York and London, 1980–2000.* 2nd ed. Lawrence: University Press of Kansas.

——. 2001b. "Inequality in Global City-Regions." In *Global City-Regions,* edited by Allen J. Scott, 285–98. New York: Oxford University Press.

——. 2005a. "Gender and Planning: Theoretical Issues." In *Gender and Planning: A Reader,* edited by S. S. Fainstein and L. Servon, 1–12. New Brunswick, N.J.: Rutgers University Press.

——. 2005b. "Planning Theory and the City." *Journal of Planning Education and Research* 25: 1–10.

——. 2005c. "The Return of Urban Renewal: Dan Doctoroff's Great Plans for New York City." *Harvard Design Magazine* no. 22 (Spring–Summer): 1–5.

——. 2008. "Mega-Projects in New York, London and Amsterdam." *International Journal of Urban and Regional Research* 32, no. 4: 768–85.

Fainstein, Susan S., and Norman Fainstein. 1974. *Urban Political Movements.* Englewood Cliffs, N.J.: Prentice-Hall.

——. 1976. "The Federally Inspired Fiscal Crisis." *Society* 13 (May/June): 27–32.

——. 1978. "National Policy and Urban Development." *Social Problems* 26: 125–46.

——. 1979. "New Debates in Urban Planning: The Impact of Marxist Theory within the United States." *International Journal of Urban and Regional Research* 3: 381–403.

——. 1986. "Regime Strategies, Communal Resistance, and Economic Forces." In *Restructuring the City: The Political Economy of Urban Redevelopment,* 2nd ed., by Susan S. Fainstein, Norman I. Fainstein, Richard Child Hill, Dennis R. Judd, and Michael Peter Smith, 245–80. White Plains, N.Y.: Longman.

———. 1994. "Urban Regimes and Racial Conflict." In *Managing Divided Cities,* edited by Seamus Dunn, 141–59. London: Keele University Press.

Fainstein, Susan S., and David Gladstone. 1999. "Evaluating Urban Tourism," in *The Tourist City,* edited by Dennis R. Judd and Susan S. Fainstein, 21–34. New Haven: Yale University Press.

Fainstein, Susan S., Ian Gordon, and Michael Harloe, eds. 1992. *Divided Cities: New York and London in the Contemporary World.* Oxford: Blackwell.

Fainstein, Susan S., and Clifford Hirst. 1995. "Urban Social Movements." In *Theories of Urban Politics,* edited by David Judge, Gerry Stoker, and Harold Wolman, 181–204. London: Sage.

Fainstein, Susan S., and Ken Young. 1992. "Politics and State Policy in Economic Restructuring." In *Divided Cities,* edited by Susan S. Fainstein, Ian Gordon, and Michael Harloe, 203–35. Oxford: Blackwell.

Faludi, Andreas, ed. 1973. *A Reader in Planning Theory.* Oxford: Pergamon.

Faludi, Andreas, and Arnold van der Valk. 1994. *Rule and Order: Dutch Planning Doctrine in the Twentieth Century.* Dordrecht: Kluwer.

Fincher, Ruth, and Kurt Iveson. 2008. *Planning and Diversity in the City.* Houndmills, Basingstoke, Hampshire, U.K.: Palgrave Macmillan.

Fischer, Frank. 1980. *Politics, Values, and Public Policy: The Problem of Methodology.* Boulder, Colo.: Westview Press.

———. 2000. *Citizens, Experts, and the Environment.* Durham, NC: Duke University Press.

———. 2003. *Reframing Public Policy.* Oxford: Oxford University Press.

———. 2009. "Discursive Planning: Social Justice as Discourse." In *Searching for the Just City,* edited by Peter Marcuse, James Connolly, Johannes Novy, Ingrid Olivo, Cuz Potter, and Justin Steil, 52–71. London: Routledge.

Fischer, Frank, and John Forester, eds. 1993. *The Argumentative Turn in Policy Analysis and Planning.* Durham, NC: Duke University Press.

Fischer, Manfred M., and Claudia Stirböck. 2004. "Regional Income Convergence in the Enlarged Europe, 1995–2000: A Spatial Econometric Perspective." ZEW—Centre for European Economic Research Discussion Paper No. 04–042. http://ssrn.com/abstract=560882.

Fisher, Peter S., and Alan H. Peters. 1998. *Industrial Incentives: Competition among American States and Cities.* Kalamazoo, Mich.: Upjohn Institute.

Flora, Peter, and Arnold J. Heidenheimer, eds. 1981. *The Development of Welfare States in Europe and America.* New Brunswick, N.J.: Transaction Books.

Florida, Richard L. 2002. *The Rise of the Creative Class.* New York: Basic Books.

Flyvbjerg, Bent. 1998. *Rationality and Power.* Translated by Steven Sampson. Chicago: University of Chicago Press.

———. 2003. "Rationality and Power." In *Readings in Planning Theory,* edited by Susan S. Fainstein and Scott Campbell, 318–29. Oxford: Blackwell.

Flyvbjerg, B., N. Bruzelius, and W. Rothengatter. 2003. *Megaprojects and Risk.* New York: Cambridge University Press.

Foglesong, Richard E. 1986. *Planning the Capitalist City.* Princeton: Princeton University Press.

Forester, John. 1993. *Critical Theory, Public Policy, and Planning Practice: Toward a Critical Pragmatism.* Albany: State University of New York Press.

———. 1999. *The Deliberative Practitioner.* Cambridge: MIT Press.

———. 2001. "An Instructive Case-Study Hampered by Theoretical Puzzles: Critical Comments on Flyvbjerg's Rationality and Power." *International Planning Studies* 6, no. 3: 263–70.

Forst, Rainer. 2000. *Contexts of Justice.* Berkeley: University of California Press.

Foster, Janet. 1999. *Docklands: Cultures in Conflict, Worlds in Collision.* London: UCL Press.

Fraser, Nancy. 1997. *Justice Interruptus.* New York: Routledge.

———. 2003. "Social Justice in the Age of Identity Politics." In *Redistribution or Recognition? A Political-Philosophical Exchange,* by Nancy Fraser and Axel Honneth. Translated by Joel Golb, James Ingram, and Christiane Wilke, 7–109. New York: Verso.

Freeman, Lance. 2006. *There Goes the Hood.* Philadelphia: Temple University Press.

Freeman, Samuel. 2000. "Deliberative Democracy: A Sympathetic Comment." *Philosophy and Public Affairs* 29, no. 4: 371–418.

Frieden, Bernard J., and Marshall Kaplan. 1975. *The Politics of Neglect.* Cambridge: MIT Press.

Frieden, Bernard J., and Lynne B. Sagalyn. 1989. *Downtown, Inc.: How America Rebuilds Cities.* Cambridge: MIT Press.

Friedland, Roger. 1983. *Power and Crisis in the City.* New York: Schocken.

Friedmann, John. 2002. *The Prospect of Cities.* Minneapolis: University of Minnesota Press.

Frug, Gerald. 1999. *City Making.* Princeton: Princeton University Press.

Fullilove, Mindy Thompson. 2004. *Root Shock.* New York: Ballantine.

Fung, Archon. 2005. "Deliberation before the Revolution: Toward an Ethics of Deliberative Democracy in an Unjust World." *Political Theory* 33, no. 2: 397–419.

GamesBid.com. 2008. "London 2016's Olympic Village Has Financial Shortfall." http://www.gamesbids.com/eng/other_news/1216133699.html.

Gans, Herbert. 1968. *People and Plans.* New York: Basic Books.

———. 1973. *More Equality.* New York: Pantheon.

Garreau, Joel. 1992. *Edge City.* New York: Anchor.

Gawande, Atul. 2008. "Annals of Public Policy: Getting There From Here; How Health Care Reform Really Happens." *New Yorker,* January 26, 26–33.

Gellner, Ernest. 1992. *Postmodernism, Reason, and Religion.* New Brunswick, N.J.: Rutgers University Press.

Geras, Norman. 1985. "The Controversy about Marx and Justice." *New Left Review* no. 150 (March–April): 47–85.

———. 1992. "Bringing Marx to Justice: An Addendum and Rejoinder." *New Left Review* no. 195 (September–October): 37–69.

Gibson, Owen. 2009. "Government Forced to Bail Out Major Olympic Projects." *Guardian.* January 21.

Giddens, Anthony. 1990. *The Consequences of Modernity.* Stanford: Stanford University Press.

Gilderbloom, John. 2009. "Amsterdam: Planning and Policy for the Ideal City?" *Local Environment: International Journal of Justice and Sustainability* 14, no. 6 (July): 473–93.

Gill, Brendan. 1990. "The Sky Line: Battery Park City." *New Yorker,* August 20, 99–106.

Gilligan, Andrew. 2008. "Credit Crunch Threatens the Olympic Plans." *Evening Standard* (London), September 30. http://www.thisislondon.co.uk/standard/article-23561567-details/Credit+crunch+threatens+the+Olympic+plans/article.do.

Gladstone, David L., and Susan S. Fainstein. 2003. "Regulating Hospitality: Tourism Workers in New York and Los Angeles." In *Cities and Visitors,* edited by Lily M. Hoffman, Susan S. Fainstein, and Dennis R. Judd, 145–66. Oxford: Blackwell.

Glickman, Norman, and Douglas P. Woodward. 1989. *The New Competitors.* New York: Basic Books.

Goetz, Edward G. 2003. *Clearing the Way.* Washington, D.C.: Urban Institute Press.

———. 2005. "Comment: Public Housing Demolition and the Benefits to Low-Income Families." *Journal of the American Planning Association* 71, no. 4: 407–10.

Goetz, Edward G., and Mara Sidney. 1994. "Revenge of the Property Owners: Community Development and the Politics of Property." *Journal of Urban Affairs* 16, no. 4: 319–34.

Gold, John R., and Margaret M. Gold. 2007. Introduction to *Olympic Cities,* edited by John R. Gold and Margaret M. Gold, 1–11. London: Routledge.

Goldberger, Paul. 2004. *Up from Zero.* New York: Random House.

Gordon, David L. A. 1997. *Battery Park City: Politics and Planning on the New York Waterfront.* Amsterdam: Gordon and Breach.

Gorz, André. 1967. *Strategy for Labor.* Boston: Beacon Press.

Gutmann, Amy, and Dennis Thompson. 1996. *Democracy and Disagreement.* Cambridge: Harvard University Press.

Habermas, Jürgen. 1986–89. *Theory of Communicative Action.* Translated by Thomas McCarthy. Cambridge: Polity Press.

Haffner, Marietta E. A. 2002. "Dutch Personal Income Tax Reform 2001: An Exceptional Position for Owner-Occupied Housing." *Housing Studies* no. 3: 521–534.

Hajer, Maarten. 1995. *The Politics of Environmental Discourse.* Oxford: Oxford University Press.

Hajer, Maarten, and Arnold Reijndorp. 2001. *In Search of New Public Domain.* Rotterdam: NAI.

Hall, Peter. 2002. *Cities of Tomorrow.* 3rd ed. Oxford: Blackwell.

Hamnett, Chris. 2003. *Unequal City: London in the Global Arena.* London: Routledge.

Hannigan, John. 1998. *Fantasy City.* New York: Routledge.

Harloe, Michael. 1977. *Captive Cities.* New York: Wiley.

———. 1995. *The People's Home.* Oxford: Blackwell.

Hartman, Chester. 2002. *Between Eminence and Notoriety: Four Decades of Radical Planning.* New Brunswick, N.J.: Center for Urban Policy Research, Rutgers University.

Hartz, Louis. 1990. *The Necessity of Choice: Nineteenth-Century Political Thought.* Edited, compiled, and prepared by Paul Roazen. New Brunswick, N.J.: Transaction.

Harvey, David. 1978. "On Planning the Ideology of Planning." In *Planning Theory in the 1980s,* edited by Robert Burchell and George Sternlieb,

213–34. New Brunswick, N.J.: Center for Urban Policy Research, Rutgers University.

———. 1988. *Social Justice and the City.* 2nd ed. Oxford: Basil Blackwell.

———. 1989. "From Managerialism to Entrepreneurialism: The Transformation in Urban Governance in Late Capitalism." *Geografiska Annaler: Series B, Human Geography* 71, no. 1: 3–17.

———. 1992. "Social Justice, Postmodernism, and the City." *International Journal of Urban and Regional Research* 16, no. 4: 588–601.

———. 1996. *Justice, Nature and the Geography of Difference.* Oxford: Blackwell.

———. 1997. "The New Urbanism and the Communitarian Trap: On Social Problems and the False Hope of Design." *Harvard Design Magazine*, no. 1 (Winter/Spring): 1–3.

———. 2002 [1993]. "Social Justice, Postmodernism, and the City." In *Readings in Urban Theory*, edited by S. S. Fainstein and S. Campbell, 2nd ed., 386–402. London: Wiley-Blackwell.

———. 2005. *A Brief History of Neoliberalism.* New York: Oxford University Press.

———. 2006. *Spaces of Global Capitalism.* London: Verso.

Harvey, David, with Cuz Potter. 2009. "The Right to the Just City." In *Searching for the Just City*, edited by Peter Marcuse, James Connolly, Johannes Novy, Ingrid Olivo, Cuz Potter, and Justin Steil, 40–51. London: Routledge.

Hays, Samuel P. 1995. *The Response to Industrialism, 1885–1914.* 2nd ed. Chicago: University of Chicago Press.

Healey, Patsy. 1996. "Planning through Debate: The Communicative Turn in Planning Theory." In *Readings in Planning Theory*, edited by Scott Campbell and Susan S. Fainstein, 234–57. Oxford: Blackwell.

———. 2003. "Collaborative Planning in Perspective." *Planning Theory* 2, no. 2: 101–24.

———. 2006. *Collaborative Planning: Shaping Places in Fragmented Societies.* 2nd ed. New York: Palgrave Macmillan.

———. 2007. *Urban Complexity and Spatial Strategies.* London: Routledge.

Held, Virginia. 1990. "Mothering versus Contract." In *Beyond Self-Interest,* edited by Jane J. Mansbridge, 287–304. Chicago: University of Chicago Press.

Hipwell, Deirdre. 2008. "Lend Lease's Nigel Hugill Resigns." *PropertyWeek.com,* September 3. http://www.propertyweek.com/story.asp?sectioncode=297&storycode=3121636&c=3.

Hirschmann, Nancy J. 1992. *Rethinking Obligation: A Feminist Method for Political Theory.* Ithaca: Cornell University Press.

Hoch, Charles. 1996. "A Pragmatic Inquiry about Planning and Power." In *Explorations in Planning Theory*, edited by Seymour J. Mandelbaum, Luigi Mazza, and Robert W. Burchell, 30–44. New Brunswick, N.J.: Center for Urban Policy Research, Rutgers University.

Hoffman, Lily M. 1989. *The Politics of Knowledge.* Albany: State University of New York Press.

Hoffman, Lily M., Susan S. Fainstein, and Dennis R. Judd, eds. 2003. *Cities and Visitors.* Oxford: Blackwell.

Honneth, Axel. 2003. "Redistribution as Recognition: A Response to Nancy Fraser." In *Redistribution or Recognition?*, by Nancy Fraser and Axel

Honneth. Translated by Joel Golb, James Ingram, and Christiane Wilke, 110–97. London: Verso.

Hu, Sinnie. 2006. "Yankees Win as Council Approves Stadium." *New York Times,* April 6.

Huxley, Margo, and Oren Yiftachel. 2000. "New Paradigm or Old Myopia? Unsettling the Communicative Turn in Planning Theory." *Journal of Planning Education and Research* 19, no. 4: 333–42.

Innes, Judith E. 1995. "Planning Theory's Emerging Paradigm: Communicative Action and Interactive Practice." *Journal of Planning Education and Research* 14, no. 3: 183–89.

——. 1996. "Group Processes and the Social Construction of Growth Management: Florida, Vermont, and New Jersey." In *Explorations in Planning Theory,* edited by Seymour J. Mandelbaum, Luigi Mazza, and Robert W. Burchell, 164–87. New Brunswick, N.J.: Center for Urban Policy, Research Rutgers University.

——. 1998. "Information in Communicative Planning." *Journal of the American Planning Association* 64, no. 1: 52–63.

Jackson, Anthony. 1976. *A Place Called Home: A History of Low-Cost Housing in Manhattan.* Cambridge: MIT Press.

Jacobs, Jane. 1961. *The Death and Life of Great American Cities.* New York: Modern Library.

Judd, Dennis R. 1999. "Constructing the Tourist Bubble." In *The Tourist City,* edited by S. S. Fainstein and D. R. Judd, 35–53. New Haven: Yale University Press.

Judd, Dennis R., and Michael Parkinson, eds. 1990. *Leadership and Urban Regeneration: Cities in North America and Europe.* Newbury Park, Calif.: Sage.

Kanter, Rosabeth Moss. 2000. "Business Coalitions as a Force for Regionalism." In *Reflections on Regionalism,* edited by Bruce Katz, 154–84. Washington: Brookings Institution.

Kayden, Jerold. 2000. *Privately Owned Public Space.* New York: John Wiley.

Keating, W. Dennis. 1994. *The Suburban Racial Dilemma.* Philadelphia: Temple University Press.

Kelso, Paul. 2008. "Parliament and Public Misled over Olympics Budget, Say MPs." *Guardian,* April 22.

Kirby, Andrew. 2004. "Metropolitics or Retropolitics? Review of Myron Orfield, *American Metropolitics: The New Suburban Reality.*" *Antipode* 36, no. 4: 753–59.

Koch, Edward. 1984. *Mayor.* New York: Simon and Schuster.

Kohn, Margaret. 2004. *Brave New Neighborhoods: The Privatization of Public Space.* New Brunswick, N.J.: Rutgers University Press.

Kramer, Jane. 2006. "The Dutch Model: Multiculturalism and Muslim Immigrants." *New Yorker,* April 3, 60–67.

Krieger, Alex. 2005. "The Costs and Benefits of Sprawl." In *Sprawl and Suburbia,* edited by William S. Saunders, 45–56. Minneapolis: University of Minnesota Press.

Kristof, Frank. 1976. "Housing and People in New York City." *City Almanac* no. 10 (February).

Krueckeberg, Donald A. 1999. "The Grapes of Rent: A History of Renting in a Country of Owners." *Housing Policy Debate* 10, no. 1: 9–30.

Krumholz, Norman, and John Forester. 1990. *Making Equity Planning Work.* Philadelphia: Temple University Press.

Kwekkeboom, Willem. 2002. "Rebuilding the Bijlmermeer, 1992–2002." In *Rebuilding the Bijlmermeer, 1992–2002: Amsterdam Southeast: Centre Area Southeast and Urban Renewal in the Bijlmermeer, 1992–2012*, edited by Dick Bruijne, Dorine van Hoogstraten, Willem Kwekkeboom, and Anne Luijten, 73–113. Bussum, Netherlands: Thoth.

Lake, Robert W. 1993. "Rethinking NIMBY." *Journal of the American Planning Association* 59, no. 1: 87–93.

Lasch-Quinn, Elizabeth. 1996. "Review: *The Suburban Racial Dilemma* by W. Dennis Keating." *Annals of the American Academy of Political and Social Science*, no. 544: 228–29.

Lawless, Paul. 1989. *Britain's Inner Cities.* 2nd ed. London: Paul Chapman.

Lawless, Paul, and Frank Brown. 1986. *Urban Growth and Change in Britain.* London: Harper and Row.

Lee, Trymaine. 2007. "Pre–Opening Day Jitters for Establishments That Live in Yankee Stadium's Shadow." *New York Times,* April 2.

Lefebvre, Henri. 1991. *The Production of Space.* Translated by Donald Nicholson-Smith. Oxford: Cambridge: Blackwell.

Lindblom, Charles E. 1959. "The Science of 'Muddling Through.'" *Public Administration Review* 19, no. 2: 79–88.

——. 1959. *Inquiry and Change.* New Haven: Yale University Press.

Lipsky, Michael. 1980. *Street-Level Bureaucracy.* New York: Russell Sage Foundation.

Locum Consulting. 2006. "Review of the Impacts of the London 2012 Olympic and Paralympic Games on the South East Region." *Report to South East of England Development Agency.* April. http://www.seeda.co.uk/publications/Strategy/docs/OlympicImpact.pdf.

Logan, John R., and Harvey L. Molotch. 1987. *Urban Fortunes: The Political Economy of Place.* Berkeley: University of California Press.

Logan, John R., and Todd Swanstrom, eds. 1990. *Beyond the City Limits.* Philadelphia: Temple University Press.

London Assembly. 2008. *Proposal for a Preliminary Investigation into the Sporting Legacy of the 2012 Olympic and Paralympic Games.* Report #5. September 3.

London Docklands Development Corporation (LDDC). 1992. *LDDC Key Facts and Figures to the 31st March 1991.* London: LDDC.

Long, Judith Grant. 2005. "Full Count: The Real Cost of Public Funding for Major League Sports Facilities." *Journal of Sports Economics* 6: 119–43.

Low, Nicholas, and Brendan Gleeson. 1998. *Justice, Society and Nature.* London: Routledge.

Luijten, Anne. 2002. "A Modern Fairy Tale." In *Amsterdam Southeast: Centre Area Southeast and Urban Renewal in the Bijlmermeer, 1992–2012*, edited by Dick Bruijne, Dorine van Hoogstraten, Willem Kwekkeboom, and Anne Luijten, 7–25. Bussum, Netherlands: Thoth.

Lukács, György. 1971. *History and Class Consciousness.* Translated by Rodney Livingstone. Cambridge: MIT Press.

Lukas, J. Anthony. 1985. *Common Ground.* New York: Knopf.

Lynch, Kevin. 1981. *Good City Form.* Cambridge: MIT Press.

Majoor, Stan. 2007. "Amsterdam Zuidas: The Dream of 'New Urbanity.'" In *Framing Strategic Urban Projects,* edited by Willem Salet and Enrico Gualini, 53–83. London: Routledge.

———. 2008. *Disconnected Innovations.* Delft: Uitgeverij Eburon.

Mak, G. 1999. *Amsterdam.* Translated by Philipp Blom. London: Harvill Press.

Mannheim, Karl. 1936. "The Sociology of Knowledge." In *Ideology and Utopia,* 264–311. New York: Harcourt, Brace, and World.

Mansbridge, Jane, ed. 1990a. *Beyond Self-Interest.* Chicago: University of Chicago Press.

———. 1990b. "The Rise and Fall of Self-Interest in the Explanation of Political Life." In *Beyond Self-Interest,* edited by Jane J. Mansbridge, 3–11. Chicago: University of Chicago Press.

———. 2009. "A 'Selection Model' of Political Representation." *Journal of Political Philosophy* 17, no. 4: 369–99.

Marcuse, Peter. 1981. "The Targeted Crisis: On the Ideology of the Urban Fiscal Crisis and Its Uses." *International Journal of Urban and Regional Research* 5, no. 2: 330–55.

———. 1987. "Neighborhood Policy and the Distribution of Power: New York City's Community Boards." *Policy Studies Journal* 16: 277–89.

———. 2002. "The Shifting Meaning of the Black Ghetto in the United States." In *Of States and Cities,* edited by Peter Marcuse and Ronald van Kempen, 109–42. New York: Oxford University Press.

———. 2009. "From Justice Planning to Commons Planning." In *Searching for the Just City,* edited by Peter Marcuse, James Connolly, Johannes Novy, Ingrid Olivo, Cuz Potter, and Justin Steil, 91–102. London: Routledge.

Marcuse, Peter, James Connolly, Johannes Novy, Ingrid Olivo, Cuz Potter, and Justin Steil, eds. 2009. *Searching for the Just City.* London: Routledge.

Marcuse, Peter, and Ronald van Kempen, eds. 2002. *Of States and Cities.* New York: Oxford University Press.

Markusen, Ann. 2006. "The Artistic Dividend: Urban Artistic Specialization and Economic Development Implications." *Urban Studies* 43, no. 1: 1661–86.

Markusen, Ann, and Susan S. Fainstein. 1993. "Urban Policy: Bridging the Social and Economic Development Gap." *University of North Carolina Law Review* 71: 1463–86.

Marris, Peter. 1987. *Meaning and Action.* 2nd ed. London: Routledge and Kegan Paul.

Marshall, T. H. 1964. *Class, Citizenship, and Social Development.* Garden City, N.Y.: Doubleday.

Martinotti, Guido. 1999. "A City for Whom? Transients and Public Life in the Second-Generation Metropolis." In *The Urban Moment,* edited by Robert A. Beauregard and Sophie Body-Gendrot, 155–84. Thousand Oaks, Calif.: Sage.

Marx, Karl, and Friedrich Engels. 1947. *The German Ideology.* New York: International Publishers.

Massey, Doreen. 2007. "The World We're In: An Interview with Ken Livingstone." *Soundings* 36 (July): 11–25.

Mayer, Margit. 2003. "The Onward Sweep of Social Capital: Causes and Consequences for Understanding Cities, Communities and Urban Movements." *International Journal of Urban and Regional Research* 27, no. 1: 110–32.

McClelland, Peter, and Alan Magdowitz. 1981. *Crisis in the Making: The Political Economy of New York State since 1945.* New York: Cambridge University Press.

McGeehan, Patrick. 2009. "In the Shadow of Yankee Stadium, an Off Year." *New York Times,* November 4.

Meagher, Sharon M. 2008. *Philosophy and the City: Classic to Contemporary Writings.* Albany: State University of New York Press.

Mencher, Samuel. 1967. *Poor Law to Poverty Program.* Pittsburgh: University of Pittsburgh Press.

Merrick, Jane. 2009. "London 2012: Stuck on the Blocks?" *Independent,* July 19.

Mier, Robert, and Laurie Alpern. 1993. *Social Justice and Local Development Policy.* Newbury Park, Calif.: Sage Publications.

Mill, John Stuart. 1951. *Utilitarianism, Liberty, and Representative Government.* New York: Dutton.

Mitchell, Don. 2003. *The Right to the City.* New York: Guilford.

Moi, Toril. 1985. *Sexual/Textual Politics.* London: Routledge.

Mollenkopf, John Hull. 1983. *The Contested City.* Princeton: Princeton University Press.

——. 1985. "The 42nd Street Development Project and the Public Interest." *City Almanac* 18, no. 4 (Summer): 12–13.

——. 1988. "The Postindustrial Transformation of the Political Order in New York City." In *Power, Culture, and Place,* edited by John Hull Mollenkopf, 223–58. New York: Russell Sage Foundation.

Mouffe, Chantal. 1999. "Deliberative Democracy or Agonistic Pluralism?" *Social Research* 66, no. 3: 745–58.

——. 2000. *The Democratic Paradox.* New York: Verso.

——. 2005. *On the Political.* London: Routledge.

Moulaert, Frank, and Katy Cabaret. 2006. "Planning, Networks and Power Relations: Is Democratic Planning under Capitalism Possible?" *Planning Theory* 5, no. 1: 51–70.

Musterd, Sako, and Wim Ostendorf. 2008. "Integrated Urban Renewal in the Netherlands: A Critical Appraisal." *Urban Research & Practice* 1, no. 1: 78–92.

Musterd, Sako, and Sjoerd de Vos. 2007. "Residential Dynamics in Ethnic Concentrations." *Housing Studies* 22, no. 3 (May): 333–53.

National Audit Office. 1988. *Department of the Environment: Urban Development Corporations; Report by the Comptroller and Auditor General.* London: HMSO.

Needleman, Martin L., and Carolyn E. Needleman. 1974. *Guerrillas in the Bureaucracy.* New York: Wiley.

Neumann, Michael. 2000. "Communicate This: Does Consensus Lead to Advocacy and Pluralism in Planning?" *Journal of Planning Education and Research* 19, no. 4: 343–50.

Newman, Peter. 2007. "Back the Bid: The 2012 Summer Olympics and the Governance of London." *Journal of Urban Affairs* 29, no. 3: 255–67.

Newton, Kenneth, and Terrence J. Karran. 1985. *The Politics of Local Expenditure.* Houndmills, Basingstoke, Hampshire: Macmillan.

New York City (NYC) Department of City Planning. N.d. *NYC2000.* New York: Population Division, Department of City Planning.

New York City (NYC), Independent Budget Office. 2006. "Testimony of Ronnie Lowenstein before the City Council Finance Committee on Financing Plans for the New Yankee Stadium." http://www.ibo.nyc.ny.us/iboreports/yanksta diumtestimony.pdf.

Nussbaum, Martha C. 1993. "Non-Relative Virtues: An Aristotelian Approach." In *The Quality of Life,* edited by Martha C. Nussbaum and Amartya Sen, 242–69. Oxford: Oxford University Press.

——. 2000. *Women and Human Development.* Cambridge: Cambridge University Press.

——. 2005. "Women and Human Development: In Defense of Universal Values." In *Gender and Planning: A Reader,* edited by S. S. Fainstein and L. J. Servon, 104–19. New Brunswick, N.J.: Rutgers University Press.

——. 2006. *Frontiers of Justice.* Cambridge: Harvard University Press.

O'Connor, James. 1973. *The Fiscal Crisis of the State.* New York: St. Martin's.

Orfield, Myron. 2002. *American Metropolitics.* Washington, D.C.: Brookings Institution.

Organization for Economic Cooperation and Development (OECD). 2008. *Growing Unequal: Income Distribution and Poverty in OECD Countries.* Paris: OECD.

Ortega y Gasset, José. 1932. *The Revolt of the Masses.* New York: Norton.

Peters, Alan H., and Peter S. Fisher. 2003. "Enterprise Zone Incentives: How Effective Are They?" In *Financing Economic Development,* edited by Sammis B. White, Richard D. Bingham, and Ned W. Hill, 113–30. Armonk, N.Y.: M. E. Sharpe.

Peterson, Paul E. 1981. *City Limits.* Chicago: University of Chicago Press.

Pickvance, Chris, and Edmond Preteceille, eds. 1990. *State Restructuring and Local Power.* London: Francis Pinter.

Pitkin, Hanna F. 1972. *The Concept of Representation.* Berkeley: University of California Press.

Piven, Frances Fox, and Richard A. Cloward. 1971. *Regulating the Poor.* New York: Pantheon.

Polanyi, Karl. 1944. *The Great Transformation.* New York: Rinehart.

Ponte, Robert. 1982. "Building Battery Park City." *Urban Design Interntional* 3 (March–April): 10–15.

Porter, Michael E. 1998. "Clusters and the New Economics of Competition." *Harvard Business Review* 76: 77–90.

Priemus, Hugo. 1995. "How to Abolish Social Housing? The Dutch Case." *International Journal of Urban and Regional Research* 19: 145–55.

——. 2006. "Regeneration of Dutch Post-War Urban Districts: The Role of Housing Associations." *Journal of Housing and the Built Environment* 21: 365–75.

Property Wire. 2008. *London Olympic Village Project Hit by Global Credit Crunch.* September 23. http://www.propertywire.com/news/europe/london-olympic-village-credit-crunch-200809231693.html.

Pruijt, Hans. 2003. "Is the Institutionalization of Urban Movements Inevitable? A Comparison of the Opportunities for Sustained Squatting in New York City and Amsterdam." *International Journal of Urban and Regional Research* 27, no. 1: 133–57.

Purcell, Mark. 2008. *Recapturing Democracy.* New York: Routledge.

——. 2009. "Resisting Neoliberalization: Communicative Planning or Counter-Hegemonic Movements." *Planning Theory* 8, no. 2: 140–65.

Putnam, Hilary. 2002. *The Collapse of the Fact/Value Dichotomy.* Cambridge: Harvard University Press.

Putnam, Robert D. 1993. *Making Democracy Work.* Princeton: Princeton University Press.

——. 2007. "E pluribus Unum: Diversity and Community in the Twenty-First Century." *Scandinavian Political Studies* 30, no. 2: 137–74.

Rawls, John. 1971. A Theory of Justice. 1st ed. Cambridge: Harvard University Press.

——. 1999. *A Theory of Justice.* 2nd ed. Cambridge: Harvard University Press.

——. 2001. *Justice as Fairness: A Restatement.* Edited by Erin Kelly. Cambridge: Harvard University Press.

Reichl, Alexander J. 1999. *Reconstructing Times Square.* Lawrence: University Press of Kansas.

——. 2007. "Rethinking the Dual City." *Urban Affairs Review* 42, no. 5: 659–87.

Rhodes, John, and Peter Tyler. 1998. "Evaluating the LDDC: Regenerating London's Docklands." *Rising East (Journal of East London Studies)* 2, no. 2: 32–41.

Robertson, Roland. 1992. *Globalization.* Thousand Oaks, Calif.: Sage.

Robinson, Jennifer. 2006. *Ordinary Cities.* London: Routledge.

Roche, Maurice. 2000. *Mega-Events and Modernity.* London: Routledge.

Rosentraub, Mark S. 1997. *Major League Losers: The Real Cost of Sports and Who's Paying for It.* New York: Basic Books.

Rousseau, Jean-Jacques. 1987. "On the Social Contract." In *The Basic Political Writings.* Translated by Donald A. Cress. Indianapolis: Hackett.

Runciman, Walter G. 1966. *Relative Deprivation and Social Justice.* Berkeley: University of California Press.

Rusk, David. 2003. *Cities without Suburbs.* 3rd ed. Washington, D.C.: Woodrow Wilson Center Press.

Sagalyn, Lynne B. 2001. *Times Square Roulette.* Cambridge: MIT Press.

Sandel, Michael J. 1996. *Democracy's Discontent: America in Search of a Public Philosophy.* Cambridge: Harvard University Press.

Sandercock, Leonie. 1998. *Towards Cosmopolis: Planning for Multicultural Cities.* New York: John Wiley.

——. 2003. *Cosmopolis II: Mongrel Cities in the 21st Century.* London: Continuum.

Sandomir, Richard. 2008. "New Stadiums: Prices, and Outrage, Escalate." *New York Times,* April 26.

Sarbib, Jean Louis. 1983. "The University of Chicago Program in Planning." *Journal of Planning Education and Research* 2, no. 2: 77–81.

Sassen, Saskia. 2001. *The Global City.* 2nd ed. Princeton: Princeton University Press.

Sassen, Saskia, and Frank Roost. 1999. "The City: Strategic Site for the Global Entertainment Industry." In *The Tourist City,* edited by Dennis R. Judd and Susan S. Fainstein, 143–54. Oxford: Blackwell.

Saunders, Peter. 1984. "Beyond Housing Classes: The Sociological Significance of Private Property Rights in Means of Consumption." *International Journal of Urban and Regional Research* 8, no. 2: 202–27.

Sayer, Andrew, and Michael Storper. 1997. "Ethics Unbound: For a Normative Turn in Social Theory." *Environment and Planning D: Society and Space* 15, no. 1: 1–18.

Sayer, Andrew, and Richard Walker. 1992. *The New Social Economy.* Oxford: Blackwell.

Schattschneider, E. E. 1975. *The Semisovereign People.* Fort Worth, Texas: Harcourt Brace Jovanovich College.

Schill, Michael H., Ingrid Gould Ellen, Amy Ellen Schwartz, and Ioan Voicu. 2002. "Revitalizing Inner-City Neighborhoods: New York City's Ten-Year Plan." *Housing Policy Debate* 13, no. 3: 529–66.

Scott, James C. 1998. *Seeing Like a State.* New Haven: Yale University Press.

Sen, Amartya. 1992. *Inequality Reexamined.* Cambridge: Harvard University Press.

——. 1993. "Capability and Well-Being." In *The Quality of Life,* edited by Martha C. Nussbaum and Amartya Sen, 30–53. New York: Oxford University Press.

Sennett, Richard. 1970. *The Uses of Disorder.* New York: Vintage.

——. 1990. *The Conscience of the Eye: The Design and Social Life of Cities.* New York: Knopf.

Shakur, Tasleem, and Jamie Halsall. 2007. "Global Cities, Regeneration, and the Translocal Communities of Europe." *Global Built Environment Review* 6, no. 1: 1–4.

Shapiro, Ian. 1999. *Democratic Justice.* New Haven: Yale University Press.

——. 2003. *The State of Democratic Theory.* Princeton: Princeton University Press.

Shefter, Martin. 1985. *Political Crisis, Fiscal Crisis.* New York: Basic Books.

Simmel, Georg. 1950. *The Sociology of Georg Simmel.* Translated and edited by Kurt H. Wolff. New York: Free Press.

Simon, Arthur. 1970. *Stuyvesant Town, U.S.A.* New York: New York University Press.

Sintomer, Yves, Carsten Herzberg, and Anja Röcke. 2008. "Participatory Budgeting in Europe: Potentials and Challenges." *International Journal of Urban and Regional Research* 32, no. 1: 164–78.

Skocpol, Theda. 2003. *Diminished Democracy.* Norman: University of Oklahoma Press.

Spragens, Tom. 2003. "Review: Justice, Consensus, and Boundaries: Assessing Political Liberalism." *Political Theory* 31, no. 4: 589–601.

Squires, Gregory D., ed. 1989. *Unequal Partnerships: The Political Economy of Urban Redevelopment in Postwar America.* New Brunswick, N.J.: Rutgers University Press.

Starr, Roger. 1975. "Effluents and Successes in Declining Metropolitan Areas." In *Post-Industrial America,* edited by George Sternlieb and James Hughes, 190–96. New Brunswick, N.J.: Center for Urban Policy Research, Rutgers University.

——. 1976. "Making New York Smaller." *New York Times Magazine,* November 14, 33–34, 99ff.

Stone, Clarence N. 1976. *Economic Growth and Neighborhood Discontent.* Chapel Hill: University of North Carolina Press.

——. 1989. *Regime Politics: Governing Atlanta, 1946–1988.* Lawrence: University Press of Kansas.

——. 2005. "Rethinking the Policy-Politics Connection." *Policy Studies* 26, nos. 3–4: 241–60.

Swanstrom, Todd. 1985. *The Crisis of Growth Politics.* Philadelphia: Temple University Press.

Taylor, Charles. 1991. *The Ethics of Authenticity.* Cambridge: Harvard University Press.

Terhorst, Pieter. 2004. "Amsterdam's Path Dependence: Still Tightly Interwoven with a National Accumulation Regime." Unpublished paper. Department of Geography, Planning and International Development Studies, University of Amsterdam.

Terhorst, P. J. F., and J. C. L. van de Ven. 1997. *Fragmented Brussels and Consolidated Amsterdam.* Amsterdam: Netherlands Geographical Society and Department of Human Geography, University of Amsterdam.

Terhorst, Pieter, Jacques van de Ven, and Léon Deben. 2003. "Amsterdam: It's All in the Mix." In *Cities and Visitors,* edited by Lily M. Hoffman, Susan S. Fainstein, and Dennis R. Judd, 75–90. Oxford: Blackwell.

Uitermark, Justus. 2004a. "The Co-optation of Squatters in Amsterdam and the Emergence of a Movement Meritocracy: A Critical Reply to Pruijt." *International Journal of Urban and Regional Research* 28, no. 3: 687–98.

——. 2004b. "Framing Urban Injustices: The Case of the Amsterdam Squatter Movement." *Space and Polity* 8, no. 2: 227–44.

Uitermark, Justus, and Jan Willem Duyvendak. 2008. "Citizen Participation in a Mediated Age: Neighborhood Governance in the Netherlands." *International Journal of Urban and Regional Research* 32, no. 1: 114–34.

UK, Department for Culture, Media and Sport (DCMS). 2007. *Our Promise for 2012—How the UK Will Benefit from the Olympic Games and Paralympic Games.* June. http://epress.lib.uts.edu.au/dspace/bitstream/2100/449/1/Ourpromise2012Forword.pdf.

——. 2008. *London 2012 Olympic and Paralympic Games Update Report.* July. London: DCMS.

UK, Department of the Environment (DOE). 1989. *Strategic Planning Guidance for London.* July. London: DOE.

UK, Prime Minister's Office. 2006. *Speech to Greater London Authority.* April 4. http://www.number10.gov.uk/Page9281.

Urry, John. 2002. *The Tourist Gaze.* 2nd ed. Thousand Oaks, Calif.: Sage.

Van der Veer, Peter. 2006. "Pim Fortuyn, Theo van Gogh, and the Politics of Tolerance in the Netherlands." *Public Culture* 18, no. 1: 111–124.

Van de Ven, Jacques. 2004. "It's All in the Mix." In *Cultural Heritage and the Future of the Historic Inner City of Amsterdam,* edited by Léon Deben, Willem Salet, and Marie-Thérèse van Thoor, 176–84. Amsterdam: Aksant.

Van Ham, Maarten, Ronald van Kempen, and Jan van Weesep. 2006. "The Changing Role of the Dutch Social Rented Sector." *Journal of Housing and the Built Environment* 21, no. 3: 315–35.

Van Kempen, Ronald, Karien Dekker, Stephen Hall, and Iván Tosics, eds. 2005. *Restructuring Large Housing Estates in Europe.* Bristol, U.K.: Policy Press.

Vlist, Arno van der, and Piet Rietveld. 2002. *The Amsterdam Metropolitan Housing Market: Research Memorandum 2002–36.* Amsterdam: Faculty of Economics and Business Administration, University of Amsterdam.

Wacquant, Loïc J. D. 2008. *Urban Outcasts.* Cambridge: Polity.

Walzer, Michael. 1984. *Spheres of Justice: A Defense of Pluralism and Equality.* New York: Basic Books.

Watson, Vanessa. 2006. "Deep Difference: Diversity, Planning and Ethics." *Planning Theory* 5, no. 1: 31–50.

Weber, Max. 1958. "Politics as a Vocation." In *From Max Weber,* edited by Hans Gerth and C. Wright Mills, 77–128. New York: Oxford University Press.

West, Cornel. 1991. *The Ethical Dimensions of Marxist Thought.* New York: Monthly Review Press.

William, Helen. 2008. "Credit Crunch 'Hitting Olympic Village Funding.'" *Independent* (London), September 25.

Wilson, William J. 1987. *The Truly Disadvantaged.* Chicago: University of Chicago Press.

———, ed. 1989. *The Ghetto Underclass.* Newbury Park, Calif.: Sage.

Wolff, Robert Paul, Barrington Moore Jr., and Herbert Marcuse. 1969. *A Critique of Pure Tolerance.* Boston: Beacon Press.

World Architecture News.com. 2008. Editorial. August 21. http://www.worldarchitecturenews.com/index.php?fuseaction=wanappln.projectview&upload_id=10227.

Wright, E. O. 2006. "Socialism as Social Empowerment." Paper presented at the symposium on "Power" organized by the *Berkeley Journal of Sociology,* March. Working draft. http://www.lse.ac.uk/collections/LSEPublicLecturesAndEvents/pdf/20060223-Wright.pdf.

Yates, Douglas. 1977. *The Ungovernable City.* Cambridge: MIT Press.

Yiftachel, Oren. 1999. "Planning Theory at the Crossroads." *Journal of Planning Education and Research* 18, no. 3: 67–69.

Young, Iris Marion. 1990. *Justice and the Politics of Difference.* Princeton: Princeton University Press.

———. 2000. *Inclusion and Democracy.* Oxford: Oxford University Press.

———. 2001. "Activist Challenges to Deliberative Democracy." *Political Theory* 29, no. 5: 670–90.

Zucker, Ross. 2001. *Democratic Distributive Justice.* Cambridge: Cambridge University Press.

Index

Page numbers in *italics* refer to illustrations.